REASSESSING REFORM

REASSESSING REFORM

A HISTORICAL INVESTIGATION INTO CHURCH RENEWAL

Edited by Christopher M. Bellitto
and David Zachariah Flanagin

THE CATHOLIC UNIVERSITY OF AMERICA PRESS
WASHINGTON, D.C.

The paper used in this publication meets the minimum requirements of American National Standards for Information Science—Permanence of Paper for Printed Library Materials, ANSI Z39.48-1984.
∞

Library of Congress Cataloging-in-Publication Data
Reassessing reform : a historical investigation into church renewal / edited by Christopher M. Bellitto and David Zachariah Flanagin.
p. cm.
Proceedings of a conference held in Oct. 2008 at Gettysburg Lutheran Seminary.
Includes bibliographical references and index.
ISBN 978-0-8132-1999-8 (cloth : alk. paper)
1. Ladner, Gerhart B. (Gerhart Burian), 1905– Idea of reform—Congresses. 2. Church renewal—Congresses. 3. Theology, Doctrinal—History—Middle Ages, 600–1500—Congresses. 4. Theology, Doctrinal—History—16th century—Congresses. 5. Theology, Doctrinal—History—17th century—Congresses. I. Bellitto, Christopher M. II. Flanagin, David Zachariah.
BV600.3.R43 2012
262.001'7—dc23
2012015763

In the name of the members of the
American Cusanus Society, we dedicate this
volume to David McGonagle, longtime director of the
Catholic University of America Press,
for his support of our work
over many years.

CONTENTS

PREFACE

JOHN HOWE

Students of Gerhart Ladner (1905–1993) find it difficult to describe him.[1] His students were American but his intellectual world was European, and much of the Europe he had known and loved was lost during the world wars. The limits of an American perspective became clear to me during the summer of 1982 when I happened to be working at the Vatican Library while Ladner was there preparing his collected articles for publication.[2] I had known the elderly, unassuming Viennese gentleman who passed largely unnoticed through the corridors of UCLA's Bunche Hall. But that summer in Rome his one public address, sponsored by the Swiss Embassy, drew hundreds of people, including knots of eager students exclaiming to each other, "That's Gerhart Ladner!" He spent evenings with Richard Krautheimer and other giants. And during coffee breaks he was

1. On Gerhart B. Ladner himself, see John Van Engen, "Images and Ideas: The Achievements of Gerhart Burian Ladner, with a Bibliography of his Published works," *Viator* 20 (1989): 85–115; Gerhart B. Ladner, *Erinnerungen*, edited by Herwig Wolfram and Walter Pohl, Österreischischen Akademie der Wissenschaften, Philosophisch-historische Klasse, Sitzungsberichte 617 (Vienna: Verlag der Österreischischen Akademie der Wissenschaften, 1994); and Robert L. Benson, Giles Constable, and John Van Engen, "Gerhart Burian Ladner," Memoirs of Fellows and Corresponding Fellows of the Medieval Academy of America, *Speculum* 71 (1996): 802–4.

2. Gerhart B. Ladner, *Images and Ideas in the Middle Ages: Selected Studies in History and Art*, 2 vols. Raccolta di studi e testi, 155–56 (Rome: Edizioni di storia e letteratura, 1983).

able to recall a Rome prior to Benito Mussolini's *Via della Conciliazione* where he had still been able to wander through the medieval *Borgo*. His world was not mine.

In 1979, when he signed off on my dissertation, I did not realize how much my scholarship had been shaped by him. He directed with a light hand, almost imperceptibly. Yet, looking back, I realize that I had learned some important lessons. First of all, Ladner emphasized that medieval historians needed to use all the relevant evidence. He was a scholar who had polished his own diplomatic and archival skills working on Paul Kehr's exhaustive documentary inventories,[3] and who had spent much of his life attempting to catalogue every known ancient and medieval papal image.[4] For my dissertation, I had initially proposed a methodology involving large representative samples of hagiographical texts that would have yielded statistically significant regional comparisons. Ladner vetoed this idea. He never wavered on "no text left behind."

Another lesson was that an understanding of medieval history had to include art and symbolism. Actually, I do not recall him teaching this explicitly—he just assumed without question the connection between art and history that much of his academic work attempted to illuminate.[5] Ladner was an art historian before he was a historian. He had begun to study papal portraits before he began to study reform. In fact, his concern about how "image and likeness" might be realized may actually have originated out of art historical

3. Ladner, *Erinnerungen*, 28–32.

4. Gerhart B. Ladner, *Die Päpstbildnisse des Altertums und des Mittelalters*, 5 vols. in 4, Monumenti di antichità cristiana, 2 ser., 4 (Vatican City: Pontificio istituto di archeologia cristiana, 1941–1984).

5. In addition to Ladner's volumes on papal portraits (see note 4 above), he published the many individual art historical studies which comprise vol. 1 of Gerhart B. Ladner, *Images and Ideas in the Middle Ages: Selected Studies in History and Art*, 2 vols. (Rome: Edizioni di Storia e Letteratura, 1983), not to mention additional works such as Gerhart B. Ladner, *Ad Imaginem Dei: The Image of Man in Mediaeval Art* (Latrobe, Pa.: Archabbey Press, 1965); and Gerhart B. Ladner, *L'immagine dell'imperatore Ottone III*, Unione internazionale degli istituti di archeologia, storia e storia dell'arte in Roma, 5 (Rome: Unione internazionale degli istituti di archeologia, storia e storia dell'arte, 1988).

questions: Was a particular human image generic or an actual individual portrait? How do we know? Was Byzantine art illusionistic? Or naturalistic? Or some carefully constructed combination? Long after his retirement, at a time when he was becoming increasingly conscious of his own mortality, the equilibrium between his two disciplines began to shift so that his final work privileges the ahistorical, eternal aspects of symbols, allowing their more ephemeral historical contexts to recede.[6] Nevertheless, his simultaneous study of art and history continues to influence his students.

Another emphasis was vocabulary. Historians of Ladner's generation were trained in textual editing and diplomatics. He had a keen eye for shifts in the use of words and for the changing worldviews they might portend. He closely studied the meanings and parameters of reform terminology.[7] Ladner did not possess the wonderful tools scholars have today. For him "cut and paste" involved notebooks, notepads, and real scissors. Punch cards were the technological basis for his and David Packard's pioneering attempt to use computer search functions to analyze vocabulary fields.[8] Yet, although the technology has changed, his students continue to be inspired by his respect for lexicography and *Quellenkritik*.

Perhaps the most influential legacy from UCLA in the 1970s, for better and for worse, was intellectual audacity. Ladner was a child of cosmopolitan Hapsburg Vienna, a man whose earliest memory was Emperor Franz Josef and King Edward VII riding together in a flower-bedecked coach and who could still recall from later occasions the old emperor's kindly smile.[9] He wrote poetry. He delighted in

6. See especially Gerhart B. Ladner's *God, Cosmos, and Humankind: The World of Early Christian Symbolism*, translated by Thomas Dunlap (Berkeley: University of California Press, 1995).

7. Note his studies on "Renewal Ideas and Movements," in Ladner, *Images and Ideas*, 2:517–763.

8. Gerhart B. Ladner, "Gregory the Great and Gregory VII: A Comparison of Their Concepts of Renewal," *Viator* 4 (1973): 1–27; David W. Packard, "A Note on the Computer Methods Used," *Viator* 4 (1973): 27–31.

9. Ladner, *Erinnerungen*, 14. The monarchs paraded through Vienna in 1908. The

grand visions of the sweeping roles ideas and symbols played in history. His intellectual imperialism was complemented and abetted by that of his colleague Lynn White Jr. Although Ladner and White differed greatly in style and life experience, they admired each other's work and were both convinced that religion shapes culture. Here were professors who dared to claim that the Christian idea of reform underpins Western ideas of progress[10] and that the dominion over the creatures which the Bible assigns to man lies at "the historical roots of our ecologic crisis."[11] Neither halted at the boundaries of disciplines or the borders of civilizations. When the editors of the 1971 *Répertoire international des médiévistes* asked medievalists to identify their research areas with a phrase, scholars generally responded with relatively limited descriptors such as "Franciscan history" or "cartography." Lynn White Jr., however, boldly claimed "history of technology" and "India and Europe." This was quite modest compared with Gerhart Ladner's "history of art" and "history"![12] The two grand old men were not intentionally arrogant—it was just that they had mastered their fields when the scholarship was more manageable and had grown up with them. The future would belong to specialists with narrower fields of vision. The great dinosaurs would no longer walk the earth. But students who knew Ladner and White learned that historians could admire not only interesting pebbles but also spectacular horizons.

Ladner family, which at times vacationed with the Sigmund Freuds, was well connected to Viennese artistic and intellectual circles.

10. Ladner, *The Idea of Reform*, passim, esp. 169–70, 185, 423–24.

11. Lynn T. White Jr., "The Historical Roots of Our Ecologic Crisis," *Science* 155 (1967): 1203–7, often reprinted, digitized, and criticized.

12. *Répertoire international des médiévistes*, ed. Edmonde-René Labande and Bernadette Laplant, 2 vols., Publications du Centre d'études supérieures de civilisation médiévale, 5 (Poitiers: C.É.S.C.M., 1960), 1:433 and 1:828. My thanks to Sheryl Mullane-Corvi of the Medieval Academy of America for helping me track down this reference.

REASSESSING REFORM

I

INTRODUCTION

CHRISTOPHER M. BELLITTO AND
DAVID ZACHARIAH FLANAGIN

At the conclusion of his groundbreaking study, *The Idea of Reform: Its Impact on Christian Thought and Action in the Age of the Fathers*, Gerhart Ladner stated that "the idea of reform ... was to remain the self-perpetuating core, the inner life spring of Christian tradition through lesser and greater times."[1] Ladner himself sought to explore the content of such a statement in the age of patristic theology and early Christian monasticism, while at the same time pointing forward to the many developments in reform ideology in the medieval period and beyond. His insights laid the foundation for a half century of scholarship, particularly bearing fruit in the study of reform in the Middle Ages. This volume seeks to reconsider his insights in a manner that both explores and critiques the enduring significance of Ladner's study and also surveys and demonstrates new avenues and insights of contemporary reform scholarship. Our hope is to reassess Ladner's historical and theological examination of the idea of

1. Gerhart B. Ladner, *The Idea of Reform: Its Impact on Christian Thought and Action in the Age of the Fathers* (Cambridge, Mass.: Harvard University Press, 1959; republished in New York: Harper Torchbooks, 1967, with brief bibliographic *addenda*), 423

reform in the Christian tradition, with a special focus on its meaning from the end of the patristic age to the dawn of modernity.

In the twin context of the fiftieth anniversaries of the publication of *The Idea of Reform* (1959) and of Vatican II (1962–1965), this volume—the ninth collection published under the aegis of the American Cusanus Society—was born at the conference "Reassessing Reform: Medieval Models of Change. Celebrating Gerhart Ladner's *The Idea of Reform* after Fifty Years," hosted by Gettysburg Lutheran Seminary in October 2008. The conference, a biennial event, was the eleventh organized by the American Cusanus Society. It was supported by the seminary's International Seminar on Pre-Reformation Theology and once again enjoyed the leadership of Gerald Christianson. As in the past, the conference especially benefited from the collaboration of scholars from a variety of fields and churches, making the event a model of intellectual and religious diversity and ecumenism.

But the conference itself was not the only effort to reconsider Gerhart Ladner's seminal study; it was the centerpiece of a larger scholarly enterprise spanning several years, informally dubbed "The Past for the Present"—so-called because many scholars work on church reform, not only remotely in the past, but immediately and intimately in their own professional and faith lives. At a number of recent conferences, such as those of the American Catholic Historical Association and the International Congress on Medieval Studies in Kalamazoo, Michigan, we organized panels to look at historical models and examples of reform, always with an eye to see how the models were applied (or not) and succeeded (or failed) in later historical periods and especially within the context of Vatican II, which emphasized, among other important topics, ecumenism, ecclesiology, and *aggiornamento*. The papers that resulted from those panels and the Gettysburg conference have produced this *festschrift* for a book: Ladner's *Idea of Reform*. We took as our lead two prior efforts. First, we modestly and on a smaller scale followed the example of a 1977 Harvard conference inspired by the fiftieth anniversary of Charles Homer Haskins's *The Renaissance of the Twelfth Century,* which resulted in a collection of essays edited by Robert L. Benson and Giles Constable. Second, and more recently, we turned to the 2004 Gettysburg conference devoted to Brian Tierney's *Foundations of the Conciliar Theory,* which resulted in the publication of *The Church, the Councils, and Reform: The Legacy of the Fifteenth Century.*[2]

Gerhart Ladner (1905–1993) was an Austrian convert to Catholicism and part of the influential exile population that fled Nazi Europe.[3] He earned his doctorate in art history at the University of Vienna, researched in Berlin and Rome in the 1930s, left Europe in 1938 to join Toronto's Pontifical Institute for Mediaeval Studies in its earliest years, taught briefly at Notre Dame and Howard universities before spending a decade at Fordham University, and then moved in 1963 to UCLA's Center for Medieval and Renaissance Studies for the rest of his long career. He carved out reform as a distinct field of intellectual history and was always interested in the power of big, important ideas, unabashedly telling an audi-

2. Charles Homer Haskins, *The Renaissance of the Twelfth Century* (Cambridge, Mass.: Harvard University Press, 1927). Robert L. Benson and Giles Constable, eds., *Renaissance and Renewal in the Twelfth Century,* with Carol D. Lanham (Toronto: University of Toronto Press, 1982), especially xvii–xxx for their planning. For the Tierney celebration, see *The Church, the Councils, and Reform: The Legacy of the Fifteenth Century,* edited by Gerald Christianson, Thomas M. Izbicki, and Christopher M. Bellitto (Washington, D.C.: The Catholic University of America Press, 2008), taking as its launching point Brian Tierney, *Foundations of the Conciliar Theory: The Contribution of the Medieval Canonists from Gratian to the Great Schism* (Cambridge: Cambridge University Press, 1955; repr. 1968; rev. ed., Leiden: Brill, 1998). On the notion of a *festschrift* for a book, see *The Church, the Councils, and Reform,* ix.

3. For a review of Ladner's career and scholarly contributions, see the article by one of his students, John Van Engen, "Images and Ideas: The Achievements of Gerhart Burian Ladner, with a Bibliography of His Published Works," *Viator* 20 (1989), 85–115. Phillip H. Stump, another of Ladner's students, looked back at *The Idea of Reform* on the fortieth anniversary of its publication to examine its reception and impact: "The Influence of Gerhart Ladner's *The Idea of Reform,*" in *Reform and Renewal in the Middle Ages and the Renaissance: Studies in Honor of Louis Pascoe, S.J.,* edited by Thomas M. Izbicki and Christopher M. Bellitto (Leiden: Brill, 2000), 3–17.

ence in 1979, "Ideas have always made history and continue to do so." Witness, too, his presidential address for the American Catholic Historical Association of 1963, titled "Greatness in Medieval History," in which he proclaimed: "It is against the background of these two great supra-individual ideas and facts of Christian history: an ever precarious pilgrim-like terrestrial destiny and a nevertheless undaunted striving for a better and more Godlike order, that individual human greatness in the Middle Ages, from Gregory the Great to Dante, should be seen."[4]

Although trained as a historian, Ladner married rigid historical methodology with a theological framework. In *The Idea of Reform,* he carefully placed the Greek and Latin vocabulary of reform in its earliest context to identify the theme of reform as a central one for Christianity from the first days of the church's history. A primary insight resulting from Ladner's research is that for most of Christianity's first millennium, the idea of reform was almost exclusively personal and, indeed, theological and even spiritual at its very core: Christians seek to restore within themselves the *imago Dei,* according to which they were created but which was diminished by Adam's fall. The salvific action of Christ offers the means of restoring this lost God-image and, primarily in the Western tradition, actually enables a *reformatio in melius* that would transcend the state of human beings in the Garden of Eden. Ladner's study was more about these ideas, images, and theories than about applications, although we should note that *The Idea of Reform* was the first of two or three volumes that he envisioned but never completed, and he brought this study only up to the period of the early Middle Ages. His later articles did at times venture into the period of the High Middle Ages and into the realm of institutional reform. These articles were

4. Gerhart B. Ladner, "The Future of Medieval Studies," in *Memory and Promise: From the Special Convocation upon the Fiftieth Anniversary of the Pontifical Institute of Mediaeval Studies, 20 October 1979* (Toronto: Pontifical Institute of Mediaeval Studies, 1980), 15–25, with quotation at 23–24; Gerhart B. Ladner, "Greatness in Medieval History," *Catholic Historical Review* 50 (1964): 1–26, with quotation at 13.

collected and republished in a 1983 collection filling two volumes, *Images and Ideas in the Middle Ages: Selected Studies in History and Art,* a title that reminds us of his first interest in the iconography of power, a subject he treated throughout his career in addition to his work on the language of reform.[5]

However, while Ladner himself did not get too far into the subject of reform during the High and late Middle Ages or the early modern period, many others—and here we find a measure of his legacy—have picked up where he left off and followed his intentions, adapting them to other emerging fields of medieval history of the last half-century. Consequently, his UCLA doctoral students, some of whom provide reminiscences and assessments in Part I, among others have pushed *The Idea of Reform* forward in many directions, both chronologically (especially into the High and late Middle Ages) and in terms of breadth by looking more closely at reform praxis; at institutional as well as personal reform; at changing notions of reform in different contexts; and at reform's impact on church and civil structures, education, social and economic developments, religious orders, and lay spirituality.[6]

We deliberately did not ask our contributors to come either to praise or to bury Ladner. Some authors here build directly on Ladner; others diverge or disagree with him; still others use his work as a jumping-off point. Because we asked our contributors to reappraise his work with an open mind, a number offer quite pointed criticisms of Ladner's methodology, particularly of his definitions

5. Gerhart B. Ladner, *Images and Ideas in the Middle Ages: Selected Studies in History and Art,* 2 vols. (Rome: Edizioni di Storia e Letteratura, 1983).

6. For a brief history of the history of reform, see Christopher M. Bellitto, *Renewing Christianity: A History of Church Reform from Day One to Vatican II* (Mahwah, N.J.: Paulist Press, 2001), 3–6; for lengthier treatment, see Christopher M. Bellitto, "The Reform Context of the Great Western Schism: Successes, Failures, and Decisions Deferred," in *A Companion to the Great Western Schism* (1378–1417), edited by Joëlle Rollo-Koster and Thomas M. Izbicki (Leiden: Brill, 2009), 303–31; and Alberto Melloni, "Christianisme et réforme," in *Réformes. Comprehendre et comparer les religions,* edited by Pier Cesare Bori, Mohamed Haddad, and Alberto Melloni (Berlin: Lit Verlag, 2007), 37–63, in a volume whose other essays on the idea of reform in many religions bear further testimony to Ladner's impact.

of reform vocabulary, which some scholars in the years since *The Idea of Reform* first appeared have found imprecise, sterile, or distant from practical application. The diversity of approaches has hopefully produced a rich setting where voices do not so much compete with or contradict each other as engage in a complementary, enriching conversation. This we take as all to the good and in the spirit of free, cordial inquiry with which Ladner himself, ever the Viennese gentleman and scholar, pursued his studies. Without presuming to speak for him, it is clear that he intended to start a conversation with some preliminary and even contingent definitions and conclusions. It is likely that he never believed his own work would do anything more than contribute to that conversation; it does not appear that he intended his work to be an end, but the beginning. The fact that he kept working on reform until the end of his life nearly thirty-five years after *The Idea of Reform* was published demonstrates that he certainly did not think he had offered his—or anyone's—last word on the idea of reform.

Through their analysis of the medieval interplay of personal, ecclesiastical, and societal reforms, the scholars in this volume offer their own contributions to Ladner's great idea. It is, in fact, in this radically altered landscape from Hildebrand to Galileo that reform most intentionally spread beyond its intrapersonal focus of the patristic era (though without renouncing it) in order to tackle the practical needs of a fallen church and society. Part I begins, deliberately, with shorter comments from three of Ladner's doctoral students who followed in his tradition, albeit applying his guidance to their own evolving interests and eras of study. We asked them to consider what they learned from Ladner, how their thinking has cohered or diverged from their initial contact with his work, in what ways they might critique their own mentor, and what the future might hold for reform studies. In Part II we intersperse case studies, from the High and late Middle Ages through the early Reformation decades, with historiographical assessments and critiques of Ladner.

One of Ladner's legacies that many of the scholars in this volume continue to strongly reaffirm is the importance of philological precision with regard to reform terminology. Such a need is only compounded by the modern ubiquity of the term "reform" with its powerful rhetorical connotations and simultaneous lack of concrete, clear meaning. The presentist—and often partisan—implications of such tendencies are treated in the essays by Lester L. Field Jr., and William V. Hudon, who lament that some scholars and most popular media are satisfied with an imprecision that serves simply to reflect and reinforce their own worldviews rather than teaching us anything about the past. The tendency to see reform backward from the present rather than forward from the past (which is the only meaning that our historical protagonists could know) creates the glaring omission of personal reform from most historical narratives. William P. Hyland and Dennis D. Martin explore this topic in their studies of the fifteenth century. While it is true that the Middle Ages introduced the idea of reform into the ecclesial and social spheres, only a post-medieval writer could conceive of such reform severed from its personal roots. Such a presentist perspective not only misrepresents the true intentions of medieval reformers but, ironically, also impoverishes the potential richness of the idea of reform for the present. Fortunately, now more than ever such imprecision need not be the case. Indeed, the advent of computers and digital databases—especially those online—has given modern historians the ability to refine their understanding of medieval vocabulary across broad reaches of time and geography with a speed and facility unimaginable to previous generations—although even here, Ladner was a pioneer.

However, while Ladner's emphasis on philology is justly praised here, some of his particular conclusions have been subject to nuance and critique. Both Louis B. Pascoe, S.J., and Phillip H. Stump raise further questions about the boundaries between reform and similar concepts, such as renewal and conversion, which appear to be far less distinct in the historical sources than Ladner's careful taxonomy would indicate. One example is the firm line that Ladner attempts to draw between reform as process or narrative, and conversion, baptism, and penance as steps of that process. As Pascoe notes, the division ignores the often extended nature of these steps (especially conversion) and their ongoing effects in the Christian life (especially baptismal grace). All indicate a complex relationship that raises interesting questions as to who is the more active agent of reform: God, by granting grace, as proposed by the Greek fathers, or humans, accepting and acting with grace, as proposed by the Latin fathers. In the end, one is tempted to conclude that Ladner's taxonomy here is deeply influenced by a Tridentine formulation of the doctrine of justification and its neat though anachronistic separation of the various stages of the Christian life.

Perhaps the imprecise distinctions in the historical sources between reform and other terms for renewal and change can point us to another lesson. If, as Ladner believed, the idea of reform is a real and enduring agent in the Christian tradition, it might be more methodologically fruitful to search for the idea itself rather than merely the occurrence of the word *reform.* That is, perhaps what is most important is not the vessel (i.e., the word "reform"), but rather the contents of that vessel (that is, the idea that the word represents). Ladner details those contents; that is, he defines reform as "the idea of free, intentional and ever perfectible, multiple, prolonged, and ever repeated efforts by man to reassert and augment values preexistent in the spiritual-material compound of the world." In other words, reform must be consciously chosen; it must be the ongoing product of human and divine effort; and it must look to restore (and, in the West, to improve) on earth that which was lost in Eden but which still exists eternally. In this conception, reform is restoration, not invention or innovation. It is Ladner's primary thesis that this "idea" is the "the self-perpetuating core, the inner life spring of Christian tradition." Furthermore, if one might continue with his aquatic image, he asserts that the Pauline notion of the personal restoration of the image of Christ in the self is the headwater of this river that nourishes two millennia of the church. Only slowly, with the rise of intentional monastic communities, does this interior transformation get applied to successively larger segments of the social order, until one speaks of reform of church and society in the Gregorian era and beyond.[7]

The majority of the essays in this volume presume this narrative of *continuity with change* in the idea of reform, exploring tributaries that flow from the great headwaters into new and varied landscapes. The concept of continuity with change has implications not only for the medieval and early modern centuries, but also for the debates concerning Vatican II, particularly whether there was a hermeneutic of continuity and-or discontinuity at work at the council itself and in the subsequent decades of interpretation and implementation. From a High Medieval perspective, Ken A. Grant examines the major transition in reform language under Gregory VII, as the success of personal reform is suddenly made contingent on a paradigmatic reform of the *ecclesia*. Gregory VII was urging free and intentional change through human and divine effort, though the object to be restored (or created anew, according to critics) is the apostolic church, not just the soul-image of Eden and eternity. Likewise, Hyland shows how Premonstratensians at the fifteenth-century councils could work to reform the church according to an ancient model—but this time the model was the community of monastic charity as described in the Rule of St. Augustine.

One important benefit of this model of continuity with change

7. Ladner, *The Idea of Reform*, 35, 423–24. If, indeed, it is this idea that is primary rather than the word "reform," the historian has the tools to create a more useful taxonomy—one that includes certain items not actually called "reform" as part of the larger history of reform and one that excludes certain items called "reform" from that very history because they no longer meet the definition. Perhaps it is only with such a refocusing that we can clear up the terminological muddle caused by a very different set of modern meanings attached to a word with a long and rich history.

is that it enables us to see particular instances of reform in light of the long histories of reform ideals, images, and models—a perspective that acts as an important control on our interpretation. In his essay on Hus, C. Colt Anderson demonstrates conclusively that the modern tendency to label the Czech reformer a (semi-)Donatist is an anachronism. Instead, Hus stood squarely in the very common Gregorian tradition of denying priestly authority to simoniacal clergy, a position quite common in the medieval period and not one associated with a fifth-century heresy. Similarly, David Albertson's examination of Heymeric de Campo's conciliarism illuminates what would otherwise be a very obscure bit of numerical speculation by locating it within the Augustinian tradition of treating numbers as anagogic agents of the soul's reform. Inigo Bocken's analysis of Nicholas of Cusa shows how the period between his conciliarism and the *Reformatio generalis* is only seen as a period of "silence" on reform issues when one limits reform to institutional and social concerns. When reform is understood in its traditional light of personal restoration to God, Cusanus's writings of this period suddenly read as "how-to" manuals for a personal reform of vision that leads us back to God, who serves as the touchstone for a vision of reform, as well. Finally, the proliferation of Carthusian tracts for lay rulers, discussed by Martin, can itself be seen as part of an ongoing effort to apply the idea of reform to more areas of human life. Indeed, one would hope that the project of studying such an applied, mundane reform program may help us to understand more deeply the ways in which the term "reform" was transferred across time and into the world of secular discourse.

Such an emphasis on models and images of reform is one of the most enduring and useful legacies of Ladner's work, as such images and models are loaded with inherent meaning (for example, the ubiquitous images of birth and rebirth) that can highlight particular aspects of the idea of reform, while changes in the use of those models and images can serve to draw attention to transformations in the understanding of reform through time. Ann W. Astell's essay on Eucharistic memory discusses how developing sacramental theology in the Middle Ages provided one such model by representing a variety of images for personal transformation and regeneration that still shared an emphasis on the dynamic and generative relationship of Christ and the church. Likewise, the Augustinian model of the loving community brings with it a certain image of reform, such that the Constance oration discussed by Hyland urges church reform while completely ignoring any possible power struggle between pope and council. However, sometimes the presence of such models can serve to highlight radical difference as much as continuity. Perhaps this is nowhere clearer than in the quite different conceptions of the apostolic church current in the medieval period, as Gerald Christianson discusses in particular. To fail to take into account novelty, difference, change, and legitimate historical development in these models may present just as serious a historical problem as imprecise presentism. Indeed, the effort to recover the past raises an important caveat concerning the accuracy of historical knowledge and reconstruction: if a reformer is wrong about models such as the *ecclesia primitiva* of Acts and the church's first few centuries, then the reformer can be wrong when using or applying those models as guides for later periods of reform.

But we cannot mention the dangers of too great an emphasis on continuity without highlighting Michael Vargas's critique of this entire narrative of reform. In his study of fourteenth-century Dominican reformers, Vargas finds the Ladnerian model of a constant, underlying idea of reform to be too simplistic to explain reality: it tends to highlight simple, external causes of a crisis rather than complex, systemic issues that exist in all organizations; it tends to polarize the parties into right reformers and wrong resisters, instead of wrestling with the ambiguous and contradictory space in the middle; and it has difficulty taking into account reform programs that are in direct contradiction to one another, as one sees especially in the sixteenth century. However, perhaps the most significant issue for Vargas is Ladner's assumption that the idea of reform exists in reality. Such an assumption indeed goes beyond what the historical evidence can prove or refute, and Vargas's contrary position argues that there is no metahistorical constant; there are only the particulars of each historical context. Such a critique has profound implications for many questions. In particular, it removes any normative standard for judging reform in the past or the present. Ladner's concerns were not only with the ancient church but with its current expression, and his work has continued to be influential in modern reforming circles. Can one still speak of true or false reform if reform has no essential characteristics?[8] It is unlikely—and, for that reason, rightly or wrongly, it is also unlikely that abandoning reform as a metahistorical category will ever be a completely dominant idea in the field.

Although the authors in this volume offer many other insights that might serve as lessons for us, perhaps the place to conclude is with the current need for synthesis. Whether one assumes, with Ladner, an Aristotelian view that the idea of reform has a metahistorical reality or, with Vargas, a nominalist view that reform is a label given to an endless stream of particulars, the fact is that a succession of Christian writers, preachers, and politicians have shared a common Christian culture and language that, despite significant changes in its history, includes among its most prevalent and powerful concepts the idea of reform. Ladner provided a historical narrative for the idea of reform in its first five centuries, and his intellectual descendants have done much to continue parts of the story through the end of the Middle Ages. However, while much has been learned in the last fifty years of reform scholarship, little has made its way into the larger historical discourse, which remains vitiated by oversimplification and anachronism. The most immediate task for historians of reform is to counter this false narrative with one

8. Yves Congar, *Vraie et fausse réforme dans l'Eglise*, rev. 2nd ed. (Paris: Editions du Cerf, 1968).

that is true—or at least as true as the provisional conclusions of history will allow. And that daunting task will require a new grand synthesis, since the antidote to a false narrative can never be simply more and more true details. Historians must provide a narrative of reform that incorporates all the complexities and nuances of recent scholarship. Gerhart Ladner's enduring legacy is the foundation of this enterprise. It is our inheritance—and our responsibility—to continue the conversation he started.

I

GERHART LADNER'S *THE IDEA OF REFORM* AFTER 50 YEARS

2

MY DEBT TO GERD

His Legacy as Teacher of History and Historian of Ideas, Fifty Years after *The Idea of Reform* and in Light of Present Research

LESTER L. FIELD JR.

What did I learn from Ladner? Having taken his last course on "The Medieval Idea of Reform," a course that he taught as an emeritus in 1980, and having served many years as his research assistant, I learned much from him both in class and in gathering material for his various projects, including his second and uncompleted volume on reform. I learned even more when he read the manuscript of my first book, on the patristic idea of *libertas*.[1] In research not very far removed from that book, or more precisely its subtitle, I am now

1. Lester L. Field Jr., *Liberty, Dominion, and the Two Swords: On the Origins of Western Political Theology (180–398)*, Publications in Medieval Studies 28, edited by John Van Engen (Notre Dame, London: University of Notre Dame Press, 1998), esp. xiii–xviii. See also Lester L. Field Jr., *My Response to T. D. Barnes: Positivistic Straw Arguments Do Not Review Books*, 2nd ed. (University, Miss.: J. D. Williams Library, 2009); Lester L. Field Jr., *On the Communion of Damasus and Meletius: Fourth-Century Synodal Formulae in the Codex Veronensis LX, with Critical Edition and Translation*, Studies and Texts 145 (Toronto: Pontifical Institute of Mediaeval Studies, 2004), esp. 93n155.

working on a book-length history of "political theology" as an analytical category. Since Erik Peterson, Ernst H. Kantorowicz, and Ladner himself historiographically pioneered its use,[2] I might well recast my initial question: "what am I still learning from Ladner?" As I explore the historiographical foundations, reception, and significance of his work, my research has made me ever more aware of my own methodological debt to him. His legacy as a teacher and as a scholar pertains to living experience as well as historical data. As a graduate student, I first read *The Idea of Reform* three decades ago. Now after many more readings and trips to archives, I realize that its research and writing also have a history—one that needs recounting, however briefly or anecdotally here.

I already knew of Ladner's close friendship with Kantorowicz but soon discovered that Kantorowicz and Peterson had also befriended one another in Rome.[3] More importantly, I later found a letter, dated 17 November 1952, from Ladner to Peterson, whose work on "monotheism as a political problem" Kantorowicz greatly admired and Ladner regarded as "fundamental."[4] Reverentially saluting Peterson, a fellow Catholic convert and fellow exile, Ladner wrote:

> I allow myself to send, enclosed, an essay of mine, which is a preliminary study for a book, the first extensive volume of which is complete. It would be of the greatest value to me—particularly in view of the book—to know

2. See, for example, Lester L. Field Jr., "Christendom before Europe? A Historiographical Analysis of 'Political Theology' in Late Antiquity," in *Plenitude of Power: The Doctrines and Exercise of Authority in the Middle Ages. Essays in Memory of Robert Louis Benson*, edited by Robert C. Figueira, Church, Faith and Culture in the Medieval West (Aldershot, U.K. and Burlington, Vt.: Ashgate, 2006), 141–70.

3. Gerhart B. Ladner, *Erinnerungen*, edited by Herwig Wolfram and Walter Pohl, Österreichische Akademie der Wissenschaften, Philosophisch-historische Klasse, Sitzungsberichte 617 (Vienna: Verlag der Österreichische Akademie der Wissenschaften, 1994), 11, 32–41, 47, 69–70; Barbara Nichtweiss, *Erik Peterson: Neue Sicht auf Leben und Werk*. 2nd ed. (Freiburg im Breisgau, Basel, Vienna: Herder, 1994), 872.

4. Gerhart B. Ladner, *The Idea of Reform: Its Impact on Christian Thought and Action in the Age of the Fathers* (Cambridge, Mass.: Harvard University Press, 1959), 267n114, citing Erik Peterson, "Monotheismus als politisches Problem," *Theologische Traktate* (Munich: Küsel-Verlag, 1951), 41–147. For Ladner's letter, I must thank Turin's Biblioteca "Erik Peterson," which granted me access to Peterson's unpublished papers and correspondence.

what you think of the essay and to have your critique. In the previous summer, I was in Austria and the Rhineland but unfortunately could not come to Rome. I have visited Father Josef Grisar in Trier, and, perhaps through him, you know of the request, which I now submit to you. As you will see from the essay, it is my endeavor to trace the idea, which establishes the foundation for the reform-movements of the Middle Ages, back to the New Testament and before all to patristics. Professor Ernst Robert Curtius, to whom I owe many fruitful critical comments, regards this fundamental view as wrong. I have now again in September discussed this with him in Bonn (we know one another since he was in Princeton at the same time as I). Yet I still believe as always that it is right to seek the roots of the medieval reform-idea there, where I seek it.[5]

Peterson likely knew Grisar, who taught at the Gregorianum. At least by reputation, Peterson had known Ladner since the 1930s[6] but

5. Translated in part in the text above, Ladner's letter to Erik Peterson, dated "17 November 1952," begins with the salutation, "Sehr verehrter Herr Professor!" and is quoted in full in Lester L. Field Jr., "Erik Peterson und Gerhart B. Ladner: 'Politische Theologie' und 'Reform,'" *Erik Peterson: Die theologische Präsenz eines Outsiders*, edited by Giancarlo Caronello (Berlin: Duncker und Humblot, 2012), 581–96 at 583. With respect to the "essay" or *Aufsatz* that Ladner's letter mentioned, I now think—despite the absence of an offprint in Turin's archive—that Ladner sent his article: Gerhart B. Ladner, "Die mittelalterliche Reform-Idee und ihr Verhältnis zur Idee der Renaissance," *Mitteilungen des Intstituts für Österreichischen Geschichtsforschung* 60 (1952): 33–59; republished in Gerhart B. Ladner, *Images and Ideas in the Middle Ages: Selected Studies in History and Art*, 2 vols., Storia e letteratura: Raccolta di Studi e Testi 155–56 (Rome: Edizioni di storia e letteratura, 1983), 2.559–93, 1030. Cf. Field, "Christendom before Europe?" 160n70.

6. For the following postcard (RW 265-10931), in which Erik Peterson criticized the anti-Semitism, paganism, and anachronism of *Der Leviathan* by his former friend Carl Schmitt, I must thank the Landesarchiv Nordrhein-Westfalen, Haupstaatsarchiv Düsseldorf for granting me access to the unpublished correspondence between Peterson and Schmitt. See Peterson, Postcard to Schmitt, July 13, 1938:

"Lieber Herr Schmitt!

Habe Ihr Buch sofort gelesen. Die Ausführungen über das Verspeisen des Leviathan bei Juden scheinen mir irrig zu sein. Grade die Frage nach dem koscheren Fleisch hört beim Leviathan auf und Leviathan = koscheres Heidenfleisch scheint mir unbelegt zu sein. Der von Ihnen beifällig zitierte Ladner ist Jude. Hobbes muss die Gleichung: Leviathan = Staat bei seinen kirchlichen Gegnern vorgefunden haben, die Apoc. 13 in dem Sinne interpretierten, dass das Tier = Reich des Antichristen ist. Mit der Staatstheorie scheint mir der Leviathan nichts zu tun zu haben. Die Staatslehre müsste beim 'grossen Menschen' und beim 'alter deus' einsetzen. Das sind doch Begriffe aus der Platonischen Kosmologie, die nicht beweisen, dass Hobbes den Staat zum Gott machen musste (p. 49), sondern nur die Fragwürdigkeit des 'Monotheismus' zeigen. Die typisch judenchristliche 'Aufspaltung der politischen Einheit' (p. 21), scheint mir auf ein Wort Jesu zurückzugehen

had also entered his own last and busiest decade[7] and—whatever his affinities with Ladner's work[8] or misgivings concerning it[9]—sent no critique worthy of mention in Ladner's "Preface," which, by contrast, did thank Curtius.[10]

---

und die Polemik gegen die potestas indirecta hat nur dann einen Sinn, wenn man darauf verzichtet, ein Christ zu sein und sich für das Heidentum entschieden hat.

Mit bestem Gruss

Ihr E.P."

Cf. Carl Schmitt, *Der Leviathan in der Staatslehre des Thomas Hobbes: Sinn und Fehlschlag eines politischen Symbols*, 2nd ed. (Cologne: Hohenheim, 1982), 83 n1, citing Gerhart B. Ladner, *Theologie und Politik vor dem Investiturstreit: Abendmahlstreit, Kirchenreform, Cluni und Heinrich III.* (Baden, 1936, repr. Darmstadt: Wissenschaftliche Buchgesellschaft, 1968), 25, 46–47. See Barbara Nichtweiss, "Apokalpyptische Verfassungslehre: Carl Schmitt im Horizont der Theologie Erik Petersons," in *Die eigentlich katholische Verschärfung … Konfession, Theologie und Politik im Werk Carl Schmitts*, edited by Bernd Wacker (Munich: W. Fink, 1994), 37–64, esp. 57–58, 60–62 (cf. n100); Micha Brumlik, "Carl Schmitts theologisch-politischer Antijudaismus," in *Die eigentlich katholische Verschärfung*, 247–56; György Geréby, "Carl Schmitt and Erik Peterson on the Problem of Political Theology: A Footnote to Kantorowicz," in *Monotheistic Kingship: The Medieval Variants*, edited by Aziz Al-Azmeh and János M. Bak (Budapest: CEU Press, 2004), 31–61. Though Peterson's Roman residence in the 1930s and association with the Pontificio Istituto di Archeologia Cristiana overlapped Ladner's, neither I nor any other student of Ladner remember his mentioning personal contact. See also Ladner, *Erinnerungen*, 50–62.

7. Nichtweiss, *Erik Peterson*, esp. 896–903. Peterson died in 1960.

8. Like Peterson, for example, Ladner regarded "political theology" as the secularization of "Christian 'imperialists.'" See Ladner, *The Idea of Reform*, 118–31, esp. nn44–46, 66–67.

9. Peterson's distrust for any historical *Entwicklung* as theologically significant kept him, unlike Ladner and Kantorowicz, from writing any monumental history. Ladner's article of 1952 cited neither Peterson's teacher, Richard Reitzenstein, who noted use of *reformatio, reformari, regneratio*, and *renasci* in the mystery religions, nor Peterson himself. Ladner ("Die mittelalterliche Reform-Idee," 580–81n88) nonetheless cited Wilhelm Kamlah and Werner Bieder, who both had criticized Peterson. See Nichtweiss, *Erik Peterson*, 6–7, 188n165, 300–305, 365–66, 478–80, 497, 505, 523, 569, 574, 752 n250, 774; Richard Reitzenstein, *Die hellenistischen Mysterienreligionen*, 3rd ed. (Leipzig/Berlin: B. G. Teubner, 1927). Without reference to Peterson's review and criticism of Edgar Salin, *Civitas Dei* (Tübingen: Mohr, 1926) in *Schmollers Jahrbuch* 50 (1926), 174–76, Ladner likewise cited Salin. Briefly anticipated where Ladner ("Die mittelalterliche Reform-Idee," 574–75) discussed Augustine's theology of the Trinity, a later footnote of particularly breathtaking erudition cited orthodox texts that redefined μία ἀρχή as Trinitarian and so qualified Peterson's otherwise magisterial demonstration of Nicene orthodoxy's destruction of μοναρχία. See Ladner, *The Idea of Reform*, 81–82n76; see also 89–90, 197–203; Field, *On the Communion of Damasus and Meletius*, 52–53, esp. note 75.

10. Peterson may have alerted Ladner to the *Physiologus* and a forthcoming article on the subject, which fascinated Ladner for the rest of his life. See Erik Peterson, "Die Spiritualität des griechischen Physiologus," *Byzantinische Zeitschrift* 47 (1954): 60–72; Ladner,

Curtius died in 1956 and so never saw *The Idea of Reform* in print. Although Ladner's conversations with him do not survive, methodological fault-lines not only divided but also defined the common ground of Ladner's and Curtius's scholarship. Though mapping them all, and in any detail, exceeds the scale of this examination, some seem particularly noteworthy. Like Ladner, Curtius attributed much to "the Latin continuity of the Middle Ages." Since no literature could "be absolutely isolated" from interpretation, philosophy, and history, Curtius's "phenomenology of literature" provided "a universal standpoint.... afforded by Latinity." Philology seemed "the foundation of all historical investigation." Like Ladner, then, Curtius heuristically distinguished renaissance and reform but, unlike Ladner, contested any enduring phenomenological identity. Both noted discrete discursive constructions linking *translatio imperii* and *translatio studii* to *renovatio.* Curtius even recognized "the phenomenon of rejuvenation" in the topos of the church as rejuvenated old woman, but Ladner showed that *reformatio ad imaginem dei* had linked beginning and end and so, in terms of past self-understanding, had pertained to the economy of salvation. Curtius had regarded creation *ad imaginem suam* as pertaining to God as *artifex* or *ideator mundi* but had ignored God as *reformator. Emendatio*—sometimes a synonym for *reformatio,* as Ladner showed—had an ancient foundation in grammar.[11]

The Idea of Reform, 314–15, 447n21; Gerhart B. Ladner, *God, Cosmos, and Humankind: The World of Early Christian Symbolism,* translated by Thomas Dunlap (Berkeley, Los Angeles, London: University of California Press, 1995), esp. 121–31. The first edition of *The Idea of Reform* missed what the second edition (499) described as "the important article by E. Peterson, 'L'immagine di Dio in S. Ireneo,' *La Scuola Cattolica* LXIX (1941) 46 ff." Ladner's heuristic "image-likeness" conveys the εἰκών or *imago* and ὁμοίωσις or *similitudo* in Genesis 1:26. 1 Cor. 11:7, 2 Cor. 4:4, Col. 1:15 used only εἰκών. James 3:9 used only ὁμοίωσις, which Plato had used to denote human assimilation to God. For Irenaean and subsequent use—especially as Ladner defined it, relative to others—see Field, *Liberty, Dominion, and the Two Swords,* 4–12, 269–76.

11. Ladner, *The Idea of Reform,* esp. 15n35, 17–18, 41n9, 91n35, 149n75, 299–301, 332n10, 415n62. Cf. Ernst Robert Curtius, *European Literature and the Latin Middle Ages,* translated by Willard R. Trask, Bollingen Series 36 (N.Y.: Pantheon Books, 1953), viii–x, 7–9, 28–30, 47–48, 64–78, 101–5, 384–85, 405–6, 439, 544–46, 587, 589, 594, 597. Cf. also Ernst Robert Curtius, "Zur Literarästhetik des Mittelalters II." *Zeitschrift für romanische Philologie* 58 (1938): 129–232, esp. 135–45, 197–99.

Given the grammatical origins and character of *historia*, Curtius, like Kantorowicz, asserted its precise but ultimately fictive character, that is, as narrative, but Ladner balanced this insight with the realism of *Historismus*—without converting to it. Since historicists from Ranke through Troeltsch had overtly simplified a "past" reality for present consumption, Ladner, Peterson, Kantorowicz, and Curtius all resisted this anachronistic reductionism and so variously analyzed a past constructed in its own language and ideological complexity.[12] Attesting to decades of collaboration, Ladner's "Preface" also thanked Kantorowicz: Ladner had himself influenced Kantorowicz's work on the "king's two bodies," so that it cross-pollinated Ladner's study. Peterson's work on "political theology" had likewise influenced Kantorowicz, whose work on the medieval "body politic" and "body natural" demonstrated their emergence as juristic secularizations of the "body of Christ," originally unique to Jesus but—by his own institution in the Eucharist—liturgically present in the historical church.[13] Since even in antiquity this body had corresponded to what Christians regarded as their ἐκκλησία, their "political assembly,"[14] Peterson, Kantorowicz, and Ladner all variously

12. Curtius, *European Literature and the Latin Middle Ages*, esp. vii–ix, 7–8, 11–15, 19, 56, 69–71, 79–105, 159–62, 436–40, 450–57, 495–500, 588–97; Ladner, *The Idea of Reform*, esp. 433–35; Otto Gerhard Oexle, "Krise des Historismus—Krise der Wirklichkeit: Eine Problemgeschichte der Moderne," *Krise des Historismus—Krise der Wirklichkeit: Wissenschaft, Kunst und Literatur 1880–1932*, edited by Otto Gerhard Oexle, Veröffentlichen des Max-Planck Instituts für Geschichte 228 (Göttingen: Vandenhoeck & Ruprecht, 2007), 11–116; Otto Gerhard Oexle, *Geschichtswissenschaft im Zeichen des Historismus: Studien zu Problemgeschichten der Moderne*, Kritische Studien zur Geschichtswissenschaft 116 (Göttingen:Vandenhoeck & Ruprecht, 1996); Joseph Mali, "'Mythenshau': Die Geschichtsphilosophie von Ernst H. Kantorowicz," in *Geschichtskörper: Zur Aktualität von Ernst H. Kantorowicz*, edited by Wolfgang Ernst and Cornelia Vismann (Munich: Wilhelm Fink Verlag, 1998), 31–46; Charles R. Bambach, *Heidegger, Dilthey, and the Crisis of Historicism* (Ithaca/London: Cornell University Press, 1995).

13. Ladner, *The Idea of Reform*, ix, xi; Ernst H. Kantorowicz, *The King's Two Bodies: A Study in Mediaeval Political Theology* (Princeton: Princeton University Press, 1957), esp. 524–25 repeatedly cited Ladner, especially his essay-length prolegomena to *The Idea of Reform*.

14. Ladner, *The Idea of Reform*, 275–76n144 citing Erik Peterson, "Von den Engeln" and "Die Kirche," *Theologische Traktate*, 323–407, 409–29 at 328–30, 422–23.

examined the public historicity of the church as well as its ancient corporate self-understandings, later secularized in the Middle Ages.

Given these public, liturgical, historical, institutional, even "political," contexts, my research into the interrelated methodologies and phenomenologies of these three historians sheds light on a historiographical problem: Ladner also followed Odo Casel, who had challenged Peterson's view of mysticism as an internalization of the public μυστήρια or sacraments, and so early favored a "personal" over a liturgical paradigm for understanding reform.[15] The heuristic utility of this distinction, which Ladner immediately and increasingly qualified, also derived from his notion of the "personal," which he never essentialized—and not just because "essence," as such, defies historical change and specificity. On the one hand, no theology seemed "private" as *opposed* to "public." Citing Peterson, for example, Ladner noted that the supposedly "'private' devotion" of the Crucifixion "in the Christian east" matched "the 'public' triumphal ... conception of the Cross."[16] Irenaeus of Lyon had likewise defined "the return to Paradise simply and without qualification as membership

15. Ladner, *The Idea of Reform*, 1n2 (on "cosmic aspects" not personal), 104–7; Nichtweiss, *Erik Peterson*, esp. 411–26. Cf. Odo Casel, *Das christliche Kultmysterium*, 2nd ed. (Regensburg: F. Pustet, 1935); also Odo Casel, "Art und Sinn der ältesten christlichen Osterfeier," *Jahrbuch für Liturgiewissenschaft* 14 (1938): 1–78, esp. 51, cited by Ladner (*The Idea of Reform*, 153n1). "A mystical theology," Ladner (82) nonetheless cautioned, "such as that developed by the Greek Fathers may fall short of the individual experiences of the mystic, but it may transcend them through its supra-individual significance." Later Ladner placed Casel's "deep symbolic notion of the 'Christian cult mystery'....above all" in "the Christocentric liturgy with its sacraments that culminated in the Eucharist"—even if it "encompassed God, the cosmos, and humankind" as "symbol and reality." See Ladner, *God, Cosmos, and Humankind*, 3. Citing Peterson and Kantorowicz, Ladner (*The Idea of Reform*, 284–318, esp. 299n7, 447n23) early regarded the liturgy and the sacramental theology derived from it, as well as conciliar affirmation of (other) normative praxis, as important and enduring fonts of reform. See Erik Peterson, *ΕΙΣ ΘΕΟΣ: Epigraphische, formgeschichtliche und religionsgeschichtliche Untersuchungen*, Forschungen zur Religion und Literatur des Alten und Neuen Testaments 24 (Göttingen: Vandenhoeck & Ruprecht, 1926), esp. 146–52; Ernst H. Kantorowicz, *Laudes Regiae: A Study of Liturgical Acclamations and Medieval Ruler Worship* (Berkeley/Los Angeles: University of California Press, 1946), esp. 68–76.

16. Erik Peterson, "La croce e la preghiera verso oriente," *Ephemerides liturgicae* 59 (1945): 52–68; Ladner, *The Idea of Reform*, 153, 155n9, also (on θεολογία) 98–105, 115–16, 330–40.

in the Church.... and for Origen, baptism" meant "entry into Paradise, namely into the Church."[17] Thus the Eucharist as well as the liturgy and the scripture that had historically flowed from it remained an important font for "reform"[18]—for the change (μεταβολή), as Basil of Caesarea put it, that made a citizen of the heavenly πολιτεία.[19]

On the other hand, Ladner placed his notion of the "personal" within Ferdinand Tönnies' distinction between *Gemeinschaft* and *Gesellschaft*, or, more precisely, within *Gemeinschaft*, which Ladner called "a supra-individual and supra-political community."[20] Since the earliest Latin theologies linked *reformatio* to baptismal regeneration, Ladner regarded reform as "a supra-individual force."[21] In

17. Ladner, *The Idea of Reform*, 70; for (heavenly) church as Kingdom or City of God, see 29, 116–18, 245–83.

18. Ladner, *The Idea of Reform*, 32, 98n59, 280–81, 285–315. See also the second edition, 494–95. Cf. Robert Markus, "Church Reform and Society in Late Antiquity," in *Reforming the Church before Modernity: Patterns, Problems and Approaches*, edited by Christopher M. Bellitto, Louis I. Hamilton, Church, Faith and Culture in the Medieval West (Aldershot, U.K./Burlington, Vt.: Ashgate, 2005), 3–19, esp. 3. For the institutional emergence, historical validation, and ecclesiastical canonization of scripture from the Eucharist, which provided the public forum for reading what Justin Martyr called "the memoirs of the apostles and the writings of the prophets," see Justin Martyr, *Apologia maior*, 65–67, edited by Miroslav Marcovich, *Apologiae pro Christianis* Patristische Texte und Studien 38 (Berlin/New York: Walter de Gruyter, 1994), 125–30; Field, *Liberty, Dominion, and the Two Swords*, 34, 293–94; François Bovon and Enrico Norelli, "Dal Kerygma al canone: Lo statuto degli scritti neotestamentari nel secondo secolo," *Cristianesimo nella storia* 15 (1994): 525–40; Romano Penna, "L'origine de *Corpus Paulinum*: Alcuni aspetti della questione," *Cristianesimo nella storia* 15 (1994): 577–607, esp. 585–89; Thomas J. Talley, "Word and Sacrament in the Primitive Eucharist," in *Eulogema: Studies in Honor of Robert Taft, S.J.*, edited by Ephrem Carr et al. Studia Anselmiana 110, Analecta liturgica 17 (Rome: Pontificio Ateneo S. Anselmo, 1993), 497–510, esp. 510.

19. Basil of Caesarea, *De spiritu sancto* 19.49, edited and translated by Benoît Pruche, *Sur le Saint-Esprit*, Sources chrétiennes 17bis, 2nd ed. (Paris: Éditions du Cerf, 1968), 420; Ladner, *The Idea of Reform*, 80.

20. Gerhart B. Ladner, "The Future of Medieval Studies," in *Memory and Promise: From the Special Convocation upon the Fiftieth Anniversary of the Pontifical Institute of Mediaeval Studies, 20 October 1979* (Toronto: Pontifical Institute of Mediaeval Studies, 1980), 15–25 at 16–17; Ladner, *Erinnerungen*, 47; John Van Engen, "Images and Ideas: The Achievements of Gerhart Burian Ladner, with a Bibliography of His Published Works," *Viator* 20 (1989): 85–115 at 91–92, 95–98.

21. Ladner, *The Idea of Reform*, 2–4 (2 for quotation), 32, 44–47, 61–62, 82, 128–31, 135, 319–424. For heuristic reasons, I use the nominal, rather than verbal, form here. Similarly in fourth century asceticism, the baptismal παλιγγενεσία and ἀνακαίνωσις of Titus 3:5

terms of historicity, then, "personal reform" emerged as a Ladnerian description, not a patristic explanation. Nor did *reformatio personalis* emerge, even in the late Middle Ages.[22] This did not occur even as a function of the fractured spiritualities that for well over a century floated in the demographic, economic, intellectual, theological, political, and ecclesiastical wake of the Black Death.[23] Personal *curiositas* and theological *singularitas*, Jean Gerson noted, impeded rather than aided *reformatio*. Pierre d'Ailly likewise located and internalized reform *in* the mystical Body of Christ.[24]

Concerning Ladner's legacy as a teacher and a scholar, on a number of levels these observations highlight another historiographical quirk. On the one hand, as Ladner's students can attest, "Ladner's *Idea of Reform* has had its most concentrated impact among scholars working in the area of late medieval reform"—all the more so, as others had framed the "medieval church ... between the early

---

had proliferated into ἀνακαινισμός and ἀναπλάσσειν, and, in the fifth century, entering the monastic state even warranted honorific description as μυστήριον, that is, as a second baptism. The West similarly valorized monastic life as *conversio*.

22. Nicolas de Clamages never used the expression. Cf. Christopher M. Bellitto, *Nicolas de Clamanges: Spirituality, Personal Reform, and Pastoral Renewal on the Eve of the Reformations* (Washington, D.C.: The Catholic University of America Press, 2001), esp. 59–90. Cf. also John M. Headley, "Introduction," in *San Carlo Borromeo: Catholic Reform and Ecclesiastical Politics in the Second Half of the Sixteenth Century*, edited by John M. Headley, John B. Tomaro (Washington, D.C.: Folger Shakespeare Library, 1988), 11–30 at 30n3. See Gerhart Niemeyer, "What Is Political Knowledge?" *Review of Politics* 23 (1961): 101–7 at 105–7; Johannes Helmrath, "Reform als Thema der Konzilien des Spätmittelalters," in *Christian Unity: The Council of Ferrara-Florence, 1438/39–1989*, edited by Giuseppe Alberigo, Bibliotheca ephemeridum theologicarum lovanensis 97 (Louvain: Leuven University Press, 1991), 75–152, esp. 93; Giles Constable, *The Reformation of the Twelfth Century* (Cambridge: Cambridge University Press, 1996), 3, 125.

23. Saverio Xeres, *La chiesa, corpo inquieto: Duemila anni di storia soto il segno della riforma*, Collana "In cammino" (Milan: Ancora, 2003), 107–56, esp. 131–32; Johannes Helmrath, *Das Basler Konzil, 1431–1449: Forschungsstand und Probleme* (Cologne: Böhlau, 1987), 327–52; Heiko A. Oberman, "From Occam to Luther: A Survey of Recent Historical Studies on the Religious Thought of the 14th and 15th Centuries," *Concilium* 17 (1966), 122–32; Ladner, "Mittelalterliche Reform-Idee," 590–93.

24. Louis B. Pascoe, *Jean Gerson: Principles of Church Reform*, Studies in Medieval and Reformation Thought 7 (Leiden: Brill, 1973), esp. 99–109; Louis B. Pascoe, *Church and Reform: Bishops, Theologians, and Canon Lawyers in the Thought of Pierre d'Ailly (1351–1420)* Studies in Medieval and Reformation Traditions 105 (Leiden: Brill, 2005), esp. 140–56.

church and reform."[25] On the other hand, one eminent patrologist notes Ladner's "little known but immensely important book." Another cites but then ignores it.[26] With respect to research into late antiquity and the Middle Ages, this disparity of influence comes with methodological and historiographical consequences. Although knowledge of Ladner's work has generally enriched studies by medievalists, ignorance of it has often impoverished the work of patrologists and late-Romanists. As Ladner, Kantorowicz, Peterson, and Curtius variously noted, ideas—whether past or present—do not exist independent of their expression. By avoiding a rigorously philological path, however, many patrologists and late-Romanists not only ignore the recombinant topoi that Ladner discovered but also ignore *past* self-understandings. Now lost on divergent paths paved with facile generalizations, an incoherent historiography not only evades specific uses of *reformatio* or related topoi but, having lost sight of them, also fails to reach any consensus about "reform," even as a presentism. As commonplace categories belie those of the past and, in the absence of historiographical engagement, one another,[27] one positivist even argues a "Constantinian Reformation" on the basis of *The Oxford English Dictionary*'s definition of "Reformation"![28]

25. Phillip H. Stump, "The Influence of Gerhart Ladner's *The Idea of Reform*," *Reform and Renewal in the Middle Ages and the Renaissance: Studies in Honor of Louis Pascoe, S.J.*, edited by Thomas M. Izbicki and Christopher M. Bellitto, Studies in the History of Christian Thought 96 (Leiden, Boston, Cologne: Brill, 2000), 3–17, esp. 17; John Van Engen, "The Future of Medieval Church History," *Church History* 71 (2002): 492–522, esp. 495.

26. Andrew Louth, *The Origins of Christian Mystical Tradition from Plato to Dionysius* (Oxford: Clarendon Press; New York: Oxford University Press, 1983), 136. Cf. Markus, "Church Reform and Society in Late Antiquity," 3.

27. Cf. Markus, "Church Reform and Society in Late Antiquity"; Rita Lizzi Testa, "Clerical Hierarchy and Imperial Legislation in Late Antiquity: The Reformed Reformers," in *Reforming the Church before Modernity*, edited by Bellitto and Hamilton, 87–103; Claire Sotinel, "The Church in the Roman Empire: Changes without Reform and Reforms without Change," in *Reforming the Church*, 155–72. Cf. also Wayne J. Hankey, "Self and Cosmos in Becoming Deiform: Neoplatonic Paradigms for Reform by Self-Knowledge from Augustine to Aquinas," in *Reforming the Church*, 39–60.

28. Cf. T. D. Barnes, "The Constantinian Reformation," in *Ernst Crake Memorial*

Others, who have followed a philological path, have nonetheless modified some of Ladner's findings. As I have suggested elsewhere, this modification rarely seems more than nuance. In some cases, however, it instructively reexamines pivotal moments in patristic tradition. To Irenaeus, for example, and in a way that Ladner hardly denied, the Incarnation did not *respond* to original sin, which somehow surprised God, but rather fulfilled his primordial intent. Assuming and assumed by his created εἰκών, however, the divine Λόγος summarized God's ὁμοίωσις—his original and final likeness or communion with humanity. In a way that modifies Ladner's conclusions, then, Paul Mattei and Réné Braun have noted how Tertullian had carefully glossed this salvific "summary" (ἀνακεφαλαίωσις), which fulfilled creation—that is, for the first time. By the same token, Tertullian's translation as *recapitulatio* imparted an iterative nuance.[29] *Renovatio* similarly nuanced ἀνακαίνωσις, and *reformatio* recast the full "transformation" of μεταμόρφωσις as "forming *again*."[30]

In *this* respect, Tertullian's *reformatio in melius*, as opposed to Augustine's, more closely *resembled* the Greek.[31] Conversely, one

Lectures 1984 (Sackville, New Brunswick: Crake Institute, 1986), 39–57; T. D. Barnes, "Was There a Constantinian Revolution?" *Journal of Late Antiquity* 2 (2009): 374–84, esp. 380–83. Ostensibly "to eschew polemic" against "ignorance, inaccuracy, misunderstanding, or blind refusal to abandon positions which have become untenable," Barnes ignored the work of Ladner, Peterson, and Kantorowicz. Cf. T. D. Barnes, *Constantine and Eusebius* (Cambridge, Mass.: Harvard University Press, 1981), esp. v–vi. See Ernst. H. Kantorowicz, "*Deus per naturam, Deus per gratiam*: A Note on Medieval Political Theology," *Selected Studies* (Locust Valley, N.Y.: J J. Augustin, 1965), 121–37; Field, "Christendom before Europe?" On positivism, see Ladner, *The Idea of Reform*, 428, 434–42.

29. Tertullian, *De monogamia* 5.2, edited and translated by Paul Mattei, *Le mariage unique*, Sources chrétiennes 343 (Paris: Éditions du Cerf, 1988), 148: "ad caput, id est ad initium reciprocare." See also Mattei's commentary, esp. 86n1, 250; Field, *Liberty, Dominion, and the Two Swords*, 4–12, 269–76; Réné Braun, *Deus christianorum: Recherches sur le vocabulaire doctrinale de Tertullien*, 2nd ed. (Paris: Études augustiniennes, 1977), 518. Cf. Ladner, *The Idea of Reform*, 68–70.

30. Cf. Ladner, *The Idea of Reform*, esp. 3, 63. See also 32, 40–47, 54–59, 83–107, 319–424. Cf. Rom. 12:2, 2 Cor. 3:18, Phil. 3:21. Similarly the pre-Christian term *renovatio* translated ἀνακαίνωσις or ἀνανέωσις in Eph. 4:23, Col. 3:10, 2 Cor. 4:16, and Titus 3:5, and *restitutio* translated ἀποκατάστασις in Mt. 17:11, Mark 9:12, Acts 1:6 and 3:21.

31. Cf. Ladner, *The Idea of Reform*, 46–48, 134–185, 377. After translation, real differences remained and grew. See Field, *Liberty, Dominion, and the Two Swords*, esp. 12, 187.

could even argue that the East never had an idea of *re*-form. In any case, moral and spiritual progress was always in the church, because it was always already Christological and eschatological. In the East it appeared in history defined by Christomimetic boundaries of monastic withdrawal from the world and imperial rule of the world.[32] In the West, as Ladner noted, "Both the Civitas Dei and the Ecclesia" remained "'social' ideas,"[33] so that every "private" imitation of Christ entailed a "social logic," again in the church.[34] For much of the Middle Ages, then, these ecclesiastical or patristic contexts defined the idea of reform. As Ladner himself discovered, however, Renaissance secularizations and vernacular-cognate pluralizations of *reformatio* not only began in the late Middle Ages but also inspired humanist attempts to re-Christianize it.[35]

Since his scholarship evinces his teaching and so reinforces what I learned from him in person, some important "lessons" bear special

32. Ladner, *The Idea of Reform,* esp. 107–52. As John Chrysostom attested, empire and church on earth already seemed radically identical. See Field, *Liberty, Dominion, and the Two Swords,* esp. 232–34, 253–56. Ladner (125, 298–320) not only recognized conciliar ἀνανέωσις or *renovatio,* which entailed an imperial summons but also noted the ways in which imperial acclamations found their way into the liturgy and protocols of the councils themselves. For the influence of Peterson and Kantorowicz, see 299n7, 447n23; Peterson, ΕΙΣ ΘΕΟΣ, 146–52; Kantorowicz, *Laudes Regiae,* esp. 68–76; Kantorowicz, *The King's Two Bodies,* 275–84.

33. Ladner, *The Idea of Reform,* 270. See also 274–77 (n144 for debt to Peterson).

34. Ladner, *The Idea of Reform,* 26, citing Gabriel de Tarde, *La logique sociale* (Paris: F. Alcan, 1895); Gabriel de Tarde, *Les lois de l'imitation: Étude sociologique,* 2nd ed. (Paris: F. Alcan, 1895); Gabriel de Tarde, *Les transformations du pouvoir* (Paris: F. Alcan, 1899). See also Gabrielle M. Spiegel, *The Past as Text: Theory and Practice of Medieval Historiography* (Baltimore, London: Johns Hopkins University Press, 1997), xvii–xix, 3–28, 44–56, 160. Ancient conversion seemed preeminently penitential, so that "conversion taken as an individual or collective act could never be more than a preparation." For ἐπιστροφή and penitential μετάνοια as *conversio* and its connection to "rebirth," see Ladner, 49–51, 377.

35. Gerhart B. Ladner, "Reform: Innovation and Tradition in Medieval Christendom," *Images and Ideas in the Middle Ages,* 2.533–58, 1030 at 552; Gerhart B. Ladner, "Vegetation Symbolism and the Concept of Renaissance," *Images and Ideas in the Middle Ages,* 2.727–73, 1033–35, 1046, at 727–28; Gerhart B. Ladner, "Religious Renewal and Ethnic-Social Pressures as Forms of Life in Christian History," in *Theology of Renewal,* edited by L. K. Shook, 2 vols. (N.Y.: Palm Publishers, 1968), 2.328–57, at 342–53; Gerhart B. Ladner, "La concezione dell'amore e della bellezza nel rinascimento italiano e la riforma cattolica," *Rivista di storia della chiesa in Italia* 40 (1986): 342–70, esp. 347, 359–70.

mention here. Methodology matters. Socially, ideas make history, even in present interpretations. Since ideas motivated, explained, and informed social action, the rhetoric of reform nonetheless signaled intentions without which any so-called "reform" remains a later judgment. Such a judgment hardly pertains to extant sources contemporary with the event that they explained, that is, in their own terms, but rather pertains to a description made after the "fact," often long after it. Whatever "reform" was socially, the past as a phenomenon survives only in its own language, itself neither private nor universal, unless, as Curtius noted, the universe pertains to its Latinity, Hellenism, or vernacularism. In Curtius's words, the past treasure philologically defies "conversion to a common currency," so that only "bartering" remains to the historian. In Ladner's words, "historical conceptions ... do not affect the phenomena as introspection does in psychology," so that "historical complementarity" neither conflates a past and a present "truth" nor reduces the one to the other. Since discrete propositions construct both past and present truths, no historical reality exists ready-made. It emerges in an interpretation. By the same token, absolutizing an interpretation as *the* historical reality ignores its philological and phenomenological limitations. It either rhetorically masks an anachronism or arrogantly postulates a transhistorical, transperspectival, metalinguistic, antihistoriographical "accuracy." Methodologically incompetent or dishonest, this still pervasive malapropism, which Ladner assiduously avoided, evades the question: "accurate" by what measure, or whose? Of limited scientific utility in quantifying natural objects and of no historiographical utility in qualifying linguistic artifacts, "accuracy" ignores what Ladner described as the "Intrusion of the Observer" or the "cut" that observers as subjects make between themselves and their "object, the *existence* of which remains a logical necessity."[36]

36. See, for example, Ladner, *The Idea of Reform*, esp. 435–37, 442; Ladner, "Future," 17–25; Curtius, *European Literature and the Latin Middle Ages*, 596–97; Field, "Christendom before Europe?"

Neither totalizing an understanding nor reducing it to a psychologism, Ladner's moderate realism rejected such objectivism and subjectivism not just as extremes of idealism and nominalism, but as presentisms. The very hermeneutics that facilitated the linguistically constructed past differed significantly from those of the interpreting present, for which the historian also remains accountable. To meet hermeneutical challenges—premodern, modern, and postmodern—Ladner's methodology evolved, but these defining insights already evident in *The Idea of Reform* not only endured but also flourished, refreshed and renewed periodically by serious engagement with other methodologies. The case for the linguistically extant past and present interpretation—mutually dependent, without confusion or separation—remains as compelling today as when Ladner made it. Little wonder that, over a vast array of fields and interests, his work not only survives the test of time but also, given current needs, now seems urgently important. "In such conditions," writes Averil Cameron, even without reference to Ladner, "to study the actual spread of ideas and social practices becomes the most pressing need for us as historians." As Hayden White saw it, "the whole of history is the history of thought."[37]

37. Helmrath, "Reform als Thema," esp. 90; Averil Cameron, "The Perception of Crisis," *Morfologie sociali e culturali in Europa fra tarda antichità e alto medievo, 3–9 aprile 1997, 1*, Settimane di studio del Centro italiano di studi sull'alto medioevo 45 (Spoleto: Presso La sede del Centro, 1998), 9–34 at 12; Hayden White, quoted and interviewed in Ewa Domańska, *Encounters: Philosophy of History after Postmodernism* (Charlottesville/London: University of Virginia Press, 1998), 30; Phillip H. Stump, "Influence."

3

GERHART LADNER'S *THE IDEA OF REFORM*

Reflections on Terminology and Ideology

LOUIS B. PASCOE, S.J.

After the Bible and *The Spiritual Exercises of St. Ignatius of Loyola*, the book that has probably most influenced me is Gerhart B. Ladner's *The Idea of Reform*.[1] I first met Ladner during the 1956–1957 academic year at Fordham University, when, as a young Jesuit scholastic in philosophical studies, I was also pursuing a master's degree in medieval history. Ladner later was a reader for my master's thesis on "St. Bernard of Clairvaux: The Doctrine of the *Imago* and Its Relationship to Cistercian Monasticism." While I was doing theological studies from 1961 to 1965, Ladner accepted a teaching position at UCLA and there was little doubt in my mind where I would be doing my doctoral studies. During my years at UCLA, from 1966 to

1. Gerhart B. Ladner, *The Idea of Reform: Its Impact on Christian Thought and Action in the Age of the Fathers* (Cambridge, Mass.: Harvard University Press, 1959; reprint with additions, New York: Harper Torchbooks, 1967).

1970, I participated in Ladner's medieval lecture and seminar courses; under his guidance as mentor, I wrote my doctoral dissertation on Jean Gerson's theory of reform.[2]

During his ten years at Fordham, 1952–1962, Ladner produced his ground-breaking study on the idea of reform, whose publication in 1959 this volume is celebrating. The reviews of Ladner's work were, as one would expect, highly laudatory and revealed little substantial criticism of any of the three parts of his book, namely, "Varieties of Renewal Ideology and the Christian Idea of Reform," "The Early Christian Idea of Reform," and "Monasticism as a Vehicle of the Christian Idea of Reform in the Age of the Fathers." Ladner's book and subsequent articles on reform have indeed engendered a distinctive school of scholarly research and writing.[3]

Before beginning my reflections, I would like to make clear that they will concentrate primarily upon the first part of his book, namely, "Varieties of Renewal Ideology and the Christian Idea of Reform."[4] This part of the book is primarily concerned with terminological and ideological categories related to renewal and reform. I was surprised that this part of Ladner's book did not engender more discussion in the scholarly reviews because of its foundational nature. While this part of his book and indeed the entire work concentrated primarily on individual and personal reform, my own reflections will not be so restricted; toward the end of the article, I will touch upon institutional reform as well. I will not, however, be dealing with the first excursus of the book which treats the epistemological dimension of the idea of reform.[5]

2. For the life and scholarly achievements of Gerhart Ladner see the article by John Van Engen, "Images and Ideas: The Achievements of Gerhart Burian Ladner with a Bibliography of His Published Works," *Viator* 20 (1989), 85–115. For Ladner's obituary see *Speculum* 71 (1996), 802–4.

3. On the influence of Ladner's book see the article by Philip Stump, "The Influence of Gerhart B. Ladner's *The Idea of Reform*," in *The Idea of Reform and Renewal in the Middle Ages and Renaissance*, edited by Thomas M. Izbicki and Christopher M. Bellitto (Leiden: Brill, 2000), 3–17.

4. Ladner, *The Idea of Reform*, 9–35.

5. Ibid., 427–32. By this dimension, I mean the question of whether or not one can

As we begin our analysis of the first part of Ladner's work, it will help greatly to recall his description of the various forms of renewal and his definition of the idea of reform. Ladner saw the idea of reform as a variant of the broader idea of renewal, which in turn was itself a variant of the even broader concepts of alteration, change, and becoming. In a sense, then, the ideas of renewal and reform can be seen as species within the genus of alteration, change, and becoming. Ladner did not deal much with the broader notions of alteration, change, and becoming but regarded his immediate task as that of describing the various types of renewal ideologies and their specific characteristics, especially noting the characteristics in each type that were incompatible with Christianity. As a result of his analysis, Ladner developed his understanding of the idea of reform, which he regarded as distinctively Christian in origin, development, and content.

Ladner began his study of renewal ideas by distinguishing four major categories of renewal ideologies that manifested themselves in the ancient and early Christian world. First in his enumeration was cosmological renewal, which he described as "perpetual, cyclical recurrences of identical or similar situations and events," and which manifested themselves in such forms as "The World Year," "The Golden Age," and diverse "Historical Ages" and "Empires." Ladner saw the deterministic dimensions inherent in such ideas as contrary to the Christian concept of personal freedom.[6] He designated a second category of renewal ideas as vitalistic since it was based on analogies to reproduction and growth in vegetative, animal, and human life. In his analysis of this category, he maintained

formulate such an idea from the disparate data available to us or whether such an idea, once formulated, ever truly relates to reality. This problem was indeed a pressing one in the historical profession at the time Ladner's book was written and has indeed intensified up to our own day. Suffice it to say that I share in Ladner's essential confidence in the Aristotelian-Thomistic theory of knowledge as well as in the confidence of human reason so admirably expressed by John Paul II in his 1998 encyclical, "Fides et Ratio," and which Benedict XVI has made a major theme of his pontificate.

6. Ibid., 10–16.

that such analogies failed to account for the Christian dimension of rational intentionality.[7] The third category of renewal ideas that Ladner delineated related to millenarian ideas, which also included messianic and utopian ideas of absolute or total perfection. By its emphasis upon total perfectibility, this category of renewal ideas, he maintained, went contrary to the Christian experience of "ineradicable terrestrial imperfection" and the belief in only a "relative perfectibility" in this life.[8] The fourth category of renewal ideas Ladner associated with the experiences of conversion, baptism, and penance. Since he regarded such experiences as primarily unique, instantaneous, and nonrepeatable, he distinguished them from the idea of reform.[9]

After delineating and analyzing the various forms of renewal, Ladner then formulated his well-known definition of reform. Reform, he maintained, was the "free, intentional, and ever perfectible, multiple, prolonged, and ever repeated efforts by man to reassert and augment values pre-existent in the spiritual-material compound of the world."[10] Ladner was well aware that the distinction between reform and renewal was not absolute because cosmological, vitalistic, and millenarian ideology and symbolism could and often were historically combined and interwoven with the idea of reform. In such cases, however, he argued that the distinctive dimensions of the idea of reform remained predominant. Finally, it must be emphasized that in insisting upon the Christian origin and dimensions of the idea of reform, Ladner was not unaware of adumbrations of that idea in the pre-Christian Greek and Roman worlds, but he regarded their manifestations as minor compared to the more compelling evidence from the Christian world.[11]

After our review of Ladner's views on renewal and reform, some personal reflection is necessary. First, I would say that Ladner's dis-

7. Ibid., 16–26.
8. Ibid., 27–31.
9. Ibid., 32–34.
10. Ibid., 35.
11. Ibid., 9.

tinction of renewal and reform ideas from the broader concepts of alteration, change, and becoming still impresses me as valid. My major area of intellectual uneasiness arises from the fact that, although Ladner discussed four major categories of renewal ideas, he did not sufficiently elaborate a more abstract definition of renewal in itself, either before or after his analysis. Thus, while there is a clear delineation of the idea of *reform*, there is no sufficiently elaborated definition of the idea of *renewal*. Furthermore, what he designated as renewal ideas are not so much ideas as metaphorical, symbolical, or analogical ways in which renewal manifested itself in early Christian thought. While this judgment is applicable in some degree to cosmological and millenarian renewal, it is especially the case with vitalistic renewal. This tendency in Ladner's approach to renewal is understandable given his early interest in early Christian art and symbolism, an interest manifested throughout his career, especially in his monumental work on papal iconography and in his final work on early Christian symbolism.[12] It must be said, however, that in a later article Ladner somewhat modified his categories of alteration, change, and becoming in terms of restoration, reform, rebellion, and renaissance, thereby clarifying renewal more in the sense of restoration.[13]

Another aspect of Ladner's views on renewal ideas that has received little attention in scholarly circles is his position with regard to conversion, baptism, and penance. As will be recalled, Ladner,

12. On this point see Gerhart B. Ladner, *Die Päpstbildnisse des Altertums und des Mittelalters*, 3 vols. (Vatican City: Pontificio Istituto di Archeologia Cristiana, 1941–1984), and Gerhart B. Ladner, *Handbook der frühchristlichen Symbolik: Gott, Kosmos, Mensch* (Stuttgart: Belser, 1992), English translation by Thomas Dunlop, *God, Cosmos, and Humankind* (Berkeley: University of California Press, 1995).

13. See Gerhart B. Ladner, "Terms and Ideas of Renewal in the Twelfth Century" in *Renaissance and Renewal in the Twelfth Century,* edited by Robert L. Benson and Giles Constable (Cambridge, Mass.: Harvard University Press, 1982), 1–33. This article and many articles of Ladner have been republished and at times updated by him in *Images and Ideas in the Middle Ages: Selected Studies in History and Art*, 2 vols. (Rome: Storia e Letteratura, 1983). Future references to the articles in this collection will be cited by the number of the article in the collection, its pagination as well as the pagination of the addenda et corrigenda. The above article is at *Images and Ideas in the Middle Ages: Selected Studies,* 29:687–726, 1032–33.

while recognizing their close relationship with the idea of reform, nevertheless kept them within the category of renewal. The basic reason he gave for not associating them with reform was that he regarded them as essentially instantaneous, unique, and nonrepeatable experiences and therefore incompatible with the notions of prolongation, multiplicity, and repetition that he ascribed to the idea of reform. The reasons Ladner gave for not including conversion, baptism, and penance in the category of reform deserve closer examination. Here, Ladner's initial judgment loses something of its strength when one considers more closely the theological dimensions of these activities.

With regard to conversion and penance, although Ladner admitted the ever repeatability of postbaptismal conversion, he did not sufficiently take into account the often gradual and prolonged stages of preparation leading up to prebaptismal conversion, stages especially evident in the lives of many prominent converts such as Augustine.[14] Even in the case of postbaptismal conversion, there is need for greater appreciation of its multiple, prolonged and ever repeatable dimensions. Clearly, conversion in its fullest sense is a lifetime process, as was implied in the Benedictine vow of *conversatio morum* (fidelity to monastic life) and made more explicit in the Franciscan understanding of conversion as a continuing process of new beginnings.[15] Understood in this context, conversion is closely associated with the idea of penance taken in its nonsacramental sense. Ladner, however, is more sensitive to this process as it relates to penance in its sacramental context, especially with regard to the decline in nonrepeatable public penance in the early Church and

14. See especially Augustine's *Confessions*, Bks. 3–8.

15. *Regula Sancti Benedicti*, 58:17–18, edited by Timothy Fry, *The Rule of St. Benedict in Latin and English with Notes* (Collegeville, Minn.: Liturgical Press, 1981), 268–69. For a survey of the various interpretations of the phrase "*conversio morum*," see 459–63. For the Franciscan view of conversion as a continual process of reform see Michael Phelps, "A Study of Renewal Ideas in the Writings of the Early Franciscans" (Ph.D. diss., University of California at Los Angeles, 1972), 63–68, 135–36. This dissertation was written under Ladner's supervision.

the gradual rise in the phenomenon of ever-repeatable private confession. Yet even here, he sees these actions more as unique starts in the long process of reform.

Baptism, while unique, instantaneous, and nonrepeatable, not only makes its recipients Christians but simultaneously provides them with sanctifying grace and the accessibility to the other sacramental sources of grace. Baptism is also a *reformatio in melius*, for the spiritual life infused into the soul at baptism is no longer the life of our first parents in paradise but the life of the resurrected and glorified Christ.[16] The grace of baptism is not therefore something static but essentially reformative and the dynamic basis for all later personal reform. Given the continued, augmentative, and ameliorative dimensions of baptism, I would personally see it as belonging more to the domain of reform than renewal. The same would necessarily be true of the parallel activities of conversion and penance.

With regard to Ladner's definition of reform, the somewhat ponderous and obscure phrase relating to the "spiritual-material compound of the world," requires some clarification. Ladner was indeed conscious of the highly compact nature of this phrase but said very little to describe its specific dimensions.[17] Among the multiform dimensions of this phrase, there is not only the issue of religious faith but there are also the distinctive elements of that faith and how they dynamically interrelate with one another. Included in these elements are the questions of original and personal sin. Ladner's definition of reform with its emphasis upon "ever perfectible, multiple, prolonged, and ever repeated efforts by man," is indeed the result of the limitations placed on human nature as a consequence of origi-

16. For patristic and especially Augustinian views on *reformatio in melius*, see Ladner, *The Idea of Reform*, 153–67. See also Ladner's earlier article on "St. Augustine's Conception of the Reformation of Man to the Image of God," in *Augustinus Magister* (Paris: Etudes augustiniennes, 1954), 867–78, *Images and Ideas in the Middle Ages: Selected Studies*, 25:595–608, 1030.

17. See Gerhart B. Ladner, *The Idea of Reform*, 433–42. In this excursus, Ladner acknowledges the theological, philosophical, and ideological preconceptions that relate to the validity of the idea of reform and to the different parts of that idea.

nal and personal sin. Another closely related element implied in the phrase "spiritual-material compound of the world" is the reformative role of the theological virtues of faith, hope, and charity. Also implied in the phrase are the reformative consequences of Word and Sacrament. While Ladner in his *The Idea of Reform* and subsequent articles did not develop to any significant degree the reform dimensions of Word and Sacrament, the seminal nature of these works have indeed opened up these relatively neglected areas of reform ideology. Finally, the reference in the definition of reform only to the "efforts by man" carries with it a slightly Pelagian tint. Obviously such was not Ladner's intent, for the limitations of human efforts and the need for grace are reasonably well treated in the later chapters of Ladner's book dealing with reform ideology in the patristic and early medieval periods. Perhaps the definition of reform should be slightly revised to read: "human efforts in conjunction with divine grace to reassert and augment spiritual values."

As a believer and theologically reflective person, Ladner was, indeed, fully aware of the complex dimensions implied in his use of the phrases "spiritual-material compound of the world" and "efforts by man." His primary goal, however, at the time of his research and writing of *The Idea of Reform* was to place that idea with its Christian roots within the broader context of the history of ideas which, together with its interdisciplinary methodology, enjoyed such considerable popularity in the mid twentieth century scholarly circles both in Europe and America. Although it is important to specify the faith elements implied in the phrases "spiritual-material compound of the world," and "efforts by man," it is also important to realize that in identifying these elements there will always be considerable debate as to the details of those elements and their interaction. Such indeed was the case in the patristic and medieval periods; the question became even more complex with the Protestant Reformation.

Another dimension of reform that has to be considered is the need to distinguish between true and false reform ideologies not only on the personal but also on the institutional level.[18] In the case of false ideologies, such aberrations can be caused by a variety of factors, especially past personal experiences, inaccurate understanding of the historical past and its models, and the excessive influence of contemporary ideologies. Reform ideologies that are true may also lead to false results because of subsequent misinterpretations and applications. Even in the case of true ideologies there is the need to discern and appreciate the frequent difference between reform ideology and its actual realization, or what one prominent scholar has called "the gap between the rhetoric and the reality."[19] Reformers are generally convinced that their reforms are fully realizable, but such is rarely the case.

Despite all our efforts to distinguish renewal and reform terminologies, we must be realistic and recognize that contemporary society and scholarship often use these terms interchangeably. Both terms are often employed in a restorative, augmentative, or ameliorative context or a combination thereof. The same interchangeability in terminology with regard to renewal and reform can also be found in our historical sources. More recent scholarly attempts to impose clearer terminological distinctions upon historical sources have also failed.[20] Perhaps the best we can do in studying and categorizing renewal and reform terms and ideologies within the Christian tradition is to make sure that whatever term is used embodies the essential Christian characteristics that Ladner delineated in his

18. On this point see Yves Congar, O.P., *Vraie et fausse réforme dans l'Eglise*, rev. 2nd ed. (Paris: Editions du Cerf, 1968). English translation by Paul Philibert, O.P., *True and False Reform in the Church* (Collegeville, Minn.: Liturgical Press, 2011).

19. Giles Constable, *The Reformation of the Twelfth Century* (Cambridge: Cambridge University Press, 1996), 125–67. What I would call the idea and models reform, Constable prefers to designate as "the rhetoric of reform," not so much in the pejorative sense of the present day usage but more to bring out the difference between the ideal striven for and the reality attained.

20. For a succinct discussion of this problem see Giles Constable, "Renewal and Reform in Religious Life: Concepts and Realities," in *Renaissance and Renewal in the Twelfth Century*, edited by Robert L. Benson and Giles Constable (Cambridge, Mass.: Harvard University Press, 1982), 37n1.

definition of reform: freedom, intentionality, ever perfectibility, and multiple, prolonged, and ever-repeated efforts to reassert and augment Christian values.

While Ladner's book dealt mainly with personal reform in the patristic period, much of that ideology, as his subsequent articles show, continued to influence later ideologies of personal reform in the medieval and modern periods of church history. As these articles also indicate, personal reform ideologies were adapted and applied to institutional reform within the church. Such indeed was the case with regard to monastic, mendicant, and canonical reform, to papal, episcopal, priestly, and lay reform, and to the whole church as institution.[21] While Ladner claims that the idea of reform, as he defines it, was originally a Christian creation and phenomenon, we must also recognize that it influenced other, more secular dimensions and institutions of Western civilization. This influence is especially the case in the field of medieval history wherein that ideology also influenced notions of imperial and nationalistic reform, the establishment of urban centers and their legislative procedures, as well as educational institutions such as monastic and cathedral schools and the universities, especially with regard to their educational theory, curricula, faculty, and administration.

In the light of the extensive influence of Christian ideas of reform and renewal within these institutions and their gradual secularization in the modern world, it might be better to incorporate ideas of renewal and reform within broader, more concrete, more contemporary, and therefore more recognizable categories, such as social, economic, political, religious, intellectual, scientific, literary, artistic, and architectural. Admittedly these categories are not as easily distinguishable in early Christian and medieval cultures as they are in today's modern culture, but there is clearly sufficient

21. Gerhart B. Ladner, "Reformatio," in *Ecumenical Dialogue at Harvard: The Roman Catholic-Protestant Colloquium* (Cambridge. Mass.: Harvard University Press, 1964), 172–90, *Images and Ideas in the Middle Ages: Selected Studies*, 22:519–531, 1030.

intellectual evidence in those earlier cultures for the employment of such categories. Only then can we delineate the strictly religious realm of reform and renewal ideologies as well as see their influence and interaction with the more secular ideologies of society. By adopting such a categorization we will be able to realize more fully the extensive contribution of Ladner's *The Idea of Reform*.

4

THE CONTINUING RELEVANCE OF *THE IDEA OF REFORM*

PHILLIP H. STUMP

In 1999, on the occasion of the fortieth anniversary of the publication of *The Idea of Reform,* I wrote about the multifaceted influence of Gerhart Ladner's classic book.[1] Since that time I have become even more convinced of the continuing relevance of his study for scholars investigating reform and related ideas of renewal in all eras. Those who have come to love *The Idea of Reform* have frequently lamented that Ladner was not able to complete his goal of publishing subsequent volumes that would trace the story through the rest of the Middle Ages. However, in recent years two fine studies, both influenced by Ladner, have surveyed the main lines of this story. Alberto Melloni relied primarily on Ladner for the patristic reform ideas in his sweeping history of Christian reform that appeared as a chapter in a volume comparing ideas of reform in different religious tradi-

1. Phillip H. Stump, "The Influence of Gerhart Ladner's *The Idea of Reform,*" in *Reform and Renewal in the Middle Ages and the Renaissance: Studies in Honor of Louis Pascoe, S.J.*, edited by Thomas Izbicki and Christopher Bellitto (Leiden: Brill, 2000).

tions.[2] Christopher Bellitto's book-length survey of Christian renewal similarly applies the method and insights of Ladner to an analysis of all the eras of Christian reform.[3] In addition to such sweeping treatments of the history of reform, there are a number of excellent recent studies of reform in its successive epochs up through the Renaissance. I will argue that among these studies, those which have drunk at the Ladnerian well have benefitted in two principal ways: (1) They have appreciated the continuing and profound influence of the biblical and patristic reform ideas on later reform ideology; and (2) they have applied three of the great strengths of Ladner's methodology—its focus on leading ideas or conceptions of reform, its close attention to reform terminology and imagery, and its clear distinction between reform and other ideas of renewal. In addition, I hope to identify a number of areas in which further research would be beneficial and would benefit from Ladner's approach, and also to mention, where appropriate, some of the manifold ways in which Ladner influenced my own development as a scholar and student of reform.

EARLY AND HIGH MEDIEVAL REFORM

In his survey of Christian renewal, Christopher Bellitto argues that the Carolingian and Gregorian Reforms both had a "top-down" character, an effort to impose reform from above, and he suggests convincingly that many of the changes made by both represent more "formation" than "reformation."[4] A recent study of Chrodegang of Metz by M. A. Claussen sheds interesting light on this tension between "forming" and "reforming."[5] His study in fact starts

2. Alberto Melloni, "Christianisme et réforme," in *Réformes: Comprendre et comparer les religions*, edited by Pier Cesare Bori, et al., Christianity and History 4 (Berlin: Lit Verlag, 2007), 37–63.

3. Christopher M. Bellitto, *Renewing Christianity: A History of Church Reform from Day One to Vatican II* (Mahwah, N.J.: Paulist Press, 2001).

4. Ibid., 90.

5. M. A. Claussen, *The Reform of the Frankish Church: Chrodegang of Metz and the "Regula canonicorum" in the Eighth Century* (Cambridge: Cambridge University Press, 2004), 1–3.

with a consideration of Ladner's *The Idea of Reform*, and he argues that while in the modern era reform generally refers to an improvement, without reference to the past, in the Middle Ages reform almost always connoted an attempt to "recapture something which has been lost." But the Carolingian reformers did not always find the past "usable" and so would often take a "pre-existing tradition [and change it] to produce a new text and a new kind of tradition." It is interesting that in doing so Chrodegang and other Carolingian reformers abandoned vibrant traditions and practices of their own time in order to reintroduce customs that they chose to believe had originated in Rome.[6] The "top-down" nature of the Gregorian reform has led Bellito and other scholars to characterize it as a revolution rather than a reform.

Such scholars have also pointed to the sometimes negative effects of the movement. Among the negative effects examined in several recent studies is the negative impact on women.[7] These studies argue, for example, that the reformers' concerns for the sexual purity of clerical men were often accompanied by negative views of women. Such unintended negative consequences of reform movements, especially the accompanying oppression of groups marginalized by the reforms, are just coming to the attention of historians, and much more work needs to be done in this area. An analogous instance is the close connection between reform and attacks on witchcraft in the fifteenth-century Dominican reformer Johannes Nider, analyzed recently by Michael Bailey.[8]

6. Ibid., 161.

7. See Bruce Vernarde, *Women's Monasticism and Medieval Society: Nunneries in France and England, 890–1215* (Ithaca, N.Y.: Cornell University Press, 1997), 160–65; and Penelope Johnson, *Equal in Monastic Profession: Religious Women in Medieval France* (Chicago: University of Chicago Press, 1991), 257.

8. Michael Bailey, *Battling Demons: Witchcraft, Heresy, and Reform in the Late Middle Ages* (University Park, Pa.: Pennsylvania State University Press, 2003). Bailey cites Ladner's *The Idea of Reform* in his bibliography and Christopher M. Bellitto's study, *Nicolas de Clamanges: Spirituality, Personal Reform and Pastoral Renewal on the Eve of the Reformations* (Washington, D.C.: The Catholic University of America Press, 2001), 60–73, for evidence of the reform concept of the *via purgativa* of adversity.

Quite a different light is shed on the relationship between women and reform in Fiona Griffiths' new study of Herrad of Landsberg, abbess of a house of Augustinian canonesses in the twelfth century.[9] Griffiths' study, strongly influenced by Ladner's *The Idea of Reform* and by his methodology, cites Herrad as an example of religious women not negatively influenced by the reform and in fact strong supporters of it.[10] Herrad's *Hortus deliciarum* is a manual of reform for her nuns, who are to reform themselves by avoiding the negative examples of male clergy.[11] In place of negative images of women Herrad often offered biting visual and textual critiques and satires of male clergy for their avarice and simony.[12]

Griffiths also points to the importance of the Augustinian monastic rule, by which Herrad's canonesses lived. (The Augustinian Rule, unlike the Benedictine, has separate male and female versions.)[13] Ladner viewed Augustinian monasticism as a primary vehicle for the transmission of reform to the Middle Ages, and he strongly emphasized the importance of Augustine's idea of the monasticization of the clergy.[14] The role of the Augustinian Rule in medieval reform movements is a topic that merits further research. It was important not only for the Augustinian canons and canonesses, but also for mendicant orders, especially the Dominicans and the Augustinian hermits, and for the Augustinian observant movements of the later Middle Ages and the Windesheim canons who were linked to the Devotio Moderna.[15]

9. Fiona Griffiths, *The Garden of Delights: Reform and Renaissance for Women in the Twelfth Century* (Philadelphia: University of Pennsylvania Press, 2007).

10. Ibid., 10–12.

11. Ibid., 194–212.

12. Ladner was very fond of Herrad of Landsberg's *Hortus deliciarum* and brought reproductions of this work to show his students in his course on medieval symbolism.

13. Griffiths, *The Garden of Delights*, 35. Griffiths also points to the "shared involvement of both men and women in many Augustinian communities."

14. Ladner, *The Idea of Reform*, 350–65, 378–85.

15. William Hyland has spoken with me about the importance of the Augustinian Rule for reform in all these contexts; Ladner's work on Augustinian monasticism led him to consider this continuity. Hyland's analysis of a reform sermon from the Council of

Important recent work has explored twelfth-century reform in Ladnerian fashion by investigating specific links between its individual and institutional dimensions and between reform conceptions and concrete reform measures. Bellitto has explored the main themes beautifully in his book, *Renewing Christianity*.[16] The fundamental study for twelfth century monastic reforms is now Giles Constable's *The Reformation of the Twelfth Century*.[17] Deeply influenced by Ladner, Constable consistently linked institutional reform to individual reform, and ideas to actions. Further research is urgently needed to explore such links, especially in the thirteenth-century reforms, above all the reforms of the mendicants. An important recent study of the reforming activity of a Franciscan archbishop of Rouen in the thirteenth century is an example of an illuminating analysis of practical reform measures without any consideration of accompanying terminology or ideology of reform.[18]

LATE MEDIEVAL REFORM

The reform era most investigated in recent years using Ladner's method is the later Middle Ages. Even though he himself wrote little about late-medieval reform, Ladner encouraged his students to study it, and he often stressed in lectures and personal conversations the deep need for reform in the later Middle Ages, sharing with us the preliminary investigations he had made, especially concerning conciliar reform. Strongly influenced by Etienne Gilson's views, Ladner believed that the disintegration of the high medieval synthesis of faith and reason, divine and natural law, posed serious challenges for late medieval reformers. Gilson had associated the breakdown with

Basel shows how strongly he has been influenced by *The Idea of Reform*. See William Hyland, "The Incarnation, Reform and the Unity of the Church: a Sermon of Master Johannes Wifflet O.Praem. for the Feast of the Annunciation at the Council of Basel (1432)," *Analecta Praemonstratensia* 83 (2007): 156–71.

16. Bellitto, *Renewing Christianity*, 63–93.

17. Giles Constable, *The Reformation of the Twelfth Century* (Cambridge: Cambridge University Press, 1996).

18. Adam Davis, *The Holy Bureaucrat: Eudes Rigaud and Religious Reform in Thirteenth-century Normandy* (Ithaca, N.Y.: Cornell University Press, 2006).

the *via moderna* of William of Ockham and his followers.[19] Ladner was, however, aware of Heiko Oberman's more nuanced interpretations of the *via moderna*,[20] and I believe it was partly for this reason that he recommended I study at Professor Oberman's *Institut für Spätmittelalter und Reformation* in Tübingen, while working on my dissertation. In turn, Oberman was more aware of the relevance of Ladner's work to late medieval reform than many German scholars of his generation. More recently, a new generation of German scholars, above all Johannes Helmrath, has benefited greatly from Ladner's approach, both directly and through studies published by American scholars of the "Ladner school" such as Louis Pascoe, S.J.

Pascoe's studies of the great conciliarists Jean Gerson and Pierre d'Ailly focused in Ladnerian manner on their reform conceptions and terminology. Pascoe was able to demonstrate the importance of ideas of hierarchy for Gerson and in this way to offer a serious challenge to earlier works that had painted the conciliar reformers as radical, laicist, or even democratic theorists. Rather than a movement that sought to reform the papacy "from below," the conciliarism of mainstream reformers like Gerson was a hierarchical reform that proceeded downward, from head to members; and the council, since it represented the entire hierarchy of the church, played a leading role and also a corrective role, when the other levels in the hierarchy were lacking.[21] Pascoe's recent study of Pierre d'Ailly similarly seeks to relate d'Ailly's conceptions of reform both to the concrete reforms he proposed as well as to legislation deliberated and enacted at the Council of Constance (1414–1418).[22]

It is only by juxtaposing concrete reform measures with the ide-

19. Gerhart B. Ladner, "Reform: Innovation and Tradition in Medieval Christendom," in *Theology and Law in Islam*, edited by Gustave E. von Grunebaum, 53–73 (Wiesbaden: Harrassowitz, 1971), repr. in *Ideas and Images in the Middle Ages: Selected Studies in History and Art*, 2 vols. (Rome: Edizione di storia e letteratura, 1983), 2:533–558 at 556–557.

20. Ladner, "Reform: Innovation and Tradition," 556n72.

21. Louis B. Pascoe, S.J., *Jean Gerson: Principles of Church Reform* (Leiden: Brill, 1973), 22–39.

22. Louis B. Pascoe, S.J., *Church and Reform: Bishops, Theologians and Canon Lawyers in the Thought of Pierre d'Ailly (1351–1420)* (Leiden: Brill, 2005).

ology of reform that we can begin to analyze the results of these reforms. This ideology needs to be analyzed in Ladnerian fashion, using close philological analysis of reform terms in their contexts, and with due consideration for the long history of the reform concepts. Only such analysis promises any hope of understanding the reforms from the viewpoint of contemporaries. In my own study of the Constance reforms I had similarly tried to juxtapose reform ideas with concrete reforms. I argued that the Constance reforms were more successful than historians have usually allowed and that lack of success was more often the result of conflicting interests and resistance to reform among the reformers themselves than of papal opposition. I found much more cooperation between the council and the new pope Martin V than earlier studies indicated. In an interesting and important recent study Birgitta Studt has demonstrated that Martin V made sincere efforts to implement reforms, often precisely those "reforms of the members" that the council had entertained but been unable to enact.[23] She found that there was considerable resistance in Germany to Martin V's attempts to implement these reforms. Johannes Helmrath has also written about the resistance of the members to reform in the conciliar period, arguing that those who were the objects of reform could be expected to resist reforms. To reform was desirable; to be reformed was less so. In conciliar reform, the same individuals were often simultaneously the agents and objects of reform. The same people who ardently supported reform in theory might very well oppose it in practice when they were the ones to be reformed.[24] Popes were perhaps more likely than councils to enact successful reforms of the members, but even they encountered difficulties, as Nicholas of Cusa discovered in his legatine reform mission in Germany.[25]

23. Birgit Studt, *Papst Martin V. (1417–1431) und die Kirchenreform in Deutschland* (Cologne: Böhlau, 2004), 3–4, 719–20.

24. Johannes Helmrath, "Theorie und Praxis der Kirchenreform im Spätmittelalter," *Rottenburger Jahrbuch für Kirchengeschichte*, 11 (1992): 41–70 at 47.

25. See Dieter Stievermann, "Klosterreform und Territorialstaat in Süddeutschland im 15. Jahrhundert," *Rottenburger Jahrbuch für Kirchengeschichte* 11 (1992): 149–60 at 155–56.

Helmrath found much continuity of conciliar reform with earlier reform ideas, going back at least to the ideas of the Gregorian reform analyzed by Ladner.[26] Jürgen Miethke and Lorenz Weinrich, also invoking Ladner, see a continuity of conciliar reform ideas reaching back several centuries to the papally initiated reform councils of the eleventh to the thirteenth century.[27] However, they see an important interlude after the Council of Vienne, after which the Avignon popes felt strong enough to carry out reform themselves rather than having to deal with the unwieldy body of a general council.

These reforming efforts of Avignon popes have been investigated in several recent studies.[28] Jan Ballweg's monograph on the reform efforts of Benedict XII explores the dynamic between conciliar and papal reform conceptions and concrete reform measures. He cites Ladner's *The Idea of Reform* at the beginning of his introduction, but it is unclear how much Ladner's analysis influenced Ballweg's theoretical consideration of reform throughout his book. Ballweg posits a model of reform that appears to owe more to empirical analysis than to any consideration of reform terminology and ideology in the Ladnerian tradition.[29] Ballweg's hypotheses concerning the relationship between reform and tradition are of great interest, and they could have been made more precise through reference to Ladner's discussion of this relationship in earlier reform literature.[30] Ballweg's hypotheses concerning the relationship between reform and correction conflict with Ladner's analysis of ideas of correction and are not anchored in an analysis of the terminology used in the texts

26. Helmrath, "Theorie und Praxis," 42.

27. Jürgen Miethke and Lorenz Weinrich, *Quellen zur Kirchenreform im Zeitalter der grossen Konzilien des 15. Jahrhunderts*, vol. 1 (Darmstadt: Wissenschaftliche Buchgesellschaft, 1995).

28. Miethke and Weinrich, *Quellen*, 12–13, and works cited there in nn29–30. See also Jan Ballweg, *Konziliare oder päpstliche Ordensreform: Benedikt XII. und die Reformdiskussion im frühen 14. Jahrhundert* (Tübingen: Mohr Siebeck, 2001); Ludwig Vones, *Urban V. (1362–1370): Kirchenreform zwischen Kardinalkollegium, Kurie, und Klientel* (Stuttgart: A. Hiersemann, 1998).

29. Ballweg, *Konziliare oder päpstliche Ordensreform*, 1–3.

30. Ibid., 317–18.

themselves.[31] In my study of the Constance reforms I found terms and images of correction to be central, and these terms and images have a long history, both in conciliar and papal reform and also in reforms carried out by secular governments. Ladner discussed their occurrence in the legislation of Justinian, and I recall it as one of the topics in his seminar on reform in church history.[32] This topic should be investigated further, with careful attention to the terms and images in their concrete contexts in both ecclesiastical and secular documents.

These parallels and connections between hierarchical church reform and secular ideas of governmental reform in the later Middle Ages are significant, and I believe that Ladner's work could be illuminating in this area as well. Hermann Heimpel demonstrated that church reform and imperial reform were intimately interconnected in the thought of Job Vener, and several studies in the volume *Reform von Kirche und Reich* explored this connection in other fifteenth-century authors.[33] The use of the word *reformatio* or of French words derived from this term in documents concerning reform by or of the royal government in France was investigated by Philippe Contamine in an incisive study that followed a philological method similar to Ladner's. Contamine points to a tradition of "réformateurs" sent out by Louis IX and later kings to bring about speedy and forceful correction of abuses.[34] Ladner had found simi-

31. Ibid., 309. Ballweg distinguishes between correction and reform, seeing correction as an attenuated reform.

32. Gerhart B. Ladner, "Justinian's Theory of Law and the Renewal Ideology of the *Leges Barbarorum*," *Proceedings of the American Philosophical Society*, 119, no. 3 (1975); repr. in *Ideas and Images*, 2:609–628, at 610–14.

33. Hermann Heimpel, *Die Vener von Gmünd und Strassburg, 1162–1447* (Göttingen: Vandenhoeck & Ruprecht, 1982); *Reform von Kirche und Reich zur Zeit der Konzilien von Konstanz (1414–1418) und Basel (1431–1449)* (Konstanz-Prager historisches Kolloquium, 11.–17. Oktober 1993), edited by Ivan Hlavácek and Alexander Patschovsky (Konstanz: Universitätsverlag Konstanz, 1996), especially the papers by Hartmut Boockmann and Carla Märtl.

34. Philippe Contamine, "Réformation: un mot, une idée," in *Des pouvoirs en France, 1300–1500* (Paris: Presses de l'École Normale Supérieure, 1992), 37–47, at 40.

lar terminology in documents of Italian communes from the later Middle Ages.[35] Interestingly, the French documents referred to a *reformatio in melius* that would result, thus employing the terminology of a change to the better which Ladner traced back to the Latin church fathers. A systematic study of the origins and development of this terminology in documents of secular governments would be of great interest.[36]

THE "REFORM IN HEAD AND MEMBERS" AND REFORM *TOPOI*

The central *topos* of hierarchical reform, the *reformatio in capite et in membris* (reform in head and members), was enriched by uses of the body metaphor in the context of secular governments, and many of the *topoi* associated with this metaphor in that context became associated with the ecclesiastical reform in head and members. The phrase "reform in head and members" had its origins in the church, in fact in papal documents calling for reform of particular churches.[37] It appears to have been first used to describe the reform of the universal church by William Durant the Younger on the eve of the Council of Vienne (1311).[38] Though in this sense the conception acknowledges the supreme role of the pope as head of the body, it also stresses the importance of the intermediate members and was thus congenial to an episcopalist conception of the church.[39] In my monograph on the Constance reforms I investigated the various understandings of the phrase at the council; and developments after

35. Ladner, "Reform: Innovation and Tradition," 551–52.

36. Justinian's legislation was probably one of the main sources; see Ladner, "Justinian's Theory of Law," 613.

37. Karl Augustin Frech, *Reform an Haupt und Gliedern: Untersuchungen zur Entwicklung und Verwendung der Formulierung im Hoch- und Spätmittelalter* (Frankfurt: P. Lang, 1992).

38. On William Durant the Younger the definitive study is Constantin Fasolt, *Council and Hierarchy: The Political Thought of William Durant the Younger* (Cambridge: Cambridge University Press, 1990).

39. See *Reform von Kirche und Reich*, 20–21.

Constance are further illuminated by a recent survey of Polish scholarship on conciliar reform.[40] During the course of the fifteenth century *reformatio in capite et in membris* was again transferred, this time to the even wider context of the reform of all Christendom. Further study of such transfers of reform *topoi* would be of great value.

The work of a research group at the Free University of Berlin directed by Professor Wilhelm Schmidt-Biggemann suggests a framework for such study. This group investigates the role of topical reasoning in the generation of new knowledge during the transition from the later Middle Ages to the early modern era. Topical reasoning is that set forth originally by Aristotle and Cicero as a form of reasoning that enjoys an intermediate degree of certainty between the rigor of logical demonstration and the persuasion of rhetorical argument.[41] The topics (*topoi*) are words, phrases, concepts, images, and arguments often referred to as *loci communes*, commonplaces. Although they often had their origin within a particular discipline or sphere of knowledge, such as law, theology, or art, during the transition from the Middle Ages to the early modern era they were often transferred to different contexts, leading to the creation of new knowledge that often transcended the old disciplinary boundaries and could be conveyed through images as well as words. Thomas Frank shows how topical learning applied to reform, specifically in the hospital reform of the early sixteenth century.[42] Although he

40. Krzystof Ozog, "La réforme de l'Église et le conciliarisme en Pologne au XVe siècle: Bilan des recherches," *Quaestiones medii aevi novae* 6 (2001): 261–76 at 275, 268–69. The concept of a two-fold structure of the church (*corpus politicum* and *corpus mysticum*) developed by these conciliarists in some ways echoes the image proposed by St. Augustine's contemporary, Tyconius, of a bi-partite body of Christ. St. Augustine had preferred the image of the two cities to suggest that not all the members of the visible church would be part of the church triumphant, the city of God. See Ladner, *The Idea of Reform*, 261–63.

41. Wilhelm Schmidt-Biggemann and Anja Hallacker, "Topik: Tradition und Erneurung," in *Topik und Tradition: Prozesse der Neuordnung von Wissensüberlieferungen des 13. bis 17. Jahrhunderts*, edited by Thomas Frank et al. (Göttingen: V&R Unipress, 2007), 17–27, at 15–17.

42. Thomas Frank, "Hospitalreformen um 1500 am Beispiel Strassburg," in *Topik und Tradition*, 105–26. See, most recently, Thomas Frank, "Spätmittelalterliche Hospitalreformen und Kanonistik," *Reti Medievali Rivista* 11.1 (2010): 1–40 <http://www.retimedievali.it>

does not cite Ladner's *The Idea of Reform,* he told me in a personal conversation that Ladner's work had strongly influenced his own thought. He follows Ladner's method of identifying leading concepts of reform, such as the concept of "compassion (misericordia)," in the discourse concerning hospital reform at Strasbourg during the early Reformation.[43]

NON-HIERARCHICAL REFORM AND ITS CONTINUITY WITH THE RENAISSANCE AND REFORMATIONS

Overemphasis on top-down, hierarchical reform in head and members tends to obscure the continuing importance of ideas of personal reform and of the many "grassroots" reforms of the later Middle Ages, as Bellitto has remarked. Bellitto points to the skepticism of reformers like Nicolas de Clamanges, the friend and colleague of Gerson and d'Ailly, who questioned the efficacy of the "top-down" reform unless the reformers first reformed themselves.[44] Pascoe emphasized the continuing importance of the theme of personal reform in Gerson's and d'Ailly's own thought.

Late medieval monastic reforms and observant movements often began in "grassroots" fashion, even though their further growth and implementation were fostered in "top-down" fashion by popes, councils, and territorial rulers.[45] Unfortunately, the excellent studies of these monastic reform movements produced over the past decades by Kaspar Elm and others have focused mostly on the practice

43. Frank treats these leading reform conceptions separately from the reform *topoi,* which are more specific and are used in the context of reform rhetoric. Further study of the relationship between reform conceptions, reform rhetoric, and reform *topoi* would be of great value.

44. Christopher M. Bellitto, "The Reform Context of the Great Western Schism," in *A Companion to the Great Western Schism (1378–1417),* edited by Joëlle Rollo-Koster and Thomas M. Izbicki (Brill's Companions to the Christian Tradition, 17; Leiden: Brill, 2009), 303–31, at 303–5, 314; Bellitto, *Nicolas de Clamanges,* 91–93.

45. Kaspar Elm, "Reform und Erneuerung des Ordenswesens im Spätmittelalter: Forschungen und Forschungsaufgaben," in *Untersuchungen zu Kloster und Stift,* Veröffentlichungen des Max-Planck-Instituts für Geschichte 68 (Göttingen: Vandenhoeck und Ruprecht, 1980), 188–238, at 219–23.

of reform rather than conceptions of reform, so few have made explicit reference to Ladner's *The Idea of Reform*. Dieter Mertens does point to a number of important guiding conceptions in the writings of reformers and historians of monastic orders from the time period, but argues that they mainly affected theory rather than practice.[46]

The role of territorial rulers in a top-down reform of monastic orders raises the question of continuity with the reformations of the sixteenth century.[47] Mertens and Elm are cautious about conclusions concerning such continuity, which often are accompanied by a tendency to focus too narrowly on the Lutheran Reformation and on theological reform.[48] Elm does, however, see continuity between the later medieval monastic reform movements and the Catholic Reformation of the sixteenth century, precisely in the area of personal reform.[49] He observes in these movements a change in piety that is new, involving especially more individual prayer and emphasis on penitence and imitation of Christ, especially in the religious houses influenced by the Devotio Moderna, but also as a result of parallel developments in other houses and lands.[50]

Again, more study is needed concerning the ways in which this new piety was conceptualized in terms of reform ideology. One of Ladner's students, John Van Engen, has recently done this for the Devotio Moderna, the Sisters and Brothers of the Common Life.[51] As Constable had done for twelfth-century reform, Van Engen relates the individual reform of the Devout to their institutional reform, in this case their "life-turn" (*conversio*) to their unusual "life-form"—

46. Dieter Mertens, "Monastische Reformbewegungen des 15. Jahrhunderts: Ideen—Ziele—Resultate," in *Reform von Kirche und Reich,* 157–81.

47. See Dieter Stievermann, "Klosterreform und Territorialstaat in Süddeutschland im 15. Jahrhundert," *Rottenburger Jahrbuch für Kirchengeschichte* 11 (1992): 149–60.

48. Mertens, "Monastische Reformbewegungen," 160.

49. Elm, "Reform und Erneuerung," 238.

50. Ibid., 233–34.

51. John Van Engen, *Sisters and Brothers of the Common Life: The* Devotio Moderna *and the World of the Later Middle Ages* (Philadelphia: University of Pennsylvania Press, 2008), 7–8.

communal life that often shared the goals of monastic spirituality, but without permanent vows.[52] How "new" was this life-form? In asking this question Van Engen is building implicitly on two of Ladner's important considerations in *The Idea of Reform*: (1) conversion as an idea of renewal that overlaps with reform; and (2) the forward and backward-looking elements in ideas of renewal. Van Engen seeks to avoid the exaggerated claims of newness posited earlier by Hyma and others; *moderna* meant simply "'of this era' as distinct from 'an earlier era'." However, he describes the Devout as people in the present animated by a heady sense of purpose, even of singularity.[53]

Although Van Engen traces the lines of continuity of the Devouts' "spiritual exercises" forward to St. Ignatius and the Jesuits,[54] he also finds among the Devout much harking back to patristic reform ideas (Augustine was their favorite Father) and to the twelfth century. While Van Engen is more concerned with the Devouts' practice of reform than with their ideas of reform, he does cite important reform terminology and concepts found in the central guidebooks written for the Devout by their leaders, especially in the *De reformatione virium* ("*On the Reform of the Human Faculties*") by Zerbolt. In these writings, the "reform in head and members" so central to late medieval reform is turned inward in an "appeal to remake the faculties of the self."[55] The faculties are those of the triune soul—intellect, memory, and will—set forth by Augustine and analyzed by Ladner in *The Idea of Reform*.[56] This self-remaking was described by one of the Devout as similar to a craftsman building a house, even to "spiritual carpentry," a peculiarly urban manifestation of the reform of monastic piety toward a greater cultivation of

52. The reform ideas of the Devout are especially tied to the concept of *conversio* in their writings. Usually in the Middle Ages conversion referred to entry into a monastic community through permanent vows analogous to marriage.

53. Van Engen, *Sisters and Brothers*, 8: Van Engen refers also to the writing of the brother Henry Pomerius, who spoke of *devotis mentibus noua sanctorum singularitas*.

54. Van Engen, *Sisters and Brothers*, 300, 318.

55. Ibid., 78–80.

56. Ladner, *The Idea of Reform*, 197–203.

the interior life, which Van Engen sees as a certain continuity with Renaissance ideas of self-fashioning.[57]

The connection of this interior piety with art in the work of Michelangelo is the subject of a recent fascinating study by Alexander Nagel, which also acknowledges its indebtedness to Ladner.[58] Nagel explores the archaizing tendencies in a series of Michelangelo's paintings and sculptures, showing how he returned to models of *trecento* art because of their evocation of interior spirituality. Nagel thus juxtaposes Michelangelo's idea of reform of art with Vasari's "progressivism." Although Michelangelo was acutely aware of change in art and saw his art as an improvement over that of his immediate predecessors, he showed a striking admiration for Giotto's art and its power "for its own time." Nagel notes that around 1500 "archaizing taste often went hand in hand with a preoccupation with reform, a preoccupation that is by definition backward-looking."[59] He observes that this idea of reform had "from the beginning been associated with the visual arts, and specifically with the work of artistic restoration," citing a passage from one of Ladner's articles which talks about the Greek fathers' comparison of reform to the cleansing of a painting.[60] Then he quotes Augustine's comparison of the reform of man to the restoration of a deformed sculpture, citing *The Idea of Reform*. In sum, Nagel's book concentrates on aspects of Michelangelo's work that reveal a consistent preoccupation with processes of excavation, recovery, and remembrance; for the exploration of these themes, Nagel is deeply indebted to the work of Ladner.[61]

57. Van Engen, *Sisters and Brothers*, 304.

58. Alexander Nagel, *Michelangelo and the Reform of Art* (Cambridge: Cambridge University Press, 2000), 1–22.

59. Ibid., 15.

60. Ibid., 16, 221n47.

61. Ibid., 221n46 and 248n79, notes parallels to the artistic developments in the humanist oratory of reform in the papal court, citing John O'Malley's studies, which in turn were deeply influenced by Ladner's *The Idea of Reform*. See Stump, "The Influence of Gerhart Ladner's *The Idea of Reform*," 15.

Ladner would have been very interested in Nagel's findings. For him the High Renaissance was the peak of Western artistic development, not least because of its central theme of the divinity of man and woman created in God's image, so important to the idea of reform. The biblical and patristic ideas of personal reform manifest an extraordinary continuity into the later Middle Ages and Renaissance. Even when reform rhetoric appears in a purely institutional context, it cannot shed the earlier connotations so redolent of hope. This is why the central late-medieval reform *topos,* reform in head and members, born in a quite limited legal setting, came to express the pent-up longing for renewal of all Christendom.

Ladner's own interests led him in directions quite different from recent analyses of institutionalized realities of reform in practice. Such analyses are of great value, but what is most urgently needed is to combine them with a fresh consideration of the shifting conceptions of reform along Ladnerian lines. Further research could be especially helpful to explore the boundaries between reform and other renewal concepts and between reform and tradition, reform and correction, reform and conversion. We should also explore further the unintended negative consequences of reform and of resistance to reform. In doing so we may find ourselves investigating reform rhetoric, reform *topoi,* and reform imaginaries alongside the "idea" of reform in the strict sense rigorously defined by Ladner. I believe he would be supportive of such new perspectives, just as he welcomed the use of computer technology to facilitate the investigation of reform terminology. (We have only begun to tap the possibilities of the latter.) In such research I believe we will continue to discover a remarkable persistence of the themes set forth in *The Idea of Reform,* such as Augustinian monasticism as a vehicle for transmission of ideas of personal reform. The most illuminating recent studies of late medieval reform have been those that were fully cognizant of these themes, and one can only hope that future research will continue to return to the Ladnerian *fontes.*

II

MODELS AND CASE STUDIES OF MEDIEVAL AND REFORMATION REFORM

5

"HE DOES NOT SAY, 'I AM CUSTOM'"

Pope Gregory VII's Idea of Reform

KEN A. GRANT

It is by no means an accident that the old statement, formulated by Tertullian and then used by Cyprian and Augustine, that Christ had *not* said, "I am custom," but that he *had* said, "I am truth," was now taken up again. The principle that truth is superior to custom was of the greatest importance for the Gregorian reform movement; but so was the rejection of untraditional innovation enunciated against Cyprian by Pope Stephen I in the baptismal controversy of the third century, and never forgotten since: *Nihil innovetur nisi quod traditum est,* "Let nothing be innovated except that which is part of tradition."[1]

It is, of course, impossible to engage the idea of reform in the Middle Ages without examining and reexamining the tempestu-

1. Gerhart B. Ladner, "Reform: Innovation and Tradition in Medieval Christendom," *Images and Ideas in the Middle Ages—Selected Studies in History and Art* (Rome: Edizione Di Storia E Letteratura, 1983), 547.

ous papacy of Pope Gregory VII. As evidenced by Gerhart Ladner's many articles on the topic, we must continually return to this confounding but central figure when broaching the issue of reform. In this quotation from his article, "Reform: Innovation and Tradition in Medieval Christendom," Ladner captured the essence of Pope Gregory VII's understanding of the idea of reform and the way in which Gregory would argue for and undertake reform.[2] In order to avoid charges of innovation, Gregory attempted to ground his reforms in appeals to the Bible and the church fathers, sources held as unassailable even by those arrayed against him. This essay examines the core of Gregory's reform ideology, the manner in which he formulated his arguments, and the sources he used to bolster them. It concludes with a brief study of the clearest example of Gregory's systematic exploration of the issue of papal authority, the second letter to Bishop Hermann of Metz (March 1081). In particular, this study examines Gregory's uses of scripture in the development and support of his reform program.

Indeed, Gregory's use of scripture provides an accessible vehicle by which we can ascertain his motivation and justification for the most innovative of his actions. Insight along this line of inquiry is provided by Maureen Miller, who suggests in "The Crisis in the Investiture Crisis Narrative" that it is time to "undertake a radical reconsideration of the papacy from a truly post-confessional perspective" and to "set aside questions of whether a belief or development was right or wrong, good or bad, and concentrate on how and why ideas and practices developed."[3] By understanding Gregory's methodological apparatus, we step closer to understanding his intentions and how he justified and rationalized his actions in Gregory's terms, not our own.

Gregory's conceptualization and attempted implementation of a

2. Ibid., 574

3. Maureen Miller, "The Crisis in the Investiture Crisis Narrative," *History Compass* 7/6 (2009): 1570, 1577.

reform program in its broadest sense was an attempt to restore what he argued was originally set forth by Christ. This goal is illustrated in the way Gregory juxtaposes the actions of religious and secular rulers. His rhetorical claim is that, while his reforms remain within tradition and articulate truth, the secular authority's activities clearly did not. Against the charge of innovation—coming not only from secular rulers but church leaders, too—Gregory argued that his reforms were not innovative and instead were clearly necessary. We should note that he was quite polemical in his rhetoric as well as revolutionary in the exercise of his authority and power over the secular rulers.

Even a cursory examination of the Register of Pope Gregory VII provides clear examples of Gregory's continuing efforts to describe his reform program as non-innovative.[4] Two letters provide a sampling of Gregory's efforts. In a letter to Archbishop Werner of Magdeburg, which calls on Werner to "more zealously … drive home the chastity of clerks," Gregory comments: "We do not set before you our own decrees (although we might freely do so if there were need), but we renew things decreed by the holy fathers, lest by our silence we should incur the condemnation of the servant who hid the Lord's money."[5]

4. H. E. J. Cowdrey, *The Register of Pope Gregory VII 1073–1085: An English Translation*, (Oxford: Oxford University Press, 2002); Erich Caspar, *Das Register Gregors VII* (Berlin: Monumenta Germaniae Historica, 1920). I will be drawing on Cowdrey's translation of the Register into English for quoted passages. In conjunction with the Cowdrey citations, I will also offer the corresponding citations from Caspar's *Das Register Gregors VII*.

5. Cowdrey, *The Register of Pope Gregory VII*, 162. Caspar, *Das Register Gregors VII*, 226. It is worth noting that the majority of Gregory's references to the non-innovative character of his reform program are found in letters during the years 1075–1081, the most contentious years of his pontificate. The timing of these references coincides with a shift in the tone and tenor in the Register, most clearly witnessed in a shift of the use of, and reference to, particular biblical passages. Prior to the Lenten Synod of 1076, Gregory regularly referenced the prophets and articulated his own prophetic call for renewal and reform. After the Lenten Synod of 1076, the references shift to Matthew 16:19 and 1 Samuel 15:22–23. Of the seventeen references to Matthew 16:19 in the Register, fourteen are used after the Lenten Synod of 1076; of the nineteen references to 1 Samuel 15:22–23, fifteen are used after the synod.

Likewise, in a letter responding to Bishop Henry of Liège's query regarding the potential posthumous release of William of Utrecht from excommunication, to which Gregory replied that the release was only possible if William repented, Gregory noted in an October 28, 1076, letter that this response, and in fact all responses regarding ecclesiastical order, was non-innovative because of its grounding in the writings of the church fathers and the activity of the Holy Spirit.

What you have asked of us about the case of William, bishop of Utrecht, your prudence can ascertain and understand as stated beyond all doubt not so much by us as by the general opinion of the holy fathers. Upholding or defending their statutes, whenever we have passed or do pass judgment about matters of ecclesiastical business we do not give voice to new things or our own, but we follow and enforce things voiced by them through the Holy Spirit.[6]

Gregory argues that the innovation emerges not from his reform efforts, but from those who have attempted to usurp the authority of the church. In a letter to generate support among the faithful of Germany immediately following the Lenten Synod of 1076, wherein Gregory excommunicated and deposed Henry IV the first time, Gregory denounces those who have acted contrary to the church, and therefore to tradition.

You have heard, brother, the novel and unheard-of presumption, you have heard the atrocious loquacity and boldness of schismatics and blasphemers of the name of the Lord in blessed Peter, you have heard the pride which has reared up to the insult and shame of the apostolic see, such as your fathers have not at any time seen or heard nor does the sequence of things written teach that the like has ever come forth from pagans or heretics. Even if any case of such an evil had previously arisen since the church was founded and the faith of Christ was spread abroad, there should still be grief and lamentation on the part of all the faith for such great scorn and contempt of apostolic—no, of divine, authority.[7]

6. Cowdrey, *The Register of Pope Gregory VII*, 215–16. Caspar, *Das Register Gregors VII*, 303–4.

7. Cowdrey, *The Register of Pope Gregory VII*, 182. Caspar, *Das Register Gregors VII*, 254–55.

Gregory offers a subtle reference to the Matthew 16:18 text, and expands on this reference:

Wherefore, if you believe that the keys of the kingdom of heaven have been given to blessed Peter by our Lord God, Jesus Christ, and if you desire that entry into the joys of eternal life should be open to you through his hands, you should consider how greatly you should now be aggrieved at the wrongs that have been inflicted upon him.[8]

Gregory claims that the argument for action derives not from a casual desire for innovation or change solely for the sake of increasing papal authority, although that is certainly a potential outcome; it grows organically out of a pressing need for a restoration to the original ordering of the church so that it might live out its mission.

Gregory repeatedly returns to the Bible to buttress his arguments, offer encouragement, and provide justification for his actions in support of the church's mission. The use of biblical references reinforces Gregory's understanding that truth, as revealed by the biblical witness, supersedes customs, in other words, those traditions that he viewed as contrary to the accepted teachings of the church. The biblical witness is both the method for developing the broader reforms as well as the standard and norm on which the reforms are based and constructed.

A good example is the May 6, 1073, letter to Duke Godfrey of Lower Lorraine, where Gregory directs the reform as he offers a summation regarding his concerns about King Henry IV:

If he shall listen to us, we rejoice for his salvation not otherwise than for our own; he will most certainly be able to gain it for himself if he falls in with our warnings and counsels in holding fast to righteousness. But if, which we hope will not be the case, he shall render to us hatred for love, and to Almighty God by ignoring his righteousness (although there is no comparison) contempt for so great an honour as has been conferred upon him, the sanction by which it is said, "Cursed be the man who withholds his sword from blood" will not, by God providence, come upon us.[9]

8. Cowdrey, *The Register of Pope Gregory VII*, 182. Caspar, *Das Register Gregors VII*, 254–55.

9. Cowdrey, *The Register of Pope Gregory VII*, 10. Caspar, *Das Register Gregors VII*, 15.

The use of Jeremiah 48:10 in the last sentence of the above quotation, one of nine uses of this particular prophetic passage in the Register, is directed not at Godfrey, nor even Henry; it is directed inward, toward Gregory, and by extension, to all those who exercise religious leadership.[10] Gregory explains to Godfrey that he is bound by the call of the prophet to right action for God's sake. By so doing, he moves himself and the papacy under the direct guidance of the prophets. Gregory is compelled to act, lest he endanger his own standing at the final judgment by not working for the reform of sinners. Gregory broadens this understanding to include all who exercise leadership in the church. This is a vital point, one Gregory reiterates throughout his pontificate: it is essential to act against those who would harm the church or who have harmed the church. Those who do not act are endangering the people in their care now; moreover, if a priest, bishop, cardinal, or pope does not act to correct sinful behavior, he will be held responsible and accountable at the final reckoning.

This prophetic voice is strong in the early years of Gregory's pontificate, and Gregory routinely references the texts to provide added weight and legitimacy for actions that might be perceived to be innovative. As Ladner notes in *The Idea of Reform*, "[T]he prophets not only foretold the coming of Christ, but they are also the great examples of authentic reformers within the church."[11] The second use of the Jeremiah passage in the Register strikes a similar chord, as Gregory writes to the "Faithful of Saint Peter," warning them of

10. There are fifty references to Jeremiah and the other Old Testament prophets in the Register: twenty-eight references made prior to the events at Canossa in January 1077, and seventeen after the second excommunication of Henry IV in 1080. The dearth of prophetic references during the intervening years corresponds to a more vigorous and coercive attempt to correct and reform Henry's behavior and actions. For additional reading regarding Gregory's use of the prophets, see Christian Schneider, *Prophetisches Sacerdotium und Heilsgeschichtliches Regnum im Dialog 1073–1077* (Munich: Willhelm Fink Verlag, 1972).

11. Gerhart B. Ladner, *The Idea of Reform: Its Impact on Christian Thought and Action in the Age of the Fathers* (Cambridge, Mass.: Harvard University Press, 1959; republished in New York: Harper Torchbooks, 1967), 52.

the excommunicated and simoniacal Archbishop Godfrey of Milan. In the body of the letter, Gregory reiterates a common theme: his compulsion to act: "I want you to know, most beloved brothers, what many of you, indeed, know—that we have been set in such a station that, whether we wish to or not, we are under constraint to announce truth and righteousness to all peoples, especially to Christians."

Gregory then provides the rationale for his compulsion to act, a rationale deeply steeped in the prophetic tradition, and one that also clearly states the responsibilities for all religious leaders.

> [A]s the Lord says, "Cry, do not cease; lift up your voice as a trumpet and announce to my people their offences"; and elsewhere, "If you shall not announce to the wicked man his wickedness, I shall require his soul from your hand." Again, the prophet says, "Cursed is the man who withholds his sword from blood," that is, the word of preaching from the reproof of the carnal.[12]

In addition to the use of Jeremiah 48:10, this section of the letter also includes references to Isaiah 58:1 and Ezekiel 3:18. Respectively, the Isaiah and Ezekiel passages reinforce the need to act when faced with those who are acting contrary to the expectations of the church, and to remind those in positions of leadership within the church that they will be held accountable for inaction. The Jeremiah text, perhaps one of the most well-known of Gregory's biblical references, provides the exclamation point as it details with startling clarity the ultimate fate reserved for those who do not act. Inaction in the face of sin is, for Gregory, the greatest danger confronting the church. Reform is proactive, not simply reactive, yet still grounded in Gregory's reading of the truth as expressed in the biblical witness and the church fathers. Gregory's reforms aimed not to simply reformulate existing ideas, but to create an environment that encouraged, or demanded, right action—action prescribed by the church.

12. Cowdrey, *The Register of Pope Gregory VII*, 15–16. Caspar, *Das Register Gregors VII*, 23.

Gregory attempted to avoid charges of innovation by appealing to sources that could not be accused of innovation. The Jeremiah passage reinforces this connection to both the biblical witness and the church fathers, offering not only a direct quote from the prophet, but also including the interpretation of the text, in the final clause of the sentence, as offered by Pope Gregory I in the *Regula Pastoralis*. Both the use of the Jeremiah text and the interpretation are appropriated directly from Gregory I, and most likely from other reformers who make use of the text, including Walo, Abbot of St. Arnulf of Metz, who sent a letter to Gregory VII on the occasion of his election, citing the Jeremiah passage among many Old Testament passages as motivation for action on Gregory's part.[13]

This appropriation calls to mind the hermeneutical advice offered by C. H. Kneepkens regarding letter writers who reference scripture in their letters. Kneepkens suggested that not only should we follow the "rule to verify quotations in the context from which they were taken,"[14] we "must take into consideration that the quoting author might have meant not only to import the context of the quotation into his own text, but also the contemporary knowledge that was commonly associated with it."[15] The implication is that when writing the letter, the author "might have intended not only to

13. I. S. Robinson, *Authority and Resistance in the Investiture Controversy* (Manchester: Manchester University Press, 1978), 24–25. Robinson elaborates, "The letter of Walo, Abbot of St. Arnulf of Metz, composed to congratulate Gregory on accession, abounds in Old Testament imagery and in particular uses the text of Jeremiah to incite the pope against those who opposed his succession to the holy see." Robinson also states that "Walo's letter has been suggested as the direct source for the pope's frequent application of Jer. 48:10," 25. To this, I would add that Gregory VII's many references to Gregory I's writings, especially the *Moralia* and the *Regula*, argue for a direct transmission of these particular ideas, as well as the indirect transmission through individuals like Walo. Of the 117 references to patristic and conciliar sources in the Register, 62 are taken from Gregory I's writings. Such prevalence of use suggests, at least, familiarity with the texts.

14. C. H. Kneepkens, "There is more in a Biblical quotation than meets the eye: On Peter the Venerable's letter of consolation to Heloise," *Media Latinitas—A Collection of Essays to Mark the Occasion of the Retirement of L. J. Engels* (Steenbrugis: Brepols Publishers, 1996), 90–91.

15. Kneepkens, *Media Latinitas*, 90–91.

call the attention of his addressee or his readership to the imported Scriptural context, but also to introduce the contemporary Biblical exegesis of a given quotation into his letter."[16] This is sound advice when reading Gregory's letters and noting his use of scripture, and is worth noting when Gregory subtly references those for whom he knows there is great respect. There is a sense of anamnesis involved in Gregory's references to Gregory I, as he attempts to appropriate Gregory I's sterling reputation, perhaps recognizing the contested and polarizing nature of his own reputation.[17]

These two references to Jeremiah 48:10, as with the seven other references to the passage, provide Gregory with the opportunity to make use of the prophets to reinforce his reforms, exclaiming that he must follow what the prophets have called him to do. The prophetic call provides Gregory with the opportunity to act in novel or innovative ways, as such action was directly tied to the prophetic call to action. In this reading, Gregory was not acting of his own accord, but simply acting as directed by the prophets.

Gregory builds on the use of Jeremiah 48:10 by concluding the letter to Duke Godfrey of Lower Lorraine with a reference to Paul's letter to the Galatians: "Nor is it open to us by way of personal favor to anyone to treat the law of God as being of secondary importance, or to depart from the path of rectitude out of human partiality; as the Apostle says, 'If I would be pleasing to men, I should not be the servant of God.'"[18]

Gregory explains to Godfrey and the "Faithful" that he cannot help but act in accordance with God's wishes, and thus, even if he could take into consideration such realities as political, social, or fa-

16. Ibid., 91.

17. See Robinson, *Authority and Resistance in the Investiture Controversy,* 32: "Gregory VII's emphasis on the model of Gregory I is apparent not only from the frequent egregious references to the doctor in his letters but also from the polemics of the schismatic cardinals, a source which, although hostile to Gregory VII, nevertheless reflects the scholarly preoccupations of Gregorian Rome."

18. Cowdrey, *The Register of Pope Gregory VII,* 10. Caspar, *Das Register Gregors VII,* 15.

milial circumstances, he is proscribed from doing so. The reform of church and society proceeds because it is God's will. Should Gregory fail to act then he would be held responsible and accountable for all of the people in his care at the seat of judgment.

As the years of Gregory's papacy grind on, the prophetic call for repentance and renewal shifts and fades, replaced by a far more demanding and coercive tone. Gregory drops the use of the prophetic passages in the immediate wake of the Lenten Synod in 1076, and only returns to them in a much more oblique fashion in the last years of his papacy. After the Lenten Synod of 1076, Gregory no longer calls people to repentance and renewal with the words of the prophets, but demands reform with repeated uses of Matthew 16:16–19 and 1 Samuel 15:22–23, the former invoking papal primacy and the latter a need for strict obedience.

Likewise, as with the shift in the use of particular biblical passages, we note a shift toward a more structural and institutional reform. A greater focus on the issue of lay investiture, stated most clearly in the synods of 1078, highlights one component of this shift. In another shift in 1078, Gregory articulated a workable model of penance—one that demanded the penitent to give up his office while performing his penance. Both the injunction against lay investiture and the strengthening of the penitential prescriptions sought not only to reform individual actions and activities, but to reform the apparatus of governance; control should lie in the hands of the centralized authority of the papacy.

The clearest expression of Gregory's idea of reform, and revelatory of the shift both in the use of scriptural references and the movement from personal to institutional reform, is articulated in his second letter to Bishop Hermann of Metz in the Register dated March 1081. This letter, far more so than the *Dictatus papae*, details in the most systematic fashion the heart of Gregory's understanding of reform. The *Dictatus papae* offers hints of Gregory's understanding of authority and is easily the most recognizable of Gregory's works because it is such a blunt document; it offers, as Kathleen Cushing notes, both seemingly revolutionary statements on papal primacy and authority, as well as statements with ample historical precedent.[19] Yet relying on the *Dictatus* to discern fully Gregory's ideology is problematic. This is not because of sentences that Cushing notes reveal a "break with canonical tradition" or because Gregory did not follow through on these provocative statements of papal prerogative, primacy, and authority. Rather, relying on the *Dictatus* is problematic because it is incomplete.[20] These are not full explications of Gregory's conceptualization of papal authority; they are likely titles, lacking the clarification necessary to accept or reject them as typical of Gregory's ideology. Gregory never explicitly returns to this list, and thus the *Dictatus,* while interesting and even tantalizing, resists attempts to extract a complete articulation of Gregory's ideology.

In contrast, the March 1081 letter to Hermann of Metz is far more efficient in unpacking Gregory's conceptualization of authority. In this letter, Gregory treats the reform issue with patience and thoughtfulness. As noted by H. E. J. Cowdrey, the second letter to Bishop Hermann of Metz is not only a "nuanced and rounded picture of papal authority,"[21] but also "achieved a wide circulation and was regarded as authoritative by papalist writers and canonists into the twelfth century."[22] In this letter, Gregory confronts the argument that his actions were innovative or even contrary to the tradition of the church. Gregory's perspective and reading of the state of affairs, his employment of biblical passages to augment and support

19. Kathleen G. Cushing, *Reform and the Papacy in the Eleventh Century—Spirituality and Social Change* (Manchester: Manchester University Press, 2005), 79.

20. Cowdrey comments, "Yet, given the importance of the theses proposed and the forthrightness with which they are expressed, it is puzzling that they should have remained largely unused and unnoticed in the subsequent years both by Gregory and by his friends and foes." Cowdrey adds that the *Dictatus papae* "left little mark on future letters of Gregory, whether registered or not; where allusions to them may be suspected, there was a tendency to tone them down and to adhere more closely to biblical or canonical precedents." H. E. J. Cowdrey, *Gregory VII* (Oxford: Clarendon Press, 1998), 502–3.

21. Ibid., 504.

22. Ibid., 504.

his argument, and his understanding of the role of the church and the papacy, are all given their fullest treatment in this lengthy defense of his positions.

The letter opens with Gregory's standard greeting, "*Gregorius episcopus servus servorum Dei ... salutem et apostolicam benedictionem,*" "Gregory, bishop, servant of the servants of God.... greeting and apostolic blessing."[23] The greeting, repeated in the vast majority of the letters of the Register, is in and of itself a twofold rhetorical device: First, the phrase is a direct appropriation of the greeting used by Pope Gregory I. This reference subtly reminds the reader that Gregory is the namesake of one of the most famous and influential doctors of the church, and thus seems to be yet another attempt to appropriate Gregory I's authority and stature. Second, the reference reinforces Gregory's self-understanding of his role. Gregory attempts to reinforce the humility he feels regarding his position in this statement, a humility that belies the standard critique of his personality and papacy, effectively summed up in the introductory paragraphs of the Decree of the Council of Brixen in 1080, the council at which the new anti-pope, Clement III, formerly Wibert, Archbishop of Ravenna, was elected:

> From the time he entered the world, this man strove to procure position for himself over men through vain glory, without the support of any merits; to set dreams and divinations, his own and those of others, ahead of divine dispensation; to appear a monk in habit and not to be one by profession; to judge himself exempt from ecclesiastical discipline, subject to no master.[24]

The regular use of *servus servorum Dei* in the Register acts as a subtle counterargument to this imperial perspective. As Gregory VII remarks in the record of the Lenten Synod of 1080:

23. Cowdrey, *The Register of Pope Gregory VII*, 387. Caspar, *Das Register Gregors VII*, 546–47.

24. Theodor E. Mommsen and Karl F. Morrison, translators, *Imperial Lives and Letters of the Eleventh Century*, edited by Robert L. Benson (New York: Columbia University Press, 2000), 157.

For you know that I did not willingly come to holy orders, and I departed unwillingly across the mountains with the lord Pope Gregory, but more unwillingly I returned with my lord Pope Leo to your special church, in which such as I am I have served you; thereafter, exceedingly unwilling, with great sorrow and groaning and complaint I, though altogether unworthy, have been placed in your throne.[25]

This is an oft-repeated theme in Gregory's letters, and we can interpret this in one of two ways: First, Gregory believed this. He remarks regularly throughout the Register that he did not want to be placed in this position and that he felt unqualified for the task; thus it is distinctly possible that Gregory actually believed that he was acting in true humility. While this reading is seemingly contradicted by his revolutionary and coercive actions, Gregory's comments on this topic are consistent throughout the Register, and thus we have to at least entertain the possibility that he meant what he articulated.[26] Second, Gregory uses this false modesty as a rhetorical device to blunt criticism regarding his extensive (over-extended?) wielding of the power and authority of the church, as exemplified by the Council of Brixen decree.

The issue of Gregory VII's humility is important, for as Edward Peters notes, Gregory I argued that the fundamental flaw of "heterodox dissenters and immoderate exegetes"[27] was pride, as they pride-

25. Cowdrey, *The Register of Pope Gregory VII*, 342.

26. John Van Engen raises a similar point in his article "The Christian Middle Ages as an Historiographical Problem," in a short discussion of Herbert Grundmann's work, *Religious Movements in the Middle Ages*. Van Engen comments that "What Grundmann taught historians above all was to take seriously both the centrality of these movements in medieval history and the religious motivation of their adherents regardless of origins, be they Cathars or Free Spirits." "The Christian Middle Ages as an Historiographical Problem," *American Historical Review* 91 (June 1986): 523–24. Whether Cathar or pope, it is vital to take seriously their religious motivation, even if seems to contradict everything we think we know of the person, group, or period. In this particular case, taking Gregory VII at his word regarding his stated religious motivation is difficult because of the extreme nature of his actions and language, yet it is imperative to do so as a part of the interpretive task.

27. Edward M. Peters, "Transgressing the Limits set by the Fathers: Authority and Impious Exegesis in Medieval Thought," in *Christendom and Its Discontents—Exclusion, Persecution, and Rebellion, 1000–1500*, edited by Scott Waugh and Peter Diehl (Cambridge: Cambridge University Press, 1996), 342.

fully believed their individual interpretation to be the correct interpretation, and therefore superseded accepted tradition. Gregory VII attempts to maintain a sense of humility, offering regular reminders to those to whom he wrote that he simply acted as directed by the prophets and St. Peter. As Uta-Renate Blumenthal reminds us, "Gregory's mystical identification with Saint Peter illuminated his whole being. Thus it seemed self-evident to him that his papal activities should be free from error on the basis of Christ's prayer for Peter and the church."[28]

The formalized greeting offered in the letter, finally, reinforces a central and crucial component of Gregory's perspective on leadership, power, and authority—that the responsibility rests on the shoulders of these leaders to work for the people, to be their servant leaders. Gregory then opens the body of the letter commending Bishop Hermann of Metz for his fortitude and willingness to act for the "defense of the truth."[29] The encouragement also includes a sign that Gregory, and his supporters, are in a far more difficult position than after the first excommunication and deposition.

> It is God's unspeakable grace and marvelous clemency that he never permits his chosen entirely to wander, and he never allows them utterly to be shaken or cast down, while he makes those who in time of persecution are assailed by a kind of useful testing, even after some faltering, more strong than themselves.[30]

H. E. J. Cowdrey notes that this comment may reference Hermann's presence at "Worms in which the German bishops renounced their obedience to Gregory."[31] I argue that this may also be a comment about his increasingly tenuous position. His increasingly terse,

28. Uta-Renate Blumenthal, *The Investiture Controversy—Church and Monarchy from the Ninth to the Twelfth Century* (Philadelphia: University of Pennsylvania Press, 1988), 117.

29. Cowdrey, *The Register of Pope Gregory VII*, 387. Caspar, *Das Register Gregors VII*, 547.

30. Cowdrey, *The Register of Pope Gregory VII*, 387. Caspar, *Das Register Gregors VII*, 547.

31. Cowdrey, *The Register of Pope Gregory VII*, 387. Caspar, *Das Register Gregors VII*, 547.

demanding, and coercive language reveals him to be fighting for his professional life.

After additional preliminary comments regarding the need to stand strong in times of great adversity, and remarking that the fearlessness of one will spread to others, Gregory asks and then proceeds to answer an important question that immediately comes to the forefront of one's thinking when examining the papacy of Gregory VII—how does Gregory justify his actions and his articulation of the power and authority of the papacy?

> Now you have asked us as it were by writings of our own to help and to fortify you against the madness of those who chatter with wicked mouth that the authority of the holy and apostolic see did not have the power to excommunicate King Henry, a man who is a despiser of the Christian law in that he is a destroyer of churches and of the empire and the author and accomplice of heretics, nor to absolve anyone from the oath of fealty: this does not appear to us very necessary, since so many and most sure proofs in this matter may be found in the pages of sacred writings.[32]

The answer, offered in the next paragraph of the letter, turns directly to the most recognizable of the papal proof texts, Matthew 16:18–19. Gregory establishes the basis for his argument on this text.

> For that we may say a few things about many, who does not know the voice of our Lord and Savior Jesus Christ who says in the gospel: "You are Peter, and upon this rock I shall build my church, and the gates of hell shall not prevail against it. And to you I shall give the keys of the kingdom of heaven, and whatsoever you shall bind upon earth shall also be bound in heaven, and whatsoever you shall loose upon earth shall also be loosed in heaven." Are kings here excepted, or are they not of the sheep that the Son of God has committed to blessed Peter?[33]

With this question, we begin to see the structure that Gregory is attempting to erect to answer the central questions of authority and papal primacy. He claims the authority to act as the vicar of St. Pe-

32. Cowdrey, *The Register of Pope Gregory VII,* 387–88. Caspar, *Das Register Gregors VII,* 547–48.

33. Cowdrey, *The Register of Pope Gregory VII,* 388. Caspar, *Das Register Gregors VII,* 548.

ter, who in turn received his authority to act directly from Jesus. Gregory asks the question as to whether kings are not a part of the flock that Peter is supposed to tend. If they are not excepted, then they are part of the flock, all of whom depend on the care offered by Peter, which places Peter's representative in the position of true authority.

Gregory then provides an examination of patristic sources that support his position, referencing Pope Gelasius I, Pope Julius, and most especially Pope Gregory I. These patristic sources possessed, as Peters notes, "the authority—as heirs and interpreters of the apostolic tradition (paradosis)—to expound the rules of Christian life and the norms of the interpretation of scripture."[34] In each instance, Gregory VII quotes directly from these popes, supporting his argument for moving against Henry by detailing the precedents that they set in their relationships to both secular and religious leaders. In each case, Gregory attempts to provide justification for both excommunicating and deposing Henry by offering evidence that these precedents exist and therefore proving that he was not acting in an innovative fashion. The strength of the argument is questionable, at best, mainly because neither the Gelasian nor the Julian quotations seems to address the issue of the actions of the pope in secular affairs. While Gregory I does explicitly state that there is the potential for papal action in the secular realm, it is an abstraction, never realized by Gregory I, thus providing only limited value for the defense against charges of innovation. That said, it does still provide Gregory VII with an argument that the conditions which Gregory I set, namely, "if any king, priest, judge, and secular person who knows the text of this enactment of ours shall venture to proceed against it, let him forfeit his office,"[35] have been met and thus action can be taken.

34. Peters, "Transgressing the Limits set by the Fathers," 342.

35. Cowdrey, *The Register of Pope Gregory VII*, 389. Caspar, *Das Register Gregors VII*, 550.

Throughout the argument, Gregory regularly references, both directly and indirectly, the biblical witness to bolster and support the development of his argument for exercising complete freedom in acting on papal prerogatives and in order to indict the secular authorities on charges of wicked behavior. These references, twenty-two scattered throughout the letter, subtly reinforce the claim that Gregory's position remains within the tradition of the church while the secular authorities stand outside of that tradition. The use of the Matthew 16:18–19 passage as noted above is a good example of the way in which Gregory uses references to scripture to bolster his claims that his actions remain within the tradition. The indictment against the secular authorities as laid out in the next paragraph of the letter, and situated within in the context of the larger argument on papal authority, displays the juxtaposition between the religious and secular authorities and their relationship to both tradition and truth. By arguing that he remains within the tradition, Gregory argues that his authority to act derives from scripture and the church fathers, both of whose connection to the true source of authority, God, is unquestioned.

While Gregory is building the case for the authority of the Holy See through references to scripture and the church fathers, he is attempting to dismantle the case for royal authority by asserting, as I. S. Robinson notes, "the startling idea that kingship originated in the prompting of the devil."[36] In this section, Gregory makes reference to Romans 8:34, Galatians 4:8, Job 41:25, and finally Matthew 4:9,[37] which illuminate the relative positions of secular and ecclesial authority.

36. I. S. Robinson, *The Papacy 1073–1198 Continuity and Innovation* (Cambridge: Cambridge University Press, 1990), 410.

37. Romans 8:34, "Who is to condemn? It is Christ Jesus, who died, yes, who was raised, who is at the right hand of God, who indeed intercedes for us." Galatians 4:8, "Formerly, when you did not know God, you were enslaved to beings that by nature are not gods." Job 41:34, "He beholds everything that is high; he is king over all the sons of pride." Matthew 4:9, "and he said to him, 'All these I will give, if you will fall down and worship me.'"

But that we may return to the subject: should not a dignity invented by men who were ignorant of God not be subject to that dignity which the providence of Almighty God has devised for his own honour and mercifully given to the world? Just as his Son is undoubtedly believed to be God and man, so he is held to be high priest, the head of all priests who is sitting at the right hand of the Father and ever interceding for us; he has despised a worldly kingdom whereby the sons of the world are puffed up and has come of his own free will to the priesthood of the cross. Who may not know that kings and dukes have had their origin from those who, being ignorant of God, by pride, rapines, treachery, murders—at length by practically all crimes whatsoever, with the devil, the prince of the world, indeed urging them on, have presumed by blind greed and insupportable presumption to lord it over their equals, namely men? To be sure, when they strive to divert the priests of the Lord to their footsteps, to whom may they more rightly be likened than to him who is head over all the sons of pride? He, when tempting the supreme pontiff himself, the head of priests, the Son of the Most High, and promising him all the kingdoms of this world says, "All things I will give to you, if you will fall down and worship me."[38]

Gregory builds on the use of the biblical references by providing a brief explication of the relationship between the church and secular rulers, by questioning the propriety of anyone in a subordinate position acting as if they held the dominant position. He once again turns to Pope Gregory I to provide the historical example, as Gregory I explains in a letter to Emperor Maurice that even Constantine at the Council of Nicea understood his place in the midst of those who would render final judgments on the issues that they addressed, and remained silent.[39]

Gregory then provides a brief compilation of occurrences when secular rulers were either excommunicated, as in the cases of Pope Innocent excommunicating Emperor Arcadius and Ambrose excommunicating Emperor Theodosius, or deposed, as when Pope Zacharias, in 751, deposed Childeric IV. These references provide Gregory

38. Cowdrey, *The Register of Pope Gregory VII*, 390. Caspar, *Das Register Gregors VII*, 552–53.

39. Cowdrey, *The Register of Pope Gregory VII*, 390. Caspar, *Das Register Gregors VII*, 553.

with the opportunity to detail Ambrose's logic regarding the relative value of religious and secular authorities.

> [H]e writes near the beginning of his book on *pastoralia*: "Brothers, the episcopal honour and dignity cannot possibly be equated to any comparisons. If your comparison is to the lustre of kings and the diadem of princes, it will be far lower than if you compare the metal to lead to the lustre of gold ... we have said all these things by way of preference in order that we might show there to be nothing in this world more pre-eminent than priests, and nothing to be found more exalted than bishops."[40]

After a dismissive statement about secular rulers having less actual power than the low ranking exorcists, Gregory develops a new component of his argument, juxtaposing the motivation of the religious and secular authorities and suggesting that the secular rulers exercise their authority out of purely base motives. "For such men, not being guided by divine love, do not aspire like religious priests to lead for the honour of God and the benefit of souls, but in order that they may display their intolerable pride and that they may fulfill the lust of their soul they aspire to dominate the rest."[41]

This argument reprises a theme first developed in the May 1073 letter to Duke Godfrey of Lower Lorraine, noting that the secular authorities find their motivation to pursue their positions not for the benefit of others but for their own benefit. Even as Gregory holds up Constantine, Theodosius, Honorius, Charlemagne, and Louis the Pious as secular exemplars, celebrating them as "lovers of righteousness, propagators of religion, and defenders of churches,"[42] the praise is blunted by the caveat that they were not "bright with so great a glory of miracles"[43] as the saints. "For which emperor or king

40. Cowdrey, *The Register of Pope Gregory VII*, 391. Caspar, *Das Register Gregors VII*, 555.

41. Cowdrey, *The Register of Pope Gregory VII*, 391. Caspar, *Das Register Gregors VII*, 555–56.

42. Cowdrey, *The Register of Pope Gregory VII*, 393. Caspar, *Das Register Gregors VII*, 559.

43. Cowdrey, *The Register of Pope Gregory VII*, 393. Caspar, *Das Register Gregors VII*, 559.

has raised the dead, cleansed lepers, and given sight to the blind?"[44] Lest any misunderstanding develop, Gregory offers a particularly stark warning against what he perceives to be the fundamental problem with lay authority by stating that the "more they rejoice to prefer themselves to other men in this life, the more they may be plunged beneath eternal fires."[45]

This point is a key to understanding Gregory's relationships to both secular and religious authorities, and his conceptualization of each. In both cases, the expectation is clear: the authority's main objective is to ensure the protection of the people in their care. For religious leaders, as noted earlier, the expectation centered on the effort to ensure the care of souls, even in the face of individuals who were recalcitrant in their sinful behavior. If the attempt is made—if the religious leaders work for the repentance and reform of the people in their care—then they have done what is necessary; they have maintained their focus on what is eternal, not temporal. Gregory understands this to be the same expectation demanded of the secular authorities, but he notes a distinct difference, as he does not recognize the secular authorities as acting in their appropriate roles for the protection of the people, nor does he think that they will, compromised as they are by a desire for "vain glory."[46] In this light, Gregory produced an argument demanding institutional reform, recognizing that the secular authorities were largely incapable or unwilling to act for the sake of others, and thus they should be subordinated to the church, whose leaders had indeed acted in the right and proper manner for the good of the people, reflecting Christ's humility and purpose.

Gregory returns to the biblical witness to provide the necessary

44. Cowdrey, *The Register of Pope Gregory VII*, 393. Caspar, *Das Register Gregors VII*, 559.

45. Cowdrey, *The Register of Pope Gregory VII*, 393. Caspar, *Das Register Gregors VII*, 559.

46. Cowdrey, *The Register of Pope Gregory VII*, 394. Caspar, *Das Register Gregors VII*, 559.

justification for this departure from the long-standing tradition of the established secular rule. Gregory references the story of Saul by directly quoting Pope Gregory I as an example of how secular authorities focus too greatly on their own interests to the detriment of the kingdom and the people, and do so through the sin of idolatry. Gregory offers a way out of this long-standing tradition of idolatrous kingship: humble obedience to the pope and to the church.

> Wherefore let those whom holy church of her own will summons by deliberate counsel to kingship or empire not for transitory glory but for salvation of many show humble obedience, and let them always guard against what blessed Gregory testifies to in the same book on the pastoral care: "For a man is made similar to the apostate angel when he disdains to be similar to men. Thus after possessing the merit of humility, Saul at the summit of power was inflated into the swelling of pride. He was indeed preferred through humility but he was made reprobate through pride, as the Lord bears witness when he says, 'Was it not when you were little in your own eyes that I set you as a head over the tribes of Israel.'" and a little way below: "Now in marvelous manner when he seemed little before himself he was great before the Lord, but indeed when he seemed great before himself he was little before the Lord." Let them also vigilantly hold fast to what the Lord says in the Gospel: "I do not seek my own glory," and: "He who would be first among you, let him be servant of all."[47]

This reference harkens back to the beginning of the letter, when through the appropriated greeting of Gregory I, Gregory VII attempted to signal his humility. This humility becomes a sign of the true authority granted to those who tend the sheep. Authority, as derived from Jesus through St. Peter, and explicated by scripture and the church fathers, provides Gregory with the ability to do as necessary for the sake of the people, including excommunicating and deposing kings. As Robinson comments, "the king must be suitable for the duties prescribed by the church; he must be 'obedient, humbly devoted and useful to holy Church.'"[48] If the king is acting

47. Cowdrey, *The Register of Pope Gregory VII,* 395. Caspar, *Das Register Gregors VII,* 561–62.

48. Robinson, *The Papacy 1073–1198: Continuity and Innovation,* 411.

for his own glory, defined by Gregory as not working directly for the glory of the church by not being obedient to the church, then the church can act for the benefit of the people.

Gregory VII's idea of reform, grounded and supported in and through the biblical witness, and likewise supported by a small collection of patristic and conciliar sources, most notably Pope Gregory I, envisions a society brought back from the brink of disaster through the leadership of the pope and the church. The secular authorities work with but are subordinate to the church. The goal of reform is a society built on the care of souls and protection of the people who depend on the care of those in leadership positions, both clerical and lay. It was imperative that the religious leaders tended to the needs of the people, or at least made the effort to do so, thereby showing that they continually focused on "spiritual and not temporal interests." For Gregory, to lose focus on the spiritual was to act like the secular authorities who devoted themselves not to the care of the people but to their own needs. The focus on the spiritual reinforced the connection to the truth, and thus blunted the charge of innovation, for truth was unchangeable and the highest authority.

Finally, when attempting to ascertain Gregory VII's motivation, it is beneficial to focus on the spiritual, on his religious beliefs and his pastoral perspective. First and foremost, Gregory was a religious leader attempting to remain faithful to his call as he understood it, a call he firmly believed to be given by Christ through St. Peter, and to a lesser extent, the prophets. Thus Gregory's language and actions, including the use of scripture as authoritative texts meant to support, develop, and articulate his pastoral ideals, were driven by this self-understanding. Gregory firmly believed that he was articulating the truth and was acting as the advocate for the necessary reform of the church based on that truth. This does not discount his rhetorical excesses, and in fact, may help to explain the excesses. As his fortunes deteriorated, his religious and pastoral ideals were more and more frustrated by those he perceived as failing to share his belief in the necessity of embracing his reform. The more they resisted, the more forceful and coercive his claims became; if the people could not be led to reform, then they would be pushed or dragged. Such intransigence in the face of failure was ultimately self-defeating, but it was consistent with Gregory's belief that he was living out his call to reform the church.

6

ADMINISTRATIVE CHANGE IN THE FOURTEENTH-CENTURY DOMINICAN ORDER

A Case Study in Partial Reforms and Incomplete Theories

MICHAEL VARGAS

Over the course of the thirteenth century the followers of Dominic of Guzmán fashioned something new, productive, and vigorous, an Order of Preachers that at its prime Innocent IV called Christianity's "public workhorse" and that friar historians in our time have called "the most perfect of the monastic organizations produced in the Middle Ages."[1] Into the 1300s, however, convents in the Order of Preachers housed lying, cheating thieves, wanton seekers of pleasure, gamblers, wanderers, and womanizers—a state of affairs

1. For a discussion of Innocent IV's bull in the context of other papal lauds, see Pierre S. Mandonnet, *St. Dominic and His Work* (St. Louis: Herder, 1944), 71–73, and Marie-Humbert Vicaire, "Dominicans: 13th Century," *The Papacy: An Encyclopedia*, edited by Philippe Levillain, (New York: Routledge, 2002), 1:506–7. William Hinnebusch, *The History of the Dominican Order* (Staten Island, N.Y.: Alba House, 1965/1973), I:169.

evinced not only in anti-mendicant literature but also in the friars' own records. If we accept the standard accounts, the decline-decay crisis that befell the order in the fourteenth century was of external origin, something affecting all the orders in a cataclysmic age of economic dislocation, plague, war, and schism. It is also part of the conventional story that the flagging discipline of the late-medieval bad-boy friars needed reform, and so it happened that by 1390 Raymond of Capua and others initiated a plan to correct errant friars and renew mission zeal. In the fifteenth century the Dominican Order "preserved by Divine Providence … sprung back to new life."[2]

Following and elaborating such rise, decline, and reform narratives, Gerhart Ladner believed he had discerned a universal Christian truth. Reform in its various contexts, Ladner theorized, manifests as a series of "free, intentional and ever perfectible, multiple, prolonged and ever repeated efforts by man to reassert and augment values pre-existent in the spiritual-material compound of the world."[3] This definition of a constant and meaningful process of change in the church makes sense to those who believe that disparate reforms all connect to Christianity's self-perpetuating core. Thus, Ladner's conception has become the basis of fifty years of research. From another perspective, however, the notion of a perennial reform action in the church is a crude device, arguably an unworkable one.

In part this essay undertakes a critique of the model of reform that Ladner and others have bequeathed to us. It also examines evidence from within the Dominican Order's Province of Aragon of an attempt at reform in the mid-fourteenth century. The sources from this province, especially the recorded acts of annual provincial chapters, have special importance for the purpose of contemplating weaknesses in Ladner's model. The province emerged as a sepa-

2. William Hinnebusch, "How the Dominican Order Faced Its Crises," *Review for Religious* 32 (1976): 1307–21, at 1307.

3. Gerhart B. Ladner, *The Idea of Reform: Its impact on Christian Thought and Action in the Age of the Fathers* (Cambridge, Mass.: Harvard University Press, 1959), 35.

rate administrative territory upon division of the larger Province of Spain in 1301. Thus, the new province came into existence at the beginning of a period of supposed decline. It is also clear, nonetheless, that during its first years the province's managers sought to bring the friars in their charge into healthy religious observance. Reform and decline, we might say, were bound together by the very real exigencies of place and time from the very start. However, despite the invigoration of zeal at the province's birth, discipline deteriorated, as it did in other provinces. By 1350 another concentrated period of reform had begun.

Historians have mostly overlooked the mid-century reform examined here because it was not entirely a robust success.[4] Still, the chapter acts available to us, by far the richest administrative sources remaining from any province in the fourteenth century, tell us in considerable detail about the reform strategies and tactics of Dominican officials. Counted among them were Bernat Sescala and Nicolas Rossell, both skilled inquisitors who led some of the most important cases against heresy in the region before serving in turn as prior of the Province of Aragon (Rossell was provincial prior from 1350 until 1356, when he left the provincialate upon being appointed Cardinal of San Sisto by Innocent VI).[5] Moreover, as a mostly unsuccessful effort, as more or less a failure, the reform effort undertaken by Dominican ad-

4. For an overview of affairs in the Province of Aragon in the fourteenth century, see P. Vito T. Gómez García, O.P., "La Provincia en el primer siglo de su Historia," in *La Provincia Dominicana de Aragón: siete siglo de vida y misión*, edited by Gómez García, Alfonso Esponera Cerdán, Lorenzo Galmés Más, and Vicente Forcada Comíns (Madrid: Edibesa, 1999), 35–68.

5. Adolfo Robles Sierra, O.P., published the twenty-six years of extant acts from 1302 through 1366, in installments published in *Escritos del Vedat* 20–26 (Valencia, 1990–1996). P. Vito T. Gómez García, O.P., subsequently published the twenty-two years of extant acts from 1368 to 1399 in *Escritos del Vedat* 27–35 (1997–2005). Hereafter I will refer to the published acts in abbreviated form, e.g., Robles Sierra, "Actas," *EV* 23 (1993), 259. For an overview of affairs in the Province of Aragon in the fourteenth century, see P. Vito T.Gómez García, O.P., "La Provincia en el primer siglo de su Historia," in *La Provincia Dominicana de Aragón*, 35–68. As indicated by Patrick Zutshi and Robert Ombres, O.P., "The Dominicans in Cambridge, 1238–1538," *Archivum fratrum praedicatorum* 60 (1990): 313–373 at 314, surviving administrative records from the Dominican Order in the fourteenth-century

ministrators in the middle of the fourteenth century has much to tell us about the complexity of organizational change in the late-medieval period and about the weakness of reform as an analytical tool.

The idea of a reform action constantly at work within the Catholic Church had great potency for Ladner and others in the crisis years leading to the Second Vatican Council. Examinations of the meaning and history of reform came in a flood preceding the Council's *aggiornamento*.[6] In the decades since Vatican II, students of reform have continued to press further, although the search for the ubiquity of reform has grown muddled. Increased attention has magnified the imprecision of the vocabulary.[7] The categories of a reform typology have multiplied without a substantiation of their analytic utility.[8] Moreover, many presentations of reform, especially those treating religious orders, exhibit a problematic circularity and cyclicality.[9]

---

present "a considerably defaced mosaic." For their limited survival, see "Bibliographiae," edited by Simon Tugwell, in *Dominican History Newsletter* (Oxford: Centrum Historicum Dominicanum, 1992), 1–20.

6. On the "crisis" leading to Vatican II, see *History of Vatican II*, 3 vols., edited by Giuseppe Alberigo and Joseph A Komonchak (Maryknoll, N.Y.: Orbis, 1995–2006), 1:60–91. Seminal works linking the church history to the call for reform are Yves-Marie Congar, *Vraie et fausse réforme dans l'Église* (Paris: Cerf, 1950); Herbert Jedin, *Geschichte des Konzils von Trient* (Freiburg: Verlag Herder, 1950); Olivier Rousseau, *Le Concile et les Conciles* (Paris: Éditions de Chevetogne, 1960); and Hans Küng, *The Council, Reform, and Reunion* (New York: Sheed and Ward, 1962).

7. Christopher Bellitto, *Renewing Christianity: A History of Church Reform from Day One to Vatican II* (Mahwah, N.J.: Paulist Press, 2001), 6–14, reviews the vocabulary of reform. Louis Hamilton's introductory comments in *Reforming the Church before Modernity: Patterns, Problems, and Approaches* edited by Christopher Bellitto and Louis Hamilton (Burlington, Vt.: Ashgate, 2005), xv, admits that reform and its analogues are "all words and concepts we scholars commonly use, even if we lack common, readily articulated definitions of what they mean." John O'Malley, *Trent and All That: Renaming Catholicism in the Early Modern Era* (Cambridge, Mass: Harvard University Press, 2000), 6–7, calls customary usage "careless."

8. Recent accounts describe reform as personal, institutional, moral, procedural, mystical, programmatic, radical, pragmatic, general, special, of head, of members, top-down, bottom-up, national, conciliar, pro-papal, anti-papal, clerical, anti-clerical, magisterial, lay, liturgical, structural, cultural, centralized, local, strategic, organic, focused or diffused, back to the better past, toward the future, true and false, etc.

9. E.g., Bruce Taylor, *Structures of Reform: The Mercedarian Order in the Spanish Golden Age* (Leiden: Brill, 2000), 413.

Some researchers have laid bare a number of practical and analytical problems that weaken the notion of reform's continuities. One such problem is periodization. There is now no period in church history that has not been treated as an age of reform.[10] This might lead one to imagine that some constant operates in reform logic or method, but the literature has not borne this out. Especially troublesome are the multiplicity of overlapping chronologies at the breakdown of Catholic primacy in the early modern era, which make a mockery of the notion of a single and essential idea of Christian reform that transcends historical eras and polemics.[11] Those multiple chronologies point instead to parallel reforms, reforms operating in cross currents, and reforms in competition with one another.[12] Our attempts to more carefully temporalize reform diminish the potency of any supposed universality by pointing instead to the unique and important particularities of time and place. If reform possesses essential attributes across the variety of historically posited reforms, those attributes remain hidden from us.

10. A few illustrative examples: On reform through the eleventh century, Ladner, *The Idea of Reform* and Gerhart B.Ladner, "Gregory the Great and Gregory VII: A Comparison of Their Concepts of Renewal," *Viator* 4 (1973): 1–26. For the twelfth century, *Renaissance and Renewal in the Twelfth Century,* edited by Robert Louis Benson, Giles Constable, Carol Dana Lanham, and Charles Homer Haskins, (Cambridge, Mass.: Harvard University Press, 1982), and Giles Constable, *The Reformation of the Twelfth Century* (Cambridge: Cambridge University Press, 1996). From the thirteenth century into the early modern era: Steven Ozment, *The Age of Reform, 1250–1550: An Intellectual and Religious History of Late Medieval and Reformation Europe* (New Haven: Yale University Press, 1981); Rudolph Heinze, *Reform and Conflict: From the Medieval World to the Wars of Religion, AD 1350–1648* (Grand Rapids: Baker Books, 2005).

11. Guy Bedouelle, *Le réforme du Catholicisme, 1480–1620* (Paris: Cerf, 2002); *The Reform of Catholicism, 1480–1620,* translated and annotated by James K. Farge (Toronto: Pontifical Institute of Mediaeval Studies, 2008); John C. Olin, *Catholic Reform: From Cardinal Ximenes to the Council of Trent, 1495–1563* (New York: Fordham University Press, 1990); R. Po-chia Hsia, *The World of Catholic Renewal, 1540–1770* (Cambridge: Cambridge University Press, 1998); Eric Nelson, *The Jesuits and the Monarchy: Catholic Reform and Political Authority in France, 1590–1615* (Burlington, Vt: Ashgate, 2005).

12. E.g., Heiko Oberman, *Forerunners of the Reformation: the Shape of late Medieval Thought* (New York: Holt, Rinehart and Winston, 1966); Jaroslav Pelikan, *Obedient Rebels: Catholic Substance and Protestant Principle in Luther's Reformation* (New York: Harper & Row, 1964). O'Malley, *Trent and All That,* offers a critical appraisal.

Agency presents another difficulty. Histories of reform regularly applaud the successes of exemplary leaders who set their course and get the job done. Historians have thus imagined Dominic of Guzmán as a man of genius, a possessor of keen intelligence, who with statesman-like vision and a talent for organization founded the Order of Preachers. "As with all great leaders," says C. H. Lawrence, "there was an inspirational quality about his strategic decisions."[13] Raymond of Capua, credited with spearheading a Dominican Observant Movement after 1390, also plays the part of the reforming saint in the order's histories. We ascribe the impetus for change to individuals, making them reform heroes, but we know that hero myths often overlook the exigencies of time and place. Success stories and hero myths work by detaching from group processes, and their purpose is often to defend against rival readings of the past.[14]

Acknowledging the imperfections of current conceptions of reform may open for us alternative means and methods of studying change in the church. Recent work in the study of organizations has been especially useful in historicizing corporate change, and some work in that field is readily applicable to the study of long-lived organizations like the church and religious orders.[15] Empirical studies of administrative heritage, for example, have shown how a corporation's earliest managerial practices can put limits on the ways that successor leaders respond to changes in their environment.[16] Recent

13. C. H. Lawrence, *The Friars: The Impact of the Early Mendicant Movement on Western Society* (New York: Longman, 1995), 65–66.

14. Christine Caldwell Ames, *Righteous Persecution: Inquisition, Dominicans and Christianity in the Middle Ages* (Philadelphia: University of Pennsylvania Press, 2009), 94–134, illustrates the construction of Dominic's saintliness as a political enterprise.

15. W. Richard Scott, *Institutions and Organizations* (Thousand Oaks, Ca.: Sage, 2001), and William Ocasio, "Organizational Change," in *International Encyclopedia of Organization Studies*, 4 vols., edited by Stewart R. Clegg and James R. Bailey (Thousand Oaks, Ca.: Sage, 2008), 3:1020–25, review recent research trends.

16. Christopher A. Bartlett and Sumantra Ghoshal, *Managing across Borders* (Boston: Harvard Business School Press, 1989), is the foundational study of the way corporations are limited by their inheritance of administrative principles and practices. The authors intended to explain the hesitancy of corporations to make a move to multinational status, but the applicability of their research has been broadly felt.

studies of the Dominican Order in its milieu have begun to adopt the view that the friars' foundational ideals and processes contributed to generational disabilities. John Van Engen has called them "creative tensions."[17] The reform paradigm generally overlooks the possibility of an imperfect starting point, assuming instead that the initial state of a religious order or other Church entity approximates an ideal from which individuals and organizations fall away over time.

Studies in human cognition and in the sociology and anthropology of organizations also make abundantly clear the uncomfortable fullness of collective experience in living and working environments.[18] Aggression, injustice, and retaliation make up a dark side of collective work and action.[19] Studies of reform mostly ignore these realities of collective encounter, assuming instead that reform is an either/or proposition in which those who are right, the reformers, and those who are wrong, the reformed, make no room for an ambiguous, conflicted, or contradictory middle ground. Personal and corporate honor also have their place in organizational history. Public relations and propaganda in the shaping of corporate identity play a

17. See esp. John Van Engen, "From Canons to Preachers: A Revolution in Medieval Governance," in *Domenico di Caleruega e la nascità dell'ordine dei frati predicatori* (Spoleto: Fondazione Centro italiano di studi sull'alto Medioevo, 2005), 261–95. Henri-Charles Chéry, "Les Dominicains," in *Les Ordres Religieux II: Les Ordres Actifs*, edited by Gabriel Le Bras (Paris: Flammarion, 1980), 375–529, also sees the germ of later problems in the order's initial successes.

18. *Individualism and Collectivism: Theory, Method, and Applications*, edited by Ulchol Kim et al. (Thousand Oaks, Ca.: Sage, 1994); Michael T. Hannan and Glenn R. Carroll, *Dynamics of Organizational Populations: Density, Legitimation, and Competition* (Oxford: Oxford University Press, 1992); Joel Baum and J. V. Singh, "Organizational Niches and the Dynamics of Organizational Mortality," *American Journal of Sociology* 100 (1994): 346–80; Alessandro Lomi and Erik Reimer Larsen, "Failure as a Structural Concept: A Computational Perspective on Age Dependence in Organizational Mortality Rates," in *Dynamics of Organizations: Computational Modeling and Organizational Theories*, edited by Alessandro Lomi and Erik Reimer Larsen (Cambridge, Mass.: MIT Press, 2001), 269–306. Also see Hayagreeva Rao, Calvin Morrill, and Mayer Zald, "Power Plays: How Social Movements and Collective Action Create New Organizational Forms," *Research in Organizational Behavior* 22 (2000): 239–82.

19. *The Dark Side of Organizational Behavior*, edited by Ricky Griffin and Anne O'Leary-Kelly (San Francisco: Jossey-Bass, 2004); Thomas Donaldson, *Corporations and Morality* (Englewood Cliffs, N.J.: Prentice-Hall, 1982).

crucial role as they spin opinion, sometimes deceptively, in ways that help corporations to take advantage of opportunities and overcome obstacles to growth.[20] A commonality among these approaches is a recognition that internal stresses typically bring more lasting devastation to an organization than external change factors. Reform is, from this vantage, an incomplete explanation of the fuller problem of corporate survival. In the case of the Dominicans, there is nothing to dissuade us from Mary Douglas's observation that "all social systems are built on contradiction, in some sense at war with themselves."[21]

Like any long-lived and deeply engaged organization, the medieval Order of Preachers faced difficult challenges. The order's "first crisis" grew acute into the 1250s after university masters joined the ranks of bishops and priests in challenging the successes of the order. Humbert of Romans and other of the order's leaders responded by seeking support from the papacy, which girded the friars with privileges and protections, assuring the order's passage through that storm of criticism even as it grew more fully committed to serving papal objectives.[22] It was in the context of this reciprocity that Innocent IV proclaimed the Order of Preachers Christendom's "public workhorse."[23]

20. David Fleming, "Narrative Leadership: Using the Power of Stories," *Strategy & Leadership* 29 (2001): 34–36, and Stephen Denning, *The Secret Language of Leadership: How Leaders Inspire Action Through Narrative* (San Francisco: Jossey-Bass, 2007), give instructions for propagating myths of corporate strength and success. For an antidote, Robert X. Cringley, *Accidental Empires: How the Boys of Silicon Valley Make Their Millions, Battle Foreign Competition, and Still Can't Get a Date* (Reading, Mass.: Addison-Wesley, 1992).

21. Mary Douglas, *Purity and Danger: An Analysis of Concepts of Pollution and Taboo* (New York: Praeger, 1966), 140.

22. On the "first crisis" see Hinnebusch, "Crises," 1308–9; Lawrence, *The Friars*, 152–65; Yves Congar, "Aspects ecclésiologiques de la querelle entre mendiants et séculiers dans la second moitié de XIIIe siècle et le début du XIVe," *Archives d'histoire doctrinal et littéraire du moyen âge* 38 (1961): 35–151; Decima Douie, *The Conflict between the Seculars and the Mendicants at the University of Paris in the Thirteenth Century* (London: Blackfriars, 1954). Francisco García-Serrano, *Preachers in the City: The Expansion of the Dominican Order in Castile (1217–1438)* (New Orleans: University Press of the South, 1997), 75–94, offers a detailed local example of the Dominicans' successful quest to wrestle spiritual and economic power from the cathedral canons of Castilian Burgos.

23. Vicaire, "Dominicans," 507.

The crisis of the fourteenth century was far more destabilizing. The friar-historian William Hinnebusch and others within the order have explained that changes in the individual and corporate disposition of the friars resulted from "world shaking events" that disfigured all church institutions. "Late in its first century," Hinnebusch insisted, "the Order entered a decline-decay crisis that reached a climax in widespread collapse of spirit and religious discipline. The crisis originated in the multiplicity of problems that characterized the times and plagued the Church and all the Orders.... The signs of decline began to appear in the order about 1290. They became notably worse by 1325 and reached their peak after the Black Death, 1348–49."[24] In this view, external factors beyond the control of Dominican leaders caused the Order its internal operational and disciplinary distress. It is clear that one objective of such a claim is to deflect responsibility for bad behavior: no fault falls upon the friars or on their corporate systems. Another is to allow reform its providential space. Crisis threatened the order, bringing it close to the point of extinction, but the reform that followed reconfirmed its providential mission. Friar-historians and others concur.[25] However, such claims hardly encompass all of the evidence. Outside the grip of the meta-narrative of rise, decline, and reform, other possibilities emerge.

The truth of Dominican dysfunction in the fourteenth century contradicts this focus on externalities. Two examples will illustrate the point. The first shows Berengar of Landora, Master General of the order in the opening decades of the fourteenth century, making

24. William Hinnebusch, *A Short History of the Dominican Order* (New York: Alba House, 1975), 71–72.

25. E.g., José-María de Garganta, "Los Dominicos de la Provincia de Aragón en la Historia de la Espiritualidad, Siglos XIV–XVII," *Teología Espiritual* 1 (1957): 89–112. M.C.M.D.P.D.S.J.D.M.E.G., *Dictionnaire historique-portatif des ordres religieux et militaires, et des congregations regulières & séculières qui ont existé jusqu'à nos jours: contenant leur origine, leur progrés, leur décadence & les différentes réformes qu'ils ont éprouvées; avec les marques qui les distinguent les uns des autres* (Amsterdam: Chez Marc-Michel Rey, 1769), 115–20, is an early example of the decline-reform thesis.

accommodations to practices recognizably out of step with Dominican law. The second demonstrates the emergence of competing values within the mainstream of Dominican corporate culture.

In 1314 Berengar came to Valencia, in the order's Province of Aragon, to participate in the annual provincial chapter meeting there. At his departure he left a long letter with the Provincial Prior, Arnau Burguet, addressed to all the friars of the province, in which he noted serious lapses and defects in behavior. These included riding horses against constitutional ordinance, eating meat without good cause, excessive excursions outside the convents, leaving candles lit for friars returning late at night, and imprudent familiarity with women. Against each inappropriate activity he authorized a punishment or a shaming episode to be exacted upon the derelict, ranging from a physical beating to various physical and mental deprivations, including removal to another convent. As further remedy and reform he offered reminders, warnings, and injunctions on a range of matters including consumption of foods and meat.[26]

Berengar is recognized as a reformer, although on the subject of meat consumption his letter shows him making some uncomfortable decisions, at once demonstrating his zeal for observance and his willingness to bend to circumstance.[27] He reiterated the constitutional prohibition of meat consumption and the constitutionally permitted exception for sick friars. However, he then granted a meat-eating privilege to lectors, teaching masters in the province's convents. Berengar rationalized this dispensation—which was plainly contrary to the letter and spirit of the law, and to the rigor his own letter sought to impose—on two grounds. First, he admitted that the work

26. Robles Sierra, "Actas," *EV* 21 (1991), 106–54, at 140–44. Berengar's long letter was copied as the concluding section of the manuscript copy of the 1314 *acta* under the rubric "Epistola Reverendissimi fratris Berengarii Rutenensis XIII Magistri Ordinis Predicatorum, ad fratres Provincie Aragonie, adnexa Actis precedentibus."

27. On Berengar's reforms, see R. P. Mortier, *Histoire des Maitres Généraux de l'Ordre des Frères Prêcheurs* (Paris: A. Picara, 1902–1920), 2:474–80. Also Thomas Kaepelli, *Scriptores Ordinis Praedicatorum Medii Aevi* (Rome: 1980–1993), 4:191–94 and Hinnebusch, *History of the Dominican Order,* 1:203–4.

of conventual lectors was difficult. Second, he acknowledged that meat-eating among lectors had become, as he put it, "a laudable custom in other provinces."[28] Lectors in the Province of Aragon lobbied him to permit them a relaxation already granted, by custom, to other members of their corporate subgroup. He felt compelled to comply. Evidence within the letter suggests that Berengar might have wanted his decision to go differently but that he felt himself incapable of making some high-ranking friars heed a call to greater rigor and austerity.[29]

Privileges rankled the underprivileged, who then argued for their share. By mid-century the order's leaders permitted meat to all friars four times each year. And still the friars pushed for more. At times the internal tug-of-war about who could eat meat when, how much, and in what form, approached what we might deem comic extremes. In the mid-1350s, for instance, the Prior Provincial Nicolas Rossell had to make it clear that meatballs in stews (*bolos notabiles in potagio*) were indeed meat, and thus prohibited outside the four permitted seasons.[30] Dominican authorities, clearly, found no reason to laugh. Master Berengar and Nicolas Rossell, along with others, showed great zeal in their efforts to correct operational and disciplinary wrongs. Nonetheless, they did not succeed at turning around more than a century's inertia in the direction of an expanding smorgasbord of friar privileges.[31]

28. Robles Sierra, "Actas," *EV* 21 (1991), 142: "carnes fratribus non concedantur.… Cum lectoribus tamen qui legunt aliquo tempore anni, propter laborem, sicut est consuetum laudabiliter in aliis Provinciis, dispensatur."

29. Berengar specifically demanded that conventual priors prevent others in their charge from eating meat. One might thus argue that Berengar was forcing conventual priors to take actions he himself was unwilling to take, that is, that they should be the chief enforcers of discipline while he, to the contrary, permitted exceptions that made the task for local priors more difficult. Administrators can be duplicitous, perhaps increasingly so the higher they are in the decision-making hierarchy.

30. Robles Sierra, "Actas," *EV* 24 (1994), 274.

31. On inertia in corporate settings, see among others Dennis Gromb, "Cultural Inertia and Uniformity in Organizations," *Journal of Law, Economics and Organization* 23 (2007): 743–71, and S. Schaefer, "Influence Costs, Structural Inertia, and Organizational Change," *Journal of Economics and Management Strategy* 7 (1998): 237–63.

Master Berengar plays a part in a second example of Dominican corporate dynamics that similarly shows the comparative simplicity of reform as an analytical tool by illustrating the complexity of the order's corporate culture. At the core of this exemplum is the operation of competing values. Ambition, in this instance, may not have been compatible with humility, but it definitely found its place as an operational reality.

At the general chapter meeting held in Bologna in 1315 Master Berengar took action to remove Arnau Burguet from the office of provincial prior of the Province of Aragon. Arnau's career to this point was already both brilliant and rocky. He had been an advanced student at the turn of the fourteenth century, schooled at Bologna and at the *studium generale* in Barcelona. The province's assignment rosters list him as Doctor in 1307, the first year in which we find him in trouble. In that year, Miquel de Estella, then Provincial Prior, harshly rebuked Burguet for decorating his habit in extravagant colors and ordered the prideful brother to re-dye his clothes immediately in the order's traditional drab.[32] Burguet, like other friar-doctors, wished to wear his reputation on his sleeves. In correcting him Estella knew that such status displays, if permitted, would demonstrate too crudely that the order was no longer an egalitarian collective.[33]

Arnau Burguet's case is especially instructive because it brought him none of the punishments typically meted out to erring friars—only, perhaps, the sting to his reputation that came with his public censure in the province's annual chapter acts. In any event, his being reprimanded on such a serious matter in no way limited his career. Despite the misdemeanor on record, Arnau Burguet went on to become prior of the convent of Mallorca in 1310; in 1312 the friars in the

32. Robles Sierra, "Actas," *EV* 20 (1990), 277–78.

33. The development of a "class system" within the order is well recognized, although not often admitted in histories by friar-historians. For an exception, Benedict Ashley, O.P., *The Dominicans* (Collegeville, Minn.: Liturgical Press, 1990), 43.

prominent convent of Barcelona elected him as their prior; later that same year he attended the provincial chapter where he received the honorific title of preacher general. These were plum offices, appointments and honors, bestowed upon him within no more than a half-decade of his censure for conceit.[34]

In 1314, Burguet's peers elected him to the priorate of the Province of Aragon, the highest office in the order excepting only the master general's. From this peak in his career, he once again fell, summarily removed, as I have indicated, by Berengar of Landora. Master Berengar's letter of absolution implicates Burguet in an election tampering scheme, of which there are many recorded. Berengar deprived Burguet of his "voice," his voting rights, for a period of ten years.[35] Because evidence indicates that loss of voice for even a year or two was a harsh penalty, reserved for serious offenders, we should consider Burguet's offense and punishment extraordinary.[36] Still, even this second confrontation with Dominican justice did not impede his career. He became a noted inquisitor. He likely composed the *Vetus vita* of his highly esteemed Catalan confrere Raymond of Penyafort. In 1321—that is, before his penance had run its course—friars in the province reelected him to the provincial prior's office once again. This time Burguet served until his death in 1325.

Despite his limited adherence to traditional Dominican principles and proscriptions, Burguet possessed a strong combination of bold character and enterprise that other friars regarded highly. Generosity and service motivated many friars who wished to act in accordance with the humility, discipline, and poverty of Dominic and the first friars, but even some of the order's leaders, the best and brightest

34. For an outline of Burguet's career, Laureano Robles, *Escritores Dominicos de la Corona de Aragón, siglos XIII–XV* (Salamanca: Calatrava, 1977), 92–93.

35. Robles Sierra, "Actas," *EV* 21 (1991), 144; cf. *Acta capitulorum generalium ordinis Praedicatorum, ab anno 1304 usque ad annum 1378,* edited by B. M. Reichert, Monumenta ordinis fratrum Praedicatorum historica (Rome: 1899), 4:85.

36. Georgina R. Galbraith, *The Constitution of the Dominican Order, 1216–1360* (Manchester: Manchester University Press, 1925), 84.

men like Arnau Burguet, acknowledged another reality, one that included avidity, status-seeking, and thirst for competitive gain.[37]

Berengar's deference to an elite clique and Burguet's ambitions to join the ranks of the elite, while only two examples of the complications of everyday administration and politics inside the fourteenth-century Order of Preachers, should be enough to suggest something richer than what the decline and reform model permits. The corporate culture of the Order of Preachers was not immutable. Out of a century and more of change a new operational reality slowly emerged, one not entirely healthy for the order but one that no friar, including the order's most reform-minded administrators, could do without or entirely rise above. The disabilities were systemic. That does not mean, however, that they went unrecognized. Berengar and other masters general took corrective action, as did Miguel de Estella, Bernat Sescala, Nicolas Rossell and others in the provinces.[38]

Four general features characterize the reforms undertaken. First, the order's leaders made unmistakably deliberate attempts at changing behaviors and at strengthening command and control. In the thirteenth century, as is well known, general and provincial

37. Earlier in the order's history Gerard of Frachet and Jordan of Saxony, among others, commented on the growing problem of friars "greedy for their own private reputation." See John Van Engen, "Dominic and His Brothers" in *Christ Among the Medieval Dominicans: Representations of Christ in the Texts and Images of the Order of Preachers,* edited by Kent Emery and Joseph P. Wawrykow (Notre Dame: University of Notre Dame Press, 1998) 11, 17–18, and Simon Tugwell, *Early Dominicans: Selected Writings* (New York: Paulist Press, 1982), 122–25.

38. As regards the competencies of reformers in the Province of Aragon, Bernat Sescala and Nicolas Rossell served their order in a variety of official capacities before election to the provincialate. Both held the post of Inquisitor General of Aragon while serving as provincial prior. Both played active roles in the controversies of their time and had ongoing contacts with popes and kings. Evidence suggests that both men, like Nicolas Eymerich and Bernat Ermengaud, who followed them into both the inquisitor's role and the office of provincial prior, had difficult temperaments and led stormy relationships. They were well placed to discern the administrative needs of their province and to advance an agenda for change. Sescala, the province's tenth provincial, served from 1343 through 1350. Rossell, who became the eleventh provincial in 1350, retired from office in 1356 to take up residence in Avignon as the cardinal of San Sisto.

chapter acts show administrators struggling to measure the aptitudes and adequacy of postulants, students, and preachers. Into the fourteenth century, admonitions addressing questions of the friars' competencies appeared with even greater frequency, treated a broader range of concerns, and became considerably more sharply focused.[39] Even a cursory reading of general and provincial chapter acts reveals the imposition of a range of competency tests and the imposition of oversight committees. Some of these sought to prevent wayward friars from covertly exiting their convents.[40] Others established minimum standards intended to keep lectors at their teaching tasks and students engaged in their studies.[41] Others kept ill-prepared friars from representing the order in public ministry. In this case it is clear that provincial administrators deliberately reworked general chapter edicts to give them teeth at the local level.[42] In each case the admonitions admit very serious problems of management and discipline, but when viewed from beyond a decline and reform paradigm they show development from year to year, becoming more carefully targeted and increasingly better-crafted with time. Administrators meant to create and direct change, not just respond to events around them.

The second general feature of fourteenth-century reforms is that they redrew lines of authority. In the Province of Aragon provincials sought to gain greater control over decisions previously left to priors of local convents. The restriction of the decision-making authorities of conventual priors is especially well expressed in the establishment of conventual committees of elders, which came to take

39. A comparison of an admonition from 1302, Robles Sierra, "Actas," *EV* 20 (1990), 247, and another from 1351, Robles Sierra, "Actas," *EV* 23 (1993), 309, illustrates their increased weightiness over time.

40. E.g., Gómez-García, "Actas," *EV* 27 (1997), 279.

41. E.g., Robles Sierra, "Actas," *EV* 23 (1993), 259–60.

42. Compare Reichert, *Acta Capitulorum Generalium,* MOPH IV, 56, to Robles Sierra, "Actas," *EV* 21 (1991), 124. By 1345, Robles Sierra, "Actas," *EV* 23 (1993), 261–62, Bernat Sescala threatened local priors with removal from office if they licensed insufficiently prepared friars for preaching.

charge, at the provincial's urging, of important decisions, including: when a friar might leave his convent to preach; when and how per diem expenses were paid to traveling friars; whether a prior had appropriately granted a dispensation from the rule and constitutions or wisely expended a convent's funds.[43] With these changes came a concomitant strengthening of notions of superior-subordinate relations. One can take a broad measure of this trend by counting the increased usage of the word "superior," which came to replace the word "prelate" in contexts deliberately meant to construct hierarchies. A more precise indicator of the rhetorical shift came in 1345 when Bernat Sescala drew upon the language of traditional monastic obedience—an institution that the early Dominicans adopted only in a very weak form for the explicit purpose of confirming a chain of command.[44] Paradoxically, as conventual priors became nominal superiors in their locales, their substantive authority diminished; provincial priors, meanwhile, augmented their own superior powers to decide, supervise, and correct.[45]

A third feature of these reforms is strengthening of a managerial logic, which is to say that reformers grew less interested in traditional means of moral persuasion bound to rewards and punishments in

43. The range of examples increases in frequency by the mid-1340s. Representative admonitions include, from 1345, Robles Sierra, "Actas," *EV* 23 (1993), 260–61: four elders must give consent when a prior wishes to license a friar to go to town during class time; from 1347, Robles Sierra, "Actas," *EV* 23 (1993), 280–81: two elders put in oversight of a trust fund for the sick; from 1366, Robles Sierra, "Actas," *EV* 26 (1996), 128: the provincial chapter requires that two elders from each convent inspect the width and length of every piece of each friar's clothing, using as a standard what was permitted in "the olden days." Many of these appear to have had the support of both masters general and provincial-level advisors (difinitors).

44. Robles Sierra, "Actas," *EV* 23 (1993), 259.

45. By the 1350s the phrase "we expressly subtract the power from presidents" appeared regularly in the acts of the Province of Aragon as a way of confirming the powers of provincials to dictate new rules to priors. Appearing twice in extant acts prior to 1345 it is witnessed on more than fifteen occasions thereafter. In one case, to make the point absolutely clear, Nicolas Rossell told local priors that if they continued to offer dispensations too liberally (the very same dispensations that a century of practice had regularized), he would punish offenders so harshly as to serve "as a terror and example to others." See Robles Serra, "Actas," *EV* 24 (1994), 253.

the hereafter than in strengthening command and control for the here and now. Evidence of this is a matter both of increased rhetorical precision and also what we can perceive as the gains that came with the repetition and intensification of a battery of administrative dictates. One objective measure of this institutional elaboration is an increase in both the number of admonitory statements and their word length. Annual admonitory items in the Province of Aragon averaged approximately 600 words in the first decade of the fourteenth century and climbed to a high of 4,200 words by the mid-1350s. The tendency to prolixity was not accidental, as the chapter acts themselves made clear to their readers.[46] The inflated number and length of recorded admonitions put forward more instructions more precisely. That precision was also a matter of rhetoric. Nicolas Rossell's pronouncement that "laws are useless unless observed," arriving as it does in the context of his assertion that obstructionist brothers constitute a "brood of vipers," is a demonstration of this rhetoric reaching its apex in the decade after 1350.[47]

Finally, a fourth general feature of Dominican efforts at corporate reorganization in the fourteenth century is the concern for defending corporate honor. The first friars built up for their organization a solid corporate reputation, but with time the order's perceived corporate abuses and the friars' lack of self-restraint began to weigh on that reputation, becoming the source of what theorists call a "legitimacy gap." General and provincial chapters made it part of their routine to call friars incautious and suspect and their behaviors criminal and reprehensible.[48] Friar subgroups, most especially young friars and local priors, became the targets of enforcement.[49]

46. In 1350 and 1358 provincial administrators explicitly recognized and attempted to minimize prolixity, while insisting upon the need to reiterate past disciplinary items. Robles Sierra, "Actas," *EV* 23 (1993), 296 and Robles Sierra, "Actas," *EV* 25 (1995), 355.

47. See Robles Sierra, "Actas," *EV* 23 (1993), 306–7, and 313.

48. E.g., Robles Serra, "Actas," *EV* 23 (1993), 306–7, and 308; Robles Serra, "Actas," *EV* 24 (1994), 238–39, and 254; Robles Serra, "Actas," *EV* 26 (1996), 111–12, and 127.

49. E.g., Robles Serra, "Actas," *EV* 23 (1993), 266, in which Rossell calls young friars unuseful (*inutiles*).

The leadership insisted that individual friars guard their reputations and act in right and honest ways, so as not to deform the order's honesty. By mid century, however, a shift was clearly underway when a number of injunctions indicated that friars must do more than avoid personal scandal by avoiding activities that "deform the honesty of our Order," or that "generate grave scandal for the Order."[50] Much of the talk about the defense of corporate honor came in the context of rectifying the problem of intrusive outsiders, mostly parents, friends, and patrons, who looked after the interests of individual friars by limiting the capabilities of the order's legitimate decision-makers to assign, move, promote or demote.[51]

Despite the gains made by reformers, ample evidence shows that very strong resistance within the friars' ranks ultimately stalled the full-scale implementation of their plans. In the Province of Aragon, after Nicolas Rossell resigned the office of provincial prior to become cardinal of San Sisto resident in the papal court at Avignon, reform efforts in the province rapidly broke down. The contest between reformers and those obstructing reforms created deepening divisions. By 1363 the shattering of the province's unity culminated in the election of two provincial priors and the refusal of a great number of friars to move to the convents to which they had been assigned.[52] Over the next decade and more the situation worsened for

50. E.g., Robles Serra, "Actas," *EV* 21 (1991), 113; Robles Serra, "Actas," *EV* 20 (1990), 277; Robles Serra, "Actas," *EV* 21 (1991), 136 and 142.

51. E.g., Robles Sierra, "Actas," *EV* 24 (1994), 238 and 254; Robles Sierra, "Actas," *EV* 25 (1995), 334, 360 and 362.

52. In 1362, the Master General, Simon of Langres, removed Provincial Prior Joan Gomir, choosing Nicolau Eymeric as the vicar of the province. In the confusion that followed, a faction led by Gomir held a provincial chapter in September and elected Bernat Ermengol as provincial prior. Later in the year, Eymeric held a competing provincial chapter. Pope Urban V interceded on account of the divisiveness (*magnam divisionem provinciae*) caused by these events. He then chose Jaume Domeneç as the province's new leader. See Petrus de Arenys, *Chronicon,* edited by José Hinojosa Montalvo (Valencia: Anubar, 1975), 16, and Francisco Diago, *Historia de la Provincia de Aragón de la Orden de Predicadores* (Barcelona: Sebastian Cormellas, 1599) ff. 47r–48v. Robles Sierra, "Actas," *EV* 26 (1996), 96–97, records the letter from the Cardinal Bishop of Avignon imposing Jaume Domeneç as

the entire order.[53] Then came the Papal Schism that tore the order into rival obediences. Reform, for the time being, had run its course. Direct, measurable outcomes appear so limited that we might consider them nil, although I want to end by suggesting otherwise.

This paper opened with the admission that in the fourteenth-century Dominican Province of Aragon reform was more or less a failure. It has become customary to deem reform an all-or-nothing enterprise: a concerted effort to change for the better within the church either succeeds in its providential purpose of correction and renewal or it is, by implication, no reform at all. However, the foregoing has shown that even a failed reform has substance. Like the events that give rise to crises, the activity of reform finds much of its success in increments and at the margins.[54] More broadly, perhaps, reform takes its place as part of the regular stuff of everyday corporate activity, just like the small and large crises to which it responds. Implied here is an absence of absolutes for either reform's victory or defeat. Such a reorientation of reform sends our concluding remarks in three directions, two regarding reform among the late-medieval Dominicans, and one treating reform as a broad arena of study in the Ladnerian tradition.

First, in the case of the reform studied here, we should ask whether the attempts at reform undertaken by Berengar of Landora, Bernat Sescala, Nicolas Rossell and others, although marginal and partial, had lasting significance. A careful reading of the Dominican Order's administrative records from the decades on either side of 1350 shows that they likely did lay some groundwork for future

---

provincial prior at the insistence of the pope. In his prefatory notes, Robles Sierra refers to the incident as the province's "first institutional conflict."

53. The order's debilities led Catherine of Siena to seek from the pope a new master general, a good surgeon, who might cut deeply into the order's wounds rather than continuing to apply the salves that had turned the limbs rotten. Catherine of Siena, Letter 183. See the discussion in Aidan Nichols, *Dominican Gallery: Portrait of a Culture* (Leominster, U. K.: Gracewing, 1997), 243–44.

54. For orientation on these possibilities, see Martin Krieger, *Marginalism and Discontinuity: Tools for the Crafts of Knowledge and Decision* (New York: Russell Sage, 1989).

developments. This becomes evident, for instance, as one tracks the evolving redefinition of *discursus*, a term of signal importance to the Dominican enterprise. At the order's origins *discursus* meant travel outside convent walls for the purpose of preaching and the care of souls. It was thus at the heart of the friars' work.[55] A century later, general and provincial administrators consistently linked friars' activities outside their convents to the potential for scandal, to such an extent that *discursus* came to connote excess, making its translation something like "running around."[56] The friars' enclosure has often been described as an element of the Dominican Observant Reform, but fourteenth-century attacks on *discursus* appear to have laid the groundwork.[57]

We will find precursors to the Dominican Observant Reform as we look for them, and these will lead us to conclude that we tell that story too neatly. A number of recent examinations have already found the movement for reform ploddingly slow, complicated by its own ambiguities, internal variants, and reversals. Internal corporate reorganization stalled during the period of the papal schism in part because Dominican leaders were hesitant to tackle internal challenges while the seemingly more pressing problem of multiple popes and conciliar agendas threatened the stability of the entire church. Even under better conditions, local, regional, and even generational interests divided observants. Rival interpretations of early Dominican observance and internal divisions among reformers continued to impede reform efforts well into the sixteenth century.[58]

55. For a number of early examples, see *Acta Capitulorum Provincialium Ordinis Fratrum Praedicatorum Première Province de Provence, Province Romaine, Province D'Espagne (1239–1302)*, edited by Celeste Douais (Toulouse: Édouard Privat, 1894), 721 and 810.

56. From 1310 to 1378 nearly forty admonitions in the extant acts of the Province of Aragon linked *discursus* to excessive travel or scandal.

57. On "*la reforma monástica dominicana*" in Aragon, see Garganta, "Los Dominicos de la Provincia de Aragón," 106–7. Ashley, *The Dominicans*, 61, admits that "Raymond's reform, though it saved the Order, also had some unhappy consequences. 'Monastic observance' came to overshadow St. Dominic's single-minded goal of an Order of Preachers."

58. Michael Tavuzzi, *Renaissance Inquisitors: Dominican Inquisitors and Inquisitorial Districts in Northern Italy, 1474–1527* (Leiden: Brill, 2007), offers discussion and examples

Where does this leave Ladner's idea of reform? Not long after the Second Vatican Council had completed its work, John O'Malley argued that the views articulated by the council's framers superseded Ladner's study by confirming, if somewhat between the lines of their conciliar documents, the revolutionary implications of modern historical consciousness. For O'Malley recognition of this new historical reality meant that the historian must treat the past as so "radically contingent and particular" that historical study becomes "desacralized," separated from consideration of any overarching providential plan while opening itself up instead to recognizing the highly specific and unrepeatable circumstances of its subjects.[59] From this perspective, to follow Ladner's "metahistorical preoccupations," to accept his "preterideological assertion" of reform's continuities, is to limit ourselves to speculation and even self-delusion. Talk of reform is in our sources, and we learn by following it; but if any constant operates within the great number and diversity of Christian reforms, it is likely to be the groping imprecision with which critics describe crises and reformers advance ways to make things better.

---

of the continuing friction between observant and conventual Dominican friars in Italy well into the sixteenth century. Two recent studies, James D. Mixson, *Poverty's Proprietors: Ownership and Mortal Sin at the Origins of the Observant Movement* (Leiden: Brill, 2009) and Michael D. Bailey, "Religious Poverty, Mendicancy, and Reform in the Late Middle Ages," *Church History* 72 (2003), 457–83, also reconsider the timing and nature of Dominican reform including its inherent ambiguities and rival interpretations. On how the symbiotic relationship between Dominican support for the papacy and papal defense of Dominican privileges worked to limit the order's internal reform, see Thomas M. Izbicki, "The Council of Ferrara-Florence and Dominican Papalism," in *Christian Unity: The Council of Ferrara-Florence 1438/39–1989*, edited by Guiseppe Alberigo (Leuven: Leuven University Press, 1991), 429–43. In his conciliar sermons, for example, Leonardo Dati displayed a willingness to admit a need for moral improvement of individual friars but showed no interest in giving the councils occasion for structural reform. Thomas M. Izbicki, "Reform and obedience in four conciliar sermons by Leonardo Dati, O.P.," in *Reform and Renewal in the Middle Ages and the Renaissance*, edited by Thomas Izbicki and Christopher Bellitto (Leiden: Brill, 2000), 174–92.

59. John O'Malley, "Reform, Historical Consciousness, and Vatican II's Aggiornamento," *Theological Studies* 32 (1971), 573–601.

7

THE SIX ERRORS

Hus on Simony

C. COLT ANDERSON

One of the most fascinating characters in the Catholic Church's long history of reform is the hero of the Czech people, John Hus. Hus was burned at the stake for heresy at the Council of Constance in 1415. Five hundred and eighty-four years later, Pope John Paul II apologized on behalf of the Catholic Church for this murderous act. Prior to Vatican II, one could easily point to Hus's advocacy for allowing the laity to receive both the body and blood during the Eucharistic celebration, for vernacular liturgies, and for encouraging the laity to read the Bible as evidence of his heresy, but when Vatican II embraced and encouraged all of these practices, Catholic theologians began to reassess his theology. These theologians had the benefit of new studies into the history of reform by individuals like Gerhart Ladner to guide their work. In his pioneering work, *The Idea of Reform,* Ladner emphasized how Catholic reformers in the past drew upon "the self-perpetuating core, the inner life spring of Christian tradition through lesser and greater times."[1] If one reads his short tract, *The Six Errors*, it becomes apparent that Hus was drawing on the then traditional theology of the Gregorian reformers in an effort to combat simony and that his denial of the authority of simoniacal clergy was rooted in this tradition.[2]

Because Hus was criticized by his contemporaries for informing the laity of clerical malfeasance and for encouraging all of the people to correct these problems, he continues to be treated as a suspect figure by many theologians, as a prophetic forerunner of the Protestant Reformation, and as a political revolutionary.[3] Hus's reputation has also been affected by his heavy dependence on the on the works of the English reformer John Wyclif.[4] Hus's position that both the clergy and the nobility are accountable to the people and that everyone should be discerning about their leadership was clearly drawn from Wyclif's writings; however, Wyclif was drawing from sources that had been used by the Gregorian reformers of the 11th and 12th centuries. Their shared position on clerical accountability has led to the charge of Donatism against both men in modern sources; however, neither was charged with Donatism by their contemporaries at the Council of Constance. Daniel DiDomizio recently suggested that Hus had moved away from the traditional Catholic teaching

1. Gerhart B. Ladner, *The Idea of Reform: Its Impact on Christian Thought and Action in the Age of the Fathers* (Cambridge, Mass.: Harvard University Press, 1959), 423.

2. John Hus, *De sex erroribus* in *Betlemské texty,* edited by B. Ryba (Prague: Orbis, 1951), 41–63. The Czech version is *O Šesti Bludiech,* in *Drobné Spisy České,* vol. 4, *Magistri Iohannis Hus Opera Omnia* (Prague: Academia Scientarum Bohemoslovaca, 1985), 271–296.

3. For a review of the historiography on Hus see Ernest Werner, *Jan Hus: Welt und Umwelt eines Prager Frühreformators* (Weimar: H. Böhlaus Nachfolger, 1991). There is a more recent study that indicates a few new sources and has a summary historiographical chapter: Peter Hilsch, *Johannes Hus: Prediger Gottes und Ketzer* (Regensburg: Verlag Friedrich Pustet, 1999), 284–98. Two older studies that have been theologically influential are Heiko Oberman, *Forerunners of the Reformation* (New York: Holt, Rinehart, and Winston, 1966), 208–12 and George Tavard, *Holy Writ or Holy Church: The Crisis of the Protestant Reformation* (London: Burns and Oates, 1959), 47–51.

4. Hus was condemned for following the teachings of Wyclif at the Council of Constance. See *Decrees of the Ecumenical Councils,* vol.1, edited by Norman P. Tanner (Washington: Georgetown University Press, 1990), 426–28.

that "separates validity of the canonical position from the moral worthiness of the individual."[5] Although Hus has been cleared of the charges of heresy by scholars like Paul de Vooght, Matthew Spinka, and Kenneth Hagen, suspicion about his understanding of ecclesiastical ministry and authority has remained.[6] In some cases, he is obliquely condemned on the principle that the perception that he was a heretic must have been grounded in reality.[7]

Ironically, if anything, Hus was too old-fashioned for the temper of his times. It was precisely his commitment to traditional Catholic teachings on simony that fomented his dispute with the conciliarist theologians at the Council of Constance. Hus's claims that the clergy can be stripped of their possessions and their privileges by secular authorities for sins such as simony and that the laity must be discerning when it comes to the commands of the clergy were in direct opposition to the theology of Jean Gerson, who took a direct role in advising the inquisitorial judges.[8] Gerson maintained that the parish clergy deserve respect and tithes regardless of the quality of their lives or of their ministry.[9] Unfortunately for Hus, Gerson's ideas were more appealing to the members of the clergy at Constance.

Hus grounded his rhetoric against simony in terms of ritual purity, which tended to understand problems such as simony as a personal fault requiring penance, but he was facing a systemic problem within the church without the proper tools to correct it. Since the clergy and the nobility saw his efforts as undermining their authority just as they were trying to resolve the problems associated with

5. Daniel DiDomizio, "Jan Hus's *De Ecclesia*, Precursor of Vatican II?" *Theological Studies* 60 (1999), 257.

6. Paul L. De Vooght, *L'hérésie de Jean Huss* (Louvain: Publications Universitaires de Louvain, 1960); Kenneth Hagen, "Hus' 'Donatism'," *Augustinianum* 11 (1971), 541–47; Matthew Spinka, *John Hus: A Biography* (Princeton: Princeton University Press, 1968).

7. For an example see Francis Oakley, *The Western Church in the Later Middle Ages* (Ithaca: Cornell University Press, 1979), 296–97.

8. Matthew Spinka, *John Hus at the Council of Constance* (New York: Columbia University Press, 1965), 171.

9. Louis Pascoe, *Jean Gerson: Principles of Church Reform* (Leiden: Brill, 1973), 153–56.

the papal schism, their opposition to his reform efforts hardened as he called more attention to simony. Because of the resistance to enforcing the canons on simony by ecclesial and secular authorities, Hus was led by both tradition and practical necessity to turn to the serious charges of heresy and impurity—the latter of which led to the anachronistic charge of Donatism.

THE CHARGE OF DONATISM

Donatism was a charge that was rarely brought up in the Middle Ages, even though there were numerous groups that denied the efficacy of the sacraments performed by impure priests or denied the authority of polluted priests, including many of the Gregorian reformers such as Cardinal Humbert and Pope Gregory VII. The way that we understand Donatism is largely a modern construct that fits in poorly with medieval sensibilities. This is why a scholar like Malcolm Lambert could identify no less than twelve different groups, theologians, and movements as being Donatist in his book *Medieval Heresy,* even though he did not provide evidence of medieval charges of Donatism.[10] Kenneth Hagen pointed out that almost all of the medieval dictionaries and encyclopedias limit the discussion of Donatism to the North African Schism and Augustine's response to it.[11] The term was so rarely used prior to Luther's career that the 1517 *Lexicon theologicum* of Johann Altenstaig, which was intended to be a comprehensive theological dictionary, does not include it.[12]

The two cases where the charge of Donatism comes up in medieval sources indicate that imposing the modern understanding

10. M. D. Lambert, *Medieval Heresy: Popular Movements from Bogomil to Hus* (London: E. Arnold, 1977). Some of the material in this paragraph and the next is from C. Colt Anderson, "Ritual Purity and Pastoral Reform in the Thirteenth Century," in *Pastoral Care in the Late Middle Ages (1200–1500)* (Leiden: Brill, forthcoming).

11. Kenneth Hagen, "What Is the True Church? The History of a Heresy from Donatism to Pietism," *Discourse: A Review of the Liberal Arts,* undated offprint available in the Marquette Library Archives, 157.

12. Johann Altenstaig, *Lexicon theologicum* (Hagenau, Germany, 1517, reprinted Lugdunum, France, 1580).

of the heresy on the medieval period is an anachronistic distortion. The first was against a priest named Tanchelm in the twelfth century. It stated:

> He shook the pillars of the church of God to their foundations; he even dared to split the rock of our faith, that is Christ, holding that the church consisted only of himself and his followers; like the Donatist heretics who argued that the church only existed in Africa, he sought to limit the church ... to Tanchelmites alone.[13]

Pope John XXII's condemnation of the spiritual Franciscans in the fourteenth century is the second. Pope John XXII declared in *Gloriosam ecclesiam* (January 1318) that the Spiritual Franciscans had fallen into the Donatist heresy because they saw holiness as only residing in themselves.[14] Thus it seems that the medieval definition of Donatism was limited to identifying one group or movement with the church. The claim that the character of the priest or bishop had an effect on his ability to perform his sacramental duties was absolutely commonplace in the thirteenth century.[15] Gregorian reformers such as Peter Damian and Cardinal Humbert also taught that the purity of the minister had an impact on their priestly functions and sacramental ministry.[16]

The two medieval charges of Donatism are consonant with Augustine's writings on the subject. There are a paucity of refer-

13. The translation is from Walter L. Wakefield and Austin P. Evans, *Heresies of the High Middle Ages* (New York and London: Columbia University Press, 1969), 98. The critical edition is "Traiectenses Fridericum I archiepiscopum Coloniensem hortantus, quod ceperit Tanchelmum haereticum eiusque socios, Manassen et Everwacherum, ne eos dimittat," in *Codex Udalrici*, edited by P. Jaffé, in *Monumenta Bambergensis* (Berlin: Dunker, 1869), 296–300.

14. The text is in Heinrich Denzinger, *Enchiridion symbolorum definitionum et declarationum de rebus fidei et morum*, 34th edition (Barcelona: Herder, 1967), 286: "... quia apud ipsos solos (ut ipsi somniant) sicut spiritualis vitiae sanctitas, sic auctoritas perseverat, in qua re Donatistarum sequuntur errorem."

15. Thomas Aquinas cited Malachi 2:2 ("I will curse your blessings"), Jerome, Pope Gelasius, and Dionysius the Areopagite as indicating deficiencies with the sacramental and priestly acts of impure priests in the *Summa Theologiae* 3.82.5–6.

16. C. Colt Anderson, *The Great Catholic Reformers: From Gregory the Great to Dorothy Day* (Mahwah, N.J.: Paulist Press, 2007), 45–49.

ences in the polemical writings against Donatism that refer to the character of the minister compared to the references to baptism, rebaptism, and the unity of the church. Augustine's primary concern in respect to the Donatists was that they restricted the Catholicity of the church throughout the world. In *De agone christiano* he cautioned against "listening to the Donatist party, who deny the one holy Catholic church to be diffused throughout the whole world, and claim to be alone in Africa, and there amongst themselves, against the plain Scripture teaching of its universality; they affirm that the prophecies of its extension have already been fulfilled, after which the whole church perished outside of their remnant."[17]

This passage is consonant with and most likely the source for the Canons of Utrecht and Pope John XXIII's respective condemnations. One of the ways that the Donatists marked off their identity was by only accepting the baptisms administered by their own clergy. This was not so much a question of individual character but about the perfection of the Donatist church as compared to the rest of the Christian world, which naturally led to the practice of rebaptism. Augustine responded by arguing that there is one baptism and one body of Christ, which will retain a mixed character until the end of time.[18] Thus, the medieval understanding of Donatism was conceived of in the very narrow sense of identifying one group, church, or movement with the *communio sanctorum* and with the practice of rebaptism.

Did Hus exhibit any of the traits of Donatism as it was understood in his time? The answer is an unequivocal no. He did not ad-

17. Augustine, *De agone Christiano* 29.31. The translation is from *St. Augustine: The Writings Against the Manichaeans and Against the Donatists*, translated by Chester D. Hartranft in *The Nicene and Post-Nicene Fathers*, vol. 4, edited by Philip Schaff (New York: Charles Scribner's Sons, 1909), 376.

18. Augustine, *De doctrina christiana* (hereafter cited as *De doctrina*), 3.32.45. The critical edition is Augustine, *De doctrina christiana*, edited by J. Martin, *Corpus Christianorum Series Latina* 32 (Turnhout: Brepols, 1962), 1–167. I am working from the new translation: Augustine, *Teaching Christianity: De doctrina christiana*, translated by Edmund Hill, O.P., edited by John E. Rotelle, O.S.A. (Hyde Park, N.Y.: New City Press, 1996).

vocate for rebaptism nor did he identify any one group with the *communio sanctorum*. Insofar as he wanted to maintain the spotless or sinless quality of the church, his ecclesiology is very similar to that espoused by Pope Benedict XVI because of their shared commitment to certain Augustinian ecclesiological traditions.[19] Yet he did so without identifying any particular church, such as the Roman or Greek Church, as the pure church or the church of the elect.

In *De ecclesia,* Hus stated that one definition of the church is the great congregation of all who are under the rule of Christ the King (*magna congregacio omnium sub regimine Regis Christi*), which he saw as being equivalent with the Catholic Church (*ecclesia katholica*). Because many people fail to follow the rule of Christ, he believed that from an eternal perspective there were two churches, namely, the church of the saints and the church of the reprobates.[20] The church of the saints (*ecclesia sanctorum*) is the Catholic Church (*ecclesia katholica*) in the sense of consisting of all the predestined: past, present, and future.[21] In fact, he refused to identify the Catholic Church with the Roman church because he believed that the Greeks and other Christians were also part of the Catholic Church.[22]

Hus believed that these two churches, which can be distinguished from an eternal or atemporal perspective, are mixed in the church militant. Thus he could maintain that the Catholic Church cannot sin even though one sees many faults within the church encountered in history. Hus used the image of the church as the body of Christ to explain the mixed nature of the church. Like a human body, the body of Christ contains spit, phlegm, excrement, and

19. For an overview of Benedict XVI's ecclesiology see Aidan Nichols, *The Thought of Benedict XVI: An Introduction to the Theology of Joseph Ratzinger* (New York: Burns & Oates, 2005, reprint of *The Theology of Joseph Ratzinger* (Edinburgh: T&T Clark, 1988)), 27–50.

20. John Hus, *Tractatus de ecclesia,* edited by Samuel Harrison Thomson (Boulder: University of Colorado Press, 1956), 2: "Ex quo patet quod una est ecclesia ovium et alia edorum, una ecclesia sanctorum et alia reproborum."

21. Ibid., 2.

22. Ibid., 44.

urine that will be expelled on the last day. Though the Catholic Church is perfect, he maintained that it will contain impurities until the Judgment. These impure fluids, which represent the reprobate, are in the body but are not part of the body.[23] While we may not find his ecclesiology appealing, he did not fall into the Donatist tendency of calling for a smaller but more pure church because he did not expect to find a pure church within the confines of history.

The reason Hus was not charged with Donatism in the fifteenth century was that he did not fit the medieval understanding of the heresy. Hus does not fit the twentieth century understanding of the heresy either, because he never denied the ability of a wicked clergyman to hold office or to perform sacramental acts. Recognizing the problem with the category of Donatism led Kenneth Hagen to label Hus a semi-Donatist. Hagen believed Hus had distinguished between two levels of concern: sacerdotal and jurisdictional. Insofar as Hus maintained the validity of the sacraments performed by immoral clergy, Hagen argued Hus was not a Donatist. However, Hagen believed that Hus' doctrine that a cleric had to fulfill the duties associated with his office to have authority was a sign of ecclesiastical Donatism, which Hus used as an axe against the authority of the hierarchy of the Catholic Church.[24]

While Hus was certainly attacking the authority of some members of the ordained clergy, there was nothing novel about either his rhetoric or his claims concerning clerical accountability and authority in the church. Hus's reform rhetoric and methods were consistent with the work of many of the greatest medieval reformers including Pope Gregory the Great, Peter Damian, Pope Gregory VII, and Ber-

23. Ibid., 14–15: "Amplius est notandum quod sicut aliquid est in humano corpore quod non est pars ipsius corporis, ut sputum, flecma, stercus, apostema vel urina, et illud non est de corpore, cum non sit pars corporis, aliud vero est in humano corpore tamquam pars eius ut omne membrum eius, sic aliquid est in corpore Christi mistico, quod est ecclesia, et tamen non est de ecclesia, cum non sit pars eius quomodo est omnis christianus prescitus de. ipso corpore tamquam stercus finaliter egerendus."

24. Hagen, "Hus' 'Donatism'," 541–47.

nard of Clairvaux.[25] The rules concerning purity and impurity that Hus pointed to were deeply embedded in medieval culture and had functioned for several centuries as a means to challenge corrupt ecclesiastical figures and practices.

RITUAL PURITY AND REFORM RHETORIC

The importance of ritual purity, whether one is considering the clergy or the laity, is ubiquitous throughout the pages of medieval penitentials, collections of canon law, and theological treatises.[26] Whereas lay people who received the Eucharist in a state of impurity were seen as eating to their own damnation, priests and bishops who performed their sacramental functions in a state of impurity were believed to be bringing damnation to their entire communities.[27] Some impurities, such as those caused by involuntary responses like nocturnal emissions, could be resolved by washing; but others, such as sodomy or simony, were assumed to render a prelate useless.[28]

25. See C. Colt Anderson, "A Reappraisal of John Hus in Light of His Medieval Predecessors," *Chicago Studies* 45 (Spring 2006): 14–29. Much of the contextual material in the next several paragraphs was abstracted from this article. My work relies heavily on Spinka, *John Hus: A Biography.*

26. Much of this material is abbreviated out of Anderson, "Ritual Purity." For some examples see Burchard of Worms, *Decretorum libri XX* 17.35; Peter Damian, *Letter* 31; Alan of Lille, *Liber poenitentialis* 1.1, and Thomas de Chobham, *Summa Confessorum* 7.2.5, 7.2.16–20, 7.6.5.

27. A good example of this idea can be found in a popular medieval text called the *Stella clericorum,* edited by Eric H. Reiter (Toronto: Pontifical Institute of Mediaeval Studies, 1997), 20. This text cited Gregory the Great, *Pastoral Care,* 3.4, to explain why wicked priests are so dangerous.

28. Medieval canonists made distinctions between impurity and sin. Gratian has a discussion of three levels of impurity associated with men who have had nocturnal emissions that illustrates how ritual impurity or pollution did not always imply sinfulness. The canons claimed that men have nocturnal emissions for one of three reasons: a superfluity of nature or illness, as a result of gluttony and drunkenness, or as a result of sexual thoughts and fantasies. See Gratian, *Decretum,* D.6 c.1. There is no critical edition of this text. There is a recent translation titled *Gratian: The Treatise on Laws (Decretum DD. 1–20) with the Ordinary Gloss,* translated by Augustine Thompson and James Gordley (Washington, D.C.: The Catholic University of America Press, 1993). The Latin text I am using is *Decretum Magistri Gratiani,* 2nd edition, edited by E. Friedberg (Leipzig, 1879). There is a better edition that is not widely available: *Decretum Gratiani Emendatum et Notationibus Illustratum una cum Glossis* (Rome, 1582).

The theology that advocated removing useless and damnable clergy was well-established by the sixth century and was tied to the cultic and symbolic role they played.

According to the anthropologist Mary Douglas, who wrote the seminal study on the meaning of purity and impurity, purity and pollution are anthropological constants that arise out of a society's symbolic systems. She used contemporary ideas around dirt as an analogy.[29] Our ideas about dirt are influenced by both health and hygiene concerns as well as by aesthetics. If we exclude the concern with medical issues, which is a relatively new phenomenon, we are left with the earlier idea of dirt as matter out of place. Douglas argued that this implies two conditions: a group of beliefs about ordered relations and a contravention of that order. She wrote, "Where there is dirt, there is system. Dirt is the by-product of a systematic ordering and classification of matter, in so far as ordering involves rejecting inappropriate elements. This idea of dirt takes us straight into the field of symbolism and promises a link up with more obviously symbolic systems of purity."[30]

Shoes are not dirty in themselves, she explained, but it is dirty to put them on the kitchen table. Douglas concluded that systems of purity naturally arise out of the human need to classify things based on patterns.[31] Given the highly ordered and symbolic imagination

29. Mary Douglas, *Purity and Danger: An Analysis of Concepts of Pollution and Taboo* (London: Routledge, 1977), 35. The earlier edition was corrected in 1969 and reprinted in 1970 and 1976. While this research was applied to scriptural studies and the early church, there is virtually no material on this subject in medieval studies. One exception is a dissertation written by Annette Höing, *Gott, der ganz Reine, will keine Unreinheit: Die Reinheitsvorstellungen Hildegards von Bingen aus religionsgeschichtlicher Perspektive* (Altenberge: Oris, 2000). Her treatment of purity is only related to sexual issues, and she uses some questionable texts when there were critical editions available. There is one volume in English that is available: *Medieval Purity and Piety: Essays on Medieval Clerical Celibacy and Religious Reform*, edited by Michael Frassetto (New York: Garland Publishers, 1998). This study is primarily concerned with the issue of celibacy. Another exception is Raffaele Savigni, "Purità rituale e ridefinizione del sacro nella cultura caronlingia: l'interpretazione del *Levitico* e dell'*Epistola agli Ebrei*," *Annali di storia dell'essegesi*, 13 (1996), 229–55. Savigni's article is helpful for seeing how these ideas were transmitted through the exegetical tradition.

30. Douglas, *Purity and Danger*, 34.

31. Ibid., 36.

of medieval cultures, matters of purity and pollution were seen as vitally important.

Douglas suggested four ways that ideas associated with purity and pollution are employed to preserve moral standards when a society faces upheaval, which can be seen in Hus's sources concerning simony. The first occurs when a situation is morally ambiguous and purity rules determine whether an infraction has taken place.[32] For example, purity rules were used to answer questions about whether or not gifts or notary fees amounted to simony. Second, purity rules can reduce confusion when moral principles are in conflict by giving a central focus for determining priority. In the case of Hus, the principles in conflict were between obedience to ecclesiastical superiors and compliance with the tradition concerning simony. Third, purity rules can be used to persuade people to see the importance of a moral teaching to which the society is indifferent by emphasizing the dangerous consequences of the offense. Many theologians and popes prior to Hus used purity rules to engender resistance to the impure clergy.[33] Fourth, rules over purity are employed to provide a deterrent to immoral behavior when there are no practical methods for sanctioning offenders, which was precisely the situation in Bohemia in the early fifteenth century.[34]

The emphasis placed on the example set by priests received increasing attention in the second half of the twelfth century as the idea of the apostolic life became more significant. The growing influence of the popular movements seeking to imitate the disciples as a means of evangelization led to increasing pressure on priests to be the example of apostolic life in their communities in the thirteenth century. Priestly purity was becoming identified with the purity of apostolic life. Both the eleventh-century rhetoric, which was pri-

32. Ibid., 133.

33. For an example of this rhetoric see R. I. Moore, *The Origins of European Dissent* (Toronto, 1994), 54–55.

34. Douglas, *Purity and Danger*, 133.

marily concerned with the sacramental acts of the impure clergy, and the rhetoric that emerged in the twelfth century, which focused on the preaching and example of the clergy, were employed throughout the thirteenth century. Both forms of rhetoric relied on the assumption that some types of impurity involving sin, such as simony or heresy, rendered priests and bishops useless in their sacramental and sacrificial duties as well as in their ability to preach and to lead.[35] To identify such positions as either Donatism or Semi-Donatism or Donatistic would be to claim that virtually every major theologian of the period had fallen into some form of the fifth-century heresy. Given his historical context, Hus had few options for trying to deter immoral behavior other than to appeal to these traditions concerning ritual impurity.

HISTORICAL CONTEXT

Hus lived during the time of the Great Schism, which is a period when the church had multiple popes. From 1378 until 1409 there were two popes, one in Rome and another in Avignon. In 1409 the Council of Pisa tried to resolve the matter and elected another pope, which raised the total number of popes to three. This situation led to turmoil throughout the church as people divided themselves between the three men claiming to be the legitimate pope. While this caused problems for the universal church, it also allowed chaos to creep into individual dioceses like that of Prague.

The diocese of Prague had been in turmoil for twenty years when Hus wrote his most important works in 1412 and 1413. The problems began when Emperor Wenceslas tortured four members of the cler-

35. Pope Innocent III, *Between God and Man: Six Sermons on the Priestly Office*, translated by Corinne J. Vause and Frank C. Gardiner (Washington, D.C.: The Catholic University of America Press, 2004), 10–14. This is sermon 1 in *Patrologiae cursus completus ... series Latina*, vol. 217, edited by J.-P. Migne (Paris, 1844–1864), 650–54. This source will be cited as *PL* hereafter. Humbert of Romans, *On the Formation of Preachers* 11.124–34. The only printed edition of the Latin can be found in *B. Humberti de Romanis Opera de Vita Regulari*, edited by J. J. Berthier (Rome, 1888; repr. Turin, 1956). See also *Stella clericorum*, edited by Eric H. Reiter (Toronto: Pontifical Institute of Medieval Studies, 1997), chapters 11–12.

gy, one of whom died. Wenceslas and Archbishop Jan of Prague were involved in a miniature replay of the investiture controversy. When Archbishop Jan appealed to the Roman pope, Boniface IX (1389–1404), the pope refused to hear the charges for fear that Wenceslas might change his allegiance to Avignon. In response to the weakness of Boniface, Archbishop Jan resigned his office in protest in 1396.

After the resignation of the archbishop, the situation quickly deteriorated. The new archbishop, Zbyněc, was guilty of buying his office. The new archbishop alternated between supporting the reformers and their opponents throughout his career, which ended with a suspicious death in 1411. He also switched his allegiances between the various papacies. As Zbyněc began to oppose the reform party, Hus undercut the authority of the archbishop and the unreformed clergy by raising the issue of simony. The problems in Prague exploded in 1412 after the Pisan pope, John XXIII, allowed the selling of indulgences in Prague for the purpose of funding a crusade against King Ladislas of Naples, who was a Christian. The bull implied that the priest granting the indulgence had the authority to grant remission from sin.[36]

Arguing that it was improper to contribute money for the purpose of shedding Christian blood, Hus preached against the bull as an insidious form of simony. When his ecclesiastical superiors commanded him stop preaching against the indulgences, he refused. He also refused to recognize King Wenceslas's decree that no one could oppose the indulgence preachers. This outright rejection of both his ecclesiastical and secular superiors led to formal action against him.

36. Spinka, *John Hus: A Biography*, 133–36. Spinka provides this translation of the formula of absolution given to the papal commissioners: "And also by apostolic authority granted me, I absolve thee of all sins, if you are truly contrite and confess them to God and me. If you cannot personally undertake the project [i.e., of joining the crusade], but wish to bring a contribution according to your ability in compliance with my and the commissioner's terms in defence and aid of the above-named project, I grant thee the fullest remission of all your sins, including punishment and guilt." Spinka's source was Hus's *De indulgentiis sive de cruciata papae Iaonnis XXIII*, but given Hus's scrupulosity I doubt he would have intentionally misrepresented the formula.

Hus was ordered to stop preaching altogether, which he blatantly ignored. By October of 1412, he had to go into hiding because he had been placed under major excommunication by the Pisan papacy and had lost the support of Wenceslas. As part of an apologetic strategy to defend his actions, Hus denied the authority of the simoniacal clergy who supported the sale of indulgences and who had excommunicated him.

THE SIX ERRORS

While Hus was in exile from Prague, he began to write a small tract in both Latin and Czech called *The Six Errors*. He said he wanted it to be a shield for the people from the errors that many of the unreformed clergy were teaching.[37] The Latin edition was inscribed onto the walls of the Bethlehem Chapel in Prague, which helps to explain its brevity and lack of rhetorical flourish. Hus later expanded and translated the tract's statements on simony into Czech to make it more accessible to the people.[38] The style of presentation in the Latin edition is simple and repetitive. Its summary nature reveals what Hus saw to be essential elements to his reform agenda. His method was simply to list the errors and to provide responses to them drawn from scripture, patristic sources, and canon law. The list of erroneous positions covers creation, faith, remission of sin, obedience, excommunication, and simony. While it is not immediately apparent from the text itself, the errors are linked and are a polemical response to the positions taken by his adversaries in the controversy over indulgences.

Perhaps the most puzzling error has to do with creation. In the Latin edition Hus simply explained that some members of the cler-

37. Jan Hus, *Von den sechs Vererungen*, in *Schriften zur Glaubensreform und Briefe der Jahre 1414–1415*, edited and translated by Walter Schamschula (Frankfurt: Allgäuer Zeitungsverlag, 1969), 27. This is a German translation of the Czech version.

38. Matthew Spinka, "John Hus, Advocate of Spiritual Reform," in *Advocates of Reform: From Wyclif to Erasmus*, edited by Matthew Spinka (Philadelphia: Westminster Press, 1953), 195.

gy claimed that they created the body of Christ on the altar during the Mass. He cited a series of primarily patristic sources to show that only God has the power to create.[39] The underlying issue was authority. Hus claimed that the Czech clergy were exalting themselves in status over the Virgin Mary because she only bore Christ once whereas they created God repeatedly. The *Stella clericorum,* which did defend the idea that priests are only subject to episcopal courts by praising the dignity of priests as those who can create the creator, has been identified as the source of this doctrine.[40] Some priests were claiming by virtue of their ordination that they could not be in a state of mortal sin and that the wickedest priest was better than the holiest layperson.[41] In other words, the clergy could not be accountable for their crimes.

The remaining errors were more directly related to the issues raised by the indulgence controversy. The claim that one should have faith in the saints, Mary, and the pope was the second error. Hus responded that one should have faith in God alone, which was his response to papal apologists in Bohemia who were claiming that the pope could do whatever he willed as head of the church.[42] The third error was that a priest, bishop, or pope had the authority to forgive sins by their own will, which was a response to the problematic formula associated with John XXIII's indulgences. To this Hus responded that the church only proclaims the forgiveness that had

39. John Hus, *De sex erroribus,* 41.

40. *Stella clericorum,* 21, 46; Jan Hus, *Von den sechs Vererungen,* 27; Spinka, *John Hus: A Biography,* 143. I have some doubts that the *Stella clericorum* was directly the source of the rhetoric to which Hus was responding. The twelfth-century editions of the *Stella clericorum* praise worthy priests in a way that that could easily support arguments for absolute clerical superiority, but it does so in order to demonstrate the perversity of unworthy priests. By the fifteenth century, the chapter that declares the hands of the priest to be like the womb of the Virgin was circulating independently in a text entitled *De dignitate sacerdotum.* The *De dignitate sacerdotum* also included the first section of chapter seventeen which discusses how priests are predestined members of the elect. Within its original context, it was clear that the priests who are predestined to heaven are only the worthy priests whose ritual purity mirrors that of Mary; but in its new context it suggested that all priests are members of the elect simply by virtue of their ordination. See the note in *Stella clericorum,* 40–41.

41. Spinka, *John Hus: A Biography,* 143.

42. John Hus, *De sex erroribus,* 41–42.

already been granted by God.[43] The fourth error, which would flow naturally from the prior errors, was that people should always obey their ecclesiastical superiors in all things. Of course, this was the primary charge that led to Hus's excommunication. Hus responded that one should be obedient as long as the commands of a superior were consonant with scripture, which was a category that may have included more than the Bible for him.[44] The final error before his treatment of simony was that ecclesiastical authorities could validly excommunicate someone for any reason. According to Hus, the only valid reason for excommunication was mortal sin.[45]

Simony, the sixth error, was the source of the various problems in the Bohemian clergy. Almost half of the entire text concentrates on this error.[46] Hus claimed that priests and bishops were preaching that they could legitimately buy and sell offices in the church. In this case, he charged his opponents with heresy rather than simple error, which represents a tactical decision. It was well established in canon law that heresy was a charge that could be used to strip even the pope of his office. By charging them with heresy, he undercut their authority to command anything. The position he staked out on simony was both fundamentally traditional in nature and devastating to ecclesial credibility in the fifteenth century.

Hus was singularly unoriginal when it came to the issue of simony. He defined simony as the inordinate desire to exchange the spiritual for the temporal.[47] To support his claim, Hus cited sources from the tradition. His argument, which is primarily presented by citing passages from Gratian's *Decretum*, began with a series of statements from three popes. The fact that he placed such emphasis on

43. Ibid., 44.

44. Hus, *De sex erroribus*, 45–47. For the fluidity of the term scripture in the late Middle Ages see Tavard, *Holy Writ or Holy Church*, 13–21, 50–51.

45. Hus, *De sex erroribus*, 48–52.

46. Out of 708 lines of text, 308 lines of *De sex erroribus* concentrate on simony.

47. Hus, *De sex erroribus*, 52: Symonia est studiosa voluntus emendi vel vendendi aliquid spirituale vel annexum spirituali. Sed brevius et melius sic: Symonia est inordinate volicio spirituale pro temporalibus commutandi."

papal statements reveals the importance he ascribed to the papal office. Hus began by citing Pope Leo the Great's declaration that grace has to be freely given and accepted in order for it to be grace. Leo insisted that this was particularly true when it came to the grace associated with ordination. Those who bought their offices received a lying spirit rather than the spirit of truth. Instead of accepting grace by ordination, Leo charged them with being convicted of having a lying spirit.[48]

At this point, Hus turned to his primary papal source, Gregory the Great, to establish that simoniacal clergy cannot legitimately exercise their offices. He began with Gregory the Great's statement that those who obtain their position by buying it are removed from the church and lose their priesthood.[49] Lest his readers miss the point, he referred to Gregory's decree that both those who buy and those who sell ordination to holy orders are not able to be priests. Gregory said that both were anathema because they were guilty of the sin of simony. He posed three questions to illustrate his point. How could a man who was anathematized and who was not holy, be able to sanctify others? If they are not part of the body of Christ, how could they either give or receive the body of Christ? Finally, if they are cursed, how are they able to bless? Hus cited several more passages from Gregory, most of which are contained in the *Decretum*, to establish that simoniacal bishops, priests, and laity are damned, like the moneychangers in the temple, and polluted, by their vanity and greed, whether they accept or offer gifts or favors or services.[50]

In a misquotation, confusing Gregory I with Gregory VII, Hus extended the meaning of simony to misappropriation of church funds. The passage, which is contained in the *Decretum*, identifies

48. Ibid., 53: "Quia si spiritus veritatis—testante ipsa Veritate, de qua procedit—gratis accipitur, proculdubio spiritus mendacii esse convincitur, qui non gratis accipitur." Hus found this in *Decretum* 2.1.1.1

49. Ibid., 53: "Presbiter, si ecclesiam per pecuniam obtinuerit, non solum ecclesia privetur, sed eciam sacerdocii ordine spolietur." His source was *Decretum* 2.1.1.3.

50. Ibid., 53–55.

bishops who distribute tithes to laity, knights, or their relatives as some of the greatest heretics and antichrists.[51] Further, it included the Council of Nicea's ruling that simoniacal Christians, whether the exchange involved either a service or a gift, are condemned to the eternal fire. After repeating Pope Alexander II's call to depose those guilty of simony from their benefices, he concluded with Gratian's statement that deacons, priests, and bishops who are guilty of simony are alienated from the priesthood.[52]

Having grounded his position in papal and conciliar authority, Hus turned to the saints or people he believed to be saints. He began with a passage ascribed to St. Remegius that repeated much of Gregory's theology. The material he drew upon, which seems to be from a corrupt manuscript, concluded: "For whenever a bishop sells the grace of the Holy Spirit, even though he shines in the sight of people by means of his pontifical robes, in the eyes of God he is already deprived of his priesthood."[53] The second saint he appealed to was Ambrose. In this case, he drew most of the material out of the *Decretum*.

Ambrose helped to highlight the pollution associated with simony by identifying it as a type of spiritual leprosy. Hus found leprosy a useful analogy for the consequences of such impurity. Because leprosy had no cure, was assumed to be highly contagious, and implied

51. Hus, *De sex erroribus*, 54: "Pervenit ad nos fama sinistra, quod quidam episcoporum non sacerdotibus proprie dyocesis decimas atque Cristianorum oblaciones offerant, sed pocius laycalibus personis, militum videlicet sive servitorum, vel—quod gravius est—eciam consangwineis. Unde si quis amodo episcopus inventus fuerit huiusmodi divni precepti transgressor, inter maximos hereticos et pessimos Anticristos non minimus habeatur. Et sicut Nicea synodus de symoniacs censuit, et qui dat episcopus, et qui ab eo recipient layci, sive pacto, sive beneficio, eterni incendii ignibus deputentur." This is from *Decretum* 2.1.3.13. Spinka identifies Wyclif as the source of the confusion between Gregory I and Gregory VII in *Advocates of Reform*, 223. See John Wyclif, *De simonia*, edited by M. H. Dziewicki (London, 1898), 72.

52. Hus, *De sex erroribus*, 55. He was drawing upon *Decretum* 2.1.7.2.

53. Ibid., 56. This is a reference to Remigius of Auxerre's *Quadragesimale*. Ryba found a manuscript of this text containing this material in the Prague University Library, but it is not contained in the Migne edition in *PL*, volume 131. Further, it is uncertain how Remigius of Auxerre attained saintly status; however, Hus may be conflating him with Remigius of Reims.

separation from the community, the natural conclusion was that those guilty of simony should be permanently excommunicated from the priesthood. He found more support for this understanding of simony as spiritual leprosy and for the conclusion that such clergymen are effectively excommunicated and deposed by their actions in the writings of Ambrose, Pope Innocent III, Pope Gelasius, Gregory of Nanzianus, St. Peter Damian, and scriptural sources. The remainder of the text concentrates on outlining different species of simony associated with preaching, sacramental services, indulgences, consecrating altars, and so on before concluding that the majority of the clergy in Bohemia was guilty of simony.[54]

Setting aside the questions related to payment for services, why was Hus so concerned about the sin of simony in terms of ordinations? First and foremost, he was responding to the simoniac archbishop, Zbyněc, who was opposing the reformers in Prague. Certainly he believed that there was a type of danger from impurity for those involved and a pollution of some of the services performed by such priests and bishops; however, the key issue behind simony was the problem of ordaining unworthy candidates to the priesthood, whether they were unworthy in terms of their intellectual and moral qualifications or in terms of their reasons for pursuing or offering ordination. For Hus the only reason for anyone to be admitted into holy orders was to serve the common good. The efforts to restore order after the Great Schism and to sort out the relationship between the authority of the popes and the councils meant that the problems associated with simony and multiple benefices would not be resolved in the fifteenth century. Of course, the failure to resolve issues related to simony was arguably the most significant factor leading to the Protestant Reformations of the sixteenth century; however, if Hus's recognition of the problem of simony makes him a forerunner of the Protestant reformers, the same would be true of Pope Gregory the Great, Pope Paschal I, and Peter Damian.

54. Ibid., 56–62.

8

CHURCH, BIBLE, AND REFORM IN THE HUSSITE DEBATES AT THE COUNCIL OF BASEL, 1433

GERALD CHRISTIANSON

A penetrating insight into the Hussite reform program comes to us from a remark by Prokop Holý, the Táborite military leader and head of a Hussite delegation to the Council of Basel in early 1433. As he walked and talked in private one evening with the papal legate and council president, Cardinal Giuliano Cesarini, they agreed to speak frankly. Prokop declared: "You have regard for the authority of the early church, but are far removed from conversation with the Holy Spirit.... We regard the early church and discover that it held our Four Articles."[1]

It is noteworthy that the warrior refers to the early church rather than to scripture as the foundation of the Four Articles that encapsulated the Hussite vision for a reformed Christendom and that his

1. *Monumenta conciliorum generalium seculi decimi quinti*, edited by František Palacký et al., 4 vols. (Vienna and Basel: Typis C.R. Officinae typographicae aulae et status, 1857–1935) [hereafter MC], 1:296.

party had come to defend at the invitation of the council. Without denying that Prokop would assert the critical importance of the Bible, one suspects that the articles had become the Hussites' hermeneutical key and served to authenticate their views about scripture.

If so, the path to understanding the Hussite reform program begins in a creative fusion of exegesis and hermeneutics in which the former involves the practical methods and the latter the often unexamined assumptions that interpreters bring to the task.[2] From the early fifteenth century this path leads us back to the *vita apostolica*. In their perception of the long-ago past the Hussites saw a church where poverty, purity, and even persecution were the hallmarks of Christian discipleship and where Prokop found confirmation of his "conversation with the Holy Spirit."[3] The same notion of a pure primitive church before the fall of Constantine also provided a degree of historical distance and a measure for judging the Roman church, the pope, and even the council.[4]

Ladner's "idea of reform" helps us to understand the origins of this late medieval–early modern spirituality with its desire for the imitation of Christ and its renewed attachment to the human Jesus.[5]

2. See Karlfried Froehlich's Warfield Lecture, "'Aminadab's Chariot': The Predicament of Biblical Interpretation," *The Princeton Seminary Bulletin* 18 (1997): 262–78, esp. 274–75.

3. See Craig Atwood, *The Theology of the Czech Brethren from Hus to Comenius* (University Park, Pa.: Pennsylvania State University Press, 2009), 47.

4. Except for its application to the Hussite sojourn in Basel, the thesis here is not new. See Gordon Leff, "The Apostolic Ideal in Later Medieval Ecclesiology," *Journal of Theological Studies* 18 (1976): 58–82; František Graus, "The Crisis of the Middle Ages and the Hussites," in *The Reformation in Medieval Perspective*, edited by Steven Ozment (Chicago: University of Chicago Press, 1971), 76–103. But note the caution that other factors also played a role in Scott Hendrix, "In Quest of the *Vera ecclesia*: The Crises of Late Medieval Ecclesiology," *Viator* 7 (1976): 347–78, here 370.

5. Christopher M. Bellitto, "The Reform Context of the Great Western Schism," in *A Companion to the Great Western Schism (1378–1417)*, edited by Joëlle Rollo-Koster and Thomas M. Izbicki (Leiden: Brill, 2009), 303–31, here 315–16. Gerhart Ladner, *The Idea of Reform: Its Impact on Christian Thought and Action in the Age of the Fathers*, rev. ed. (Cambridge, Mass.: Harvard University Press, 1959; reprinted New York: Harper & Row, 1967). An intellectual biography is in John Van Engen, "Images and Ideas: The Achievements of Gerhart Burian Ladner, with a Bibliography of His Published Works," *Viator* 20 (1989): 85–115. Phillip Stump, "The Influence of Gerhart Ladner's *The Idea of Reform*," in *Reform*

But Ladner was more comfortable with beginnings than with endings. He correctly observed that the foundational principles for the fifteenth-century reform councils—a public, institutional expression of a renewed spirituality—go back at least to Gregory VII in the eleventh century. But he was further from the mark when he concluded that a faltering confidence in the divine order, prompted by an emphasis on God's unpredictability in Occam and the *via moderna,* caused a crisis of the reform idea and the decline of Christendom.[6] In the decades since Ladner's seminal work, other scholars, including Ladner's own students, have carried on the enterprise,[7] but rather than straighten out this rough and tumble period of transition, they have faced its complexities and contradictions head on. For Berndt Hamm this means giving value both to unity and diversity,[8] while Heiko Oberman commends a search for continuity and discontinuity.[9] This more dynamic approach allows us to concentrate on the changing concepts of reform in different contexts, including social and economic developments, religious orders, and lay piety—all of which were important in Bohemia.[10]

This is not to say that everything is relative in this period or that no distinctions can be made. Scott Hendrix suggests that many urged reform of the church "in head and members" prior to the sixteenth century, but "no comprehensive restructuring of Western Christianity occurred that is comparable to the Reformation."[11] Yet,

---

and Renewal in the Middle Ages and the Renaissance: Studies in Honor of Louis Pascoe, S.J., edited by Thomas M. Izbicki and Christopher M. Bellitto (Leiden: Brill, 2000), 3–17.

6. Gerald Christianson, "Annates and Reform at the Council of Basel," in Izbicki and Bellitto, *Reform and Renewal,* 192–207, here 192, 206–7.

7. Bellitto, "The Reform Context of the Great Western Schism," 308–9.

8. Berndt Hamm, "Einheit und Vielfalt der Reformation—order: was die Reformation zur Reformation machte," in Berndt Hamm et al., *Reformationstheorien: Ein kirchenhistorischer Disput über Einheit und Vielfalt der Reformation* (Göttingen: Vandenhoeck & Ruprecht, 1995), 127.

9. Heiko Oberman, *Forerunners of the Reformation* (New York: Holt, Rinehart and Winston, 1966; reprinted, Philadelphia: Fortress, 1981), 42.

10. Bellitto, "The Reform Context of the Great Western Schism," 308.

11. Scott H. Hendrix, *Recultivating the Vineyard: The Reformation Agendas of Christianization* (Louisville, Ky.: Westminster John Knox, 2004), xxi.

one large-scale defection did occur, and this large-scale defection, the Hussite movement, stands somewhere between reform and Reformation. This gives the movement its special significance.

Our purpose here is to add further specificity to the late medieval idea of reform by giving attention to the conference between the Hussites and the Council of Basel during a fourteen-and-a-half week period in 1433, from January 4 to April 14.[12] Few other episodes in this era can boast such a breadth of options for reform initiatives. Often we hear only the story of the conflict between pope and council, but here the plot thickens. Add the Hussite "heretics" to this volatile mix, and the results are even more interesting and instructive.

Here the debates become a story within a story. If the papacy saw danger in a reforming assembly like the Council of Basel, the Hussites and their sometimes anti-papal and radical reform program were particularly anathema. And if the conciliarists found themselves forced to consider the question of their own authority, the multifaceted Hussites represent an early rehearsal of questions more successfully raised, if not answered, by the Reformation, both Catholic and Protestant. Fortunately, the Hussite delegation has left us clues in their Four Articles which, when taken together with their speeches and certain asides to their friends and opponents, amount

12. A good introduction are the brief but balanced chapters on the Hussites and Basel in F. M. Bartoš, *The Hussite Revolution 1424–1437*, edited and translated by John Klassen (New York: Columbia University Press, 1986) which has the advantage of using Czech sources. Also see notes 21–22 below and Gerald Christianson, *Cesarini: the Conciliar Cardinal* (St. Ottilien: EOS Verlag, 1979), Chap. IV. For general context see Howard Kaminsky, *A History of the Hussite Revolution* (Berkeley: University of California Press, 1967); Frederick Heymann, *John Žižka and the Hussite Revolution* (Princeton: Princeton University Press, 1955); and two recent, helpful works: Atwood, *Theology of the Czech Brethren*, and Thomas A. Fudge, *The Magnificent Ride: The First Reformation in Hussite Bohemia* (Aldershot, Vt.: Ashgate, 1998). Thomas Fudge, "The Law of God: Reform and Religious Practice in Late Medieval Bohemia," in *The Bohemian Reformation and Religious Practice*, vol. 1, edited by Zdeněk David and David Holeton (Prague: Academy of Sciences of the Czech Republic, 1996), 49–72. Related documents in Thomas Fudge, *The Crusade against Heretics in Bohemia, 1418–1437* (Aldershot, Vt.: Ashgate, 2002). Also useful is Thomas Fudge, "The State of Hussite Historiography," *Mediaevistik* 7 (1994): 93–117.

to a confession of faith.[13] These clues allow us to reconstruct, if still only imperfectly, the inner drama of a movement conflicted over its own vision and permit us to glimpse the creative impulses of a reform program in action.

While the underlying hermeneutical theme of the Four Articles is the nature of the *vita apostolica* and the primitive church as the model for reform, a closely related issue concerns the specific proposals that each party put forward as the proper expression of apostolic life. The Hussite debates are especially intriguing because they illustrate a wide spectrum of models, not just conciliar and papal, but within the Hussite movement itself. United in their Four Articles, the Hussites had to deal with several, often sharply divided, parties—some with radical revisions of church and society; others closer to the ideals of the Second Vatican Council than might be expected.

A second closely related issue involved ecclesiology. Who properly interprets the scripture that determines genuine apostolic life, especially when positions conflict? What puzzled the Hussites, Thomas Izbicki astutely observes, was that the Council of Basel "could resist the power of the pope and yet condemn the dissidents of Bohemia for rejecting the same power."[14] Behind the questions of doctrine and practice, the quest for the true church and the locus of authority—a constant concern since the days of the Great Schism in 1378—had taken on new significance.[15] Yet, since the debates occurred in a period that is of great significance for an understanding

13. MC 1:147.

14. Thomas M. Izbicki, "The Authority of Peter and Paul: The Use of Biblical Authority during the Great Schism," in Rollo-Koester and Izbicki, *Companion to the Great Western Schism*, 375–393, here 393.

15. On Basel's ecclesiology, see Werner Krämer, *Konsens und Rezeption: Verfassungsprinzipien der Kirche im Basler Konziliarismus* (Münster: Aschendorff, 1980), 369–83. In general see Hendrix, "In Quest of the *Vera ecclesia*," 347–78; and David Zachariah Flanagin, "*Extra ecclesiam salus non est—sed quae ecclesia*?: Ecclesiology and Authority in the Later Middle Ages," in Rollo-Koester and Izbicki, *Companion to the Great Western Schism*, 333–74.

of the history of biblical hermeneutics,[16] our primary focus will be on a third issue: not so much exegetical methods as how the various parties sought to authenticate their reforms in the Bible and Christian antiquity with central interpretive principles that helped unlock their message.

Scholarly emphasis on exegesis and ecclesiology in the late medieval church is not new, but we can note a trend in recent historiography to narrow the focus of study on hermeneutical principles. While denying that one can easily divide scripture and tradition, George Tavard (in a vein similar to Ladner) charged the later Middle Ages with a break-down in the balance between the two.[17] Yves Congar at first adopted a similar view, but when he surveyed the breadth of biblical passages used in various discussions at Basel on the nature of the church, he later confessed that he had "underestimated the members of the council and the council itself."[18]

Hermann Schüssler did much to concentrate the field on the problem of infallibility,[19] and while Johannes Helmrath's bibliographical study of the council stresses ecclesiology in the Hussite deliberations, he takes Schüssler even further by stressing the contrast between infallible scripture against infallible council.[20] Although one can agree with Schüssler and Helmrath that, in contrast

16. Karlfried Froehlich, "'Always to Keep the Literal Sense in Holy Scripture Means to Kill One's Soul': The State of Biblical Hermeneutics at the Beginning of the Fifteenth Century," in *Literary Uses of Typology from the Late Middle Ages to the Present,* edited by Earl Miner (Princeton: Princeton University Press, 1977), 20–48, here 27.

17. George Tavard, *Holy Writ or Holy Church: The Crisis of the Protestant Reformation* (London: Burns and Oates, 1959).

18. Yves Congar, *La Tradition et les traditions,* 2 vols. (Paris: Arthème Fayard, 1960–1963), 1:128–30.

19. Hermann Schüssler, "Sacred Doctrine and the Authority of Scripture in Canonistic Thought on the Eve of the Reformation," in *Reform and Authority in the Medieval and Reformation Church,* edited by Guy Lytle (Washington, D.C.: The Catholic University of America Press, 1981), 55–68, esp. 61; and Hermann Schüssler, "Scripture and Tradition in the Later Middle Ages: The Canonist 'Panormitanus' and the Problem of Scriptural Authority," *Concordia Theological Monthly* 38 (1967): 234–41.

20. Johannes Helmrath, *Das Basler Konzil, 1431–1449: Forschungsstand und Probleme* (Cologne: Böhlau, 1987), 353–72.

to Tavard, *sola scriptura* is an anachronism at Basel in 1433, a concentration on infallibility—whether of Bible, council, church, or papacy—is probably as anachronistic as *sola scriptura* if colored by modern presuppositions. As to the story of the debates themselves, E. F. Jacob provided a brief but basic account, including the intricate negotiations leading to the Hussite agreement to attend.[21] The Belgian Benedictine Paul de Vooght, as part of his effort to resuscitate the Hussite reputation, focused on the debates alone. De Vooght's interest was Wyclif's doctrine of the church as the community of the predestined, but he also emphasized that the moderate Hussite wing was in line with the Catholic tradition of the day.[22]

Interestingly, Jacob wrote his essay in 1949 during a period of renewed interest in Czechoslovakia as a result of the Communist takeover, while de Vooght published his essay in 1970 during the afterglow of the Second Vatican Council. Yet since Jacob covers the context but not the content of the debates and de Vooght the content of the debates but not the context, a need remains to combine the two in order to have a fuller picture and attempt to determine underlying principles that drove the Hussite engine of reform. The search for an authentic church, which this essay argues is one of these principles, did not hang on a single abstract idea like infallibility or predestination, as important as they were, but on a dialectic between exegesis and ideology as this played out among the three major actors—pope, council, and Hussites.

21. E. F. Jacob, "The Bohemians at the Council of Basel," in *Prague Essays,* edited by R. W. Seton-Watson (Oxford: Clarendon Press, 1949), 81–123. Hermann Hallauer, "Das Glaubensgespräch mit den Hussiten," *Mitteilungen und Forschungsbeiträge der Cusanus-Gesellschaft* 9 (1971): 53–75, deals with Nicholas of Cusa's role in the deliberations.

22. Paul De Vooght, "La confrontation des thèses hussites et romaines au concile de Bâle (Janvier–Avril, 1433)," *Recherches de Théologie ancienne et médiévale* 37 (1970): 97–137, 254–91; Paul De Vooght, "La notion d' 'Église-assemblé des prédestinées' dans la théologie Hussite primitive," *Communio Viatorum* 13 (1970): 119–36. On the other hand, William Cook, "La transubstantiation, clef théologique de la fragmentation du movement Hussite," *Irenikon* 49 (1976): 223–35, argues that transubstantiation was the key to Hussite disagreements. To the degree that the Hussites reflect Wyclif, Ann Hudson, *English Wycliffite Writings* (Cambridge: Cambridge University Press, 1978), 4–5, sees a combination of dominion and predestination as fundamental to the English reformer.

The papacy was clear where it stood. Pope Eugenius IV first tried to transfer or even close the council after it opened in 1431, and a major reason he cited was the council's desire, in the wake of several disastrous crusades against Bohemia, to discuss doctrine with condemned heretics. Among the defenders of the papacy the term "apostolic" in *vita apostolica* and in the creedal affirmation "one holy, catholic, and apostolic Church" meant "papal." This was apparent in the very name "Apostolic See."[23]

The reforming Council of Basel, on the other hand, was a *via media* between papacy and Hussites. Despite papal resistance, the cry for reform in head and members increased sharply and joined the demand for unity after the Great Schism (1378) divided the papacy among two and then three incumbents. Unity and reform became the center of attention at the Council of Constance (1414–1418) which finally healed the breach.[24] But since Constance allowed the task of reform to revert to the recently elected pope Martin V, the issue took on an entirely new dimension at Basel (1431–1449): who would lead reform in the church, a legitimately assembled council or a single, undoubted pope?[25]

Whether deserved or not, Basel's reputation as schismatic and radical because it eventually deposed Eugenius has overshadowed its considerable reform efforts, comparable to those of Constance.[26]

23. Flanagin, "*Extra ecclesiam salus non est*," 363.

24. Bellitto, "The Reform Context of the Great Western Schism," 327. On Constance, see Phillip H. Stump, "The Council of Constance (1414–18) and the End of the Schism," in Rollo-Koester and Izbicki, *Companion to the Great Western Schism*, 395–42. For an overview of the late medieval–early modern reform councils, with extensive bibliography, see Nelson H. Minnich, "Councils of the Catholic Reformation: A Historical Survey," in *The Church, the Councils, and Reform: The Legacy of the Fifteenth Century*, edited by Gerald Christianson, Thomas M. Izbicki, and Christopher M. Bellitto (Washington, D.C.: The Catholic University of America Press, 2009), 27–59.

25. On the significance of conciliar theory and its role in Basel's resistance to Eugenius, see Flanagin, "*Extra ecclesiam salus non est*," 362–73; Gerald Christianson, "The Conciliar Tradition and Ecumenical Dialogue," in Christianson, Izbicki and Bellitto, *The Church, the Councils, and Reform*, 1–24.

26. Phillip Stump, *The Reforms of the Council of Constance (1414–1418)* (Leiden: Brill, 1994). No comparable study of Basel's reform yet exists, but see Christianson, "Annates and Reform at the Council of Basel," with further bibliography.

Among other proposals, the council debated or enacted substantial decrees on regular episcopal elections, frequent diocesan and provincial synods, an end to keeping concubines, an equitable representation of cardinals, and—most controversially—the suppression of simony and papal annates.[27] Yet while this reforming perspective made the Council of Basel cautiously open to the Hussites, most conciliarists adhered to the papacy even while refuting its more absolutist tendencies.[28] The conciliar participants in the debates had little interest in finding scriptural support for papal primacy, but their cohesion on the teaching authority of the church did not wander far from those who defended Eugenius against the council.

The last of the three major players in the drama, the Hussites, best exemplifies a reform that coincided with experiments in reshaping a culture, including nation building, and that took place in a period of turmoil in Bohemia around the turn of the century.[29] With support from the nobility who could flex their political muscle during the long absence of their king-in-waiting, Sigismund of Luxembourg,[30] the clearest sign of a changing order was a lay sacramental spirituality that urged frequent participation in the Eucharist. This spirituality reflected a determination that lay men and women could experience a devotional life in their own right,[31] and led them to more frequent communions, to the desire for both bread and wine, and later to the communion of infants.[32] In fact, although modern usage refers to the movement as "Hussite," adherents usually identified themselves as "Utraquists," advocates of communion in both kinds.

27. Christianson, *Cesarini: the Conciliar Cardinal*, 125–48.

28. Flanagin, "*Extra ecclesiam salus non est*," 373.

29. Fudge, *The Magnificent Ride*, 59.

30. Fudge, *The Magnificent Ride*, 9–10, 18–33; John M. Klassen, *The Nobility and the Making of the Hussite Revolution* (New York: Columbia University Press, 1978), 1–4.

31. Bellitto, "The Reform Context of the Great Western Schism," 318–19.

32. William Cook, "The Eucharist in Hussite Theology," *Archive for Reformation History* 66 (1975): 23–35. Zdeněk David and David Holeton, "The Bohemian Eucharistic Movement in Its European Context," in David Holeton, *The Bohemian Reformation and Religious Practice*, 23–47. Thomas A. Fudge, "Hussite Infant Communion," *Lutheran Quarterly* 10 (1996): 179–93, with further bibliography.

All these elements of a Eucharistic spirituality encouraged a greater sense of cohesiveness and community both with God and with one another, and led to the demand for specific reforms in church and society.[33] One of the first and most significant was to establish a consistory in Prague which, apart from Rome, began to regulate benefices, insist that monks serve parishes, and reduce clerical wealth and ostentation.[34] Modern scholars caution us not to romanticize the communitarian tendencies and such issues as civil dominion, especially in the Táborite wing of the movement. Yet, the observation that these practices—not counting the remarkable effort to militarize them—were not exclusive to Tábor but cut across the landscape of fifteenth century religion leans toward strengthening the argument that the conflict between the church as the *congregatio fidelium* and as an ecclesiastical body was central to all late medieval ecclesiology—not exclusive to the Hussites.

One should also not romanticize Bohemian unity. Little agreement could be reached over the extent of reform, so to achieve a semblance of consensus (and later to provide a basis for negotiation with the Council of Basel) the sometimes bitterly divided parties forged a broad alliance. This alliance reflected the teachings of Wyclif and Hus, a lay piety focused on the Eucharist, contact with the Waldensians,[35] and perhaps also the influence of a nascent humanism that encouraged return to the sources. The result was the Four Articles, first published in 1420 as an authoritative witness to Hussite faith and as a demand for significant reforms:

(1) That the most divine sacrament of the body and blood should be administered by the ministers of the church to the faithful.

(2) That civil dominion, like a deadly poison, should be taken away from the clergy.

33. Fudge, *Crusade against Heretics in Bohemia*, 1.

34. Atwood, *Theology of the Czech Brethren*, 88.

35. Ibid., 44.

(3) That the Word of God should be freely, publicly, and truthfully preached by those whose concern it is to preach.

(4) That public and more notable sins should be suppressed through lawful power by the faithful people.[36]

Although the articles reflect a Hussite desire to return to the *vita apostolica* and the primitive church, they caused fear in pope and council alike, notably the expectation that humble lay folk could punish their superiors or remove their sources of income. The anxiety only increased when the Táborite vision began to shift from prophetic to apocalyptic.[37] Given the strife out of which these four "verities" emerged and its cost in human bloodshed, not to mention what had happened to Hus at the Council of Constance, the Bohemians remained wary about conciliar motives until, led by the Prague Utraquist John Rokycana, they had wrung an agreement from the council's representatives at Cheb on May 18, 1432.[38] The Cheb Compacts, remarkable because largely unprecedented, not only assured a free and open hearing in the assembly, but in Paragraph Seven laid down a principle that came to be known as the "Cheb judge": the Articles could be judged by nothing other than "evangelical law (*lex divina*), the practice of Christ, the apostles and the primitive church, together with the councils and doctors who truly conform to them." All other authorities would be subordinate, including papal pronouncements and canon law. Although *lex divina* contained an ambiguity between scripture and a body of moral laws, the "Cheb judge" would do yeoman's duty for the Hussites in Basel. They invoked it over two dozen times. Moreover, the compacts themselves assured that the interpretation of scripture and early tra-

36. MC 1:147. This is the second major redaction. It was presented to Basel in 1433. For a translation of the earliest version of 1420, see Fudge, *Crusade against the Heretics in Bohemia*, No. 39. A third redaction was incorporated in the agreement known as the *Compactata* adopted in 1436: MC 1:495–98; Fudge, *Crusade against the Heretics in Bohemia*, No. 190. For detailed analysis, see Heymann, *John Žižka*, 148–57.

37. Atwood, *Theology of the Czech Brethren*, 94–95.

38. MC 1:220. Fudge, *Crusade against the Heretics in Bohemia*, No. 180.

dition would remain at the forefront of discussions when the Hussites entered Basel to considerable curiosity on Sunday, January 4, 1433.[39]

In addition to brief notices in the council's official "minutes" or protocols and John of Segovia's otherwise comprehensive history, we are fortunate to have a collection of three Hussite speeches and a number of observers who carefully followed the debates. John of Ragusa (Jan Stoiković), an active participant in the negotiations and the debates, provides us with two tracts, one on the opening of Basel and another on the conference itself. In addition, an anonymous "Daily Journal" (*Liber diurnus*) by someone within the Hussite delegation allows us to listen in on their internal discussions, disagreements, and decisions.[40]

In preparation for the visit, members of the council agreed to their own local reforms so as not to offend Bohemian sensibilities. They forbade public dancing, gambling, prostitution, and drunkenness.[41] They also chose an international cast of speakers to address the Articles: a Croatian, Ragusa, the procurator of the Dominican order; a Frenchman, Giles Charlier, Dean of Cambrai; a German, Henry Kalteisen, a theologian at Cologne; and a Spaniard, John of Palomar, whom Cesarini had deputized along with Ragusa to open

39. MC 1:258, 289.

40. The Bohemian speeches were published by František Bartoš in two volumes, *Orationes Nicolaus de Pelhřimov et Ulricus de Znojmo* (Tábor: Jihoceská spolecnost, 1935) and *Petri Payne Anglici* (Tábor: Taboriensis ecclesia evangelica fratrum Bohemorum, 1949). The latter is the only source we have for Payne's address. The conciliar rebuttals are in vol. 29 of *Sacrorum conciliorum nova et amplissima collectio,* edited by G. D. Mansi, 53 vols. (reprinted Graz: Akademische Druck- und Verlagsanstalt, 1960–61) [hereafter Mansi]. The protocols are in Johannes Haller, *Consilium Basiliense,* 8 vols. (Basel: R. Reich, 1896–1936; reprinted Nendeln: Kraus Reprint, 1971). Segovia's perceptive assessment of the Hussite challenge to the council: MC 2:423. But more helpful for the inner workings of the conference are John of Ragusa's *Initium et prosecutio Basiliensis concilii* in MC 1:1–131, his *Tractatus quomodo Bohemi reducti sunt ad unitatem ecclesiae* in MC 1:135–286; and *Liber diurnus de gestis Bohemorum in concilio Basileensi* in MC 1:289–357. František Palacký theorized that a Hussite priest Peter of Žatec was the author of the *Liber diurnus,* but Bartoš later suggested a German, Laurence of Reichenbach who came to Basel as Prokop's secretary. (I am grateful to Thomas Fudge for this information.)

41. MC 1:258.

the council in the cardinal's absence. All were learned; two, Ragusa and Kalteisen, were Dominicans. So that little would be left to chance, the team held practice sessions.[42]

The Hussites had far more trouble with their decision, especially on who should handle the controversial Third Article on the free preaching of the Word—a moderate like the Utraquist leader and future archbishop of Prague, John Rokycana, or someone more provocative.[43] Theological differences aside, Rokycana claimed he could speak faster and louder than the others. Nevertheless, the Third Article went to Ulrich (Oldřich) of Znojmo.[44] Ulrich was perhaps less caustic than his Táborite colleagues. He was a priest and member of the Orphan Brotherhood, followers of John Žižka, the late military genius who was largely responsible for the Bohemian victories over the crusaders, and the predecessor of Prokop Holý.

The decision about Ulrich was part of a larger compromise. The speakers would represent each of the four "societies" within the delegation: the aforementioned Rokycana on the First Article and Ulrich on the Third; Rokycana's rival, the Taborite Bishop Nicholas (Mikuláš) Biskupec of Pelhřimov on the Second; and on the Fourth, Peter Payne, a Wyclifite and transplant to Bohemia known simply as "English."[45] Still, disagreements remained even after the delegation arrived in Basel. During Cesarini's after-dinner meeting with Prokop, the warrior admitted that his delegation had differences, a fact that the council, especially its president, would later exploit.[46]

Not without some bumps in the road, the proceedings finally got under way with the First Article on January 16. "Then occurred," says the venerable A. C. Flick, "one of the wordiest debates on re-

42. MC 1:257–58.

43. See Frederick Heymann, "John Rokycana: Church Reformer between Hus and Luther," *Church History* 28 (1959): 240–80.

44. MC 1:291, 294.

45. MC 1:291–95.

46. MC 1:311. On Cesarini's conciliar theology, see Krämer, *Konsens und Rezeption,* Chap. 3, and Christianson, *Cesarini: the Conciliar Cardinal,* Epilogue.

cord, which consumed 50 days with speeches eight days long,"[47] but rich in indications of late medieval hermeneutics, ecclesiology, and reform ideas. Although each side delivered their speeches seriatim, beginning with the Hussites, we will set them side by side for purposes of direct comparison. In a relatively brief and tightly argued speech, Rokycana began with a straightforward defense of the Utraquist position on lay access to the chalice.[48] The practice had grown out of an increase in frequent communions initiated by Jakoubek of Stříbro after Hus, ill-advisedly, had left for Constance in 1414.[49] Rokycana insisted that the practice derived from the Lord himself and was not only salutary—it was necessary for salvation.

For biblical support Rokycana cited Matthew 14 (the feeding of the 5,000) and Luke 22 (the Last Supper) and their references to distribution in both kinds. He also cited John 6 which he assumed was the Johannine parallel to these narratives. But he did not end here. Perhaps alarming to those council members who thought these "Bible men" were unlearned country folk, Rokycana also appealed to a large number of non-biblical authorities reaching from Augustine to Aquinas. A famous Hussite nemesis, John of Capistrano, once admitted to Nicholas of Cusa that he avoided debate with the Bohemians because they had studied the scriptures, and "more than that they have a perfect knowledge of these numerous texts that favor communion in both kinds."[50] Capistrano's comment was more than an observation about Hussite biblical literacy. Proponents like Rokycana had actually assembled a large dossier of authorities that included Wyclif and Hus—although less than we might expect—as well as passages from the Bible, Gratian's *Decretum*, and the early Fathers. Moreover, while Rokycana's brevity followed the guidelines of the Cheb Compacts, it demonstrated that he assumed his hearers

47. Alexander Clarence Flick, *The Decline of the Medieval Church*, 2 vols. (New York: Alfred A. Knopf, 1930), 2:164.

48. MC 1:264–68, 292–93. The full speech in Mansi 29:269–306.

49. Atwood, *Theology of the Czech Brethren*, 77–80.

50. Quoted in Fudge, *The Magnificent Ride*, 112.

would see the merit of his case and agree that the divinely ordained lay chalice would provide fullness and completion to the sacrament.

Since the lay chalice was not central to Hus's preaching, recent research has turned our attention to why it became central to the Hussite reform program as well as its art—displayed, for example, on the banners carried into battle with the words, "Truth conquers all."[51] If Miri Rubin is correct that the medieval Catholic Mass—focused on the priest, the miracle of transubstantiation, and the withholding of the cup—could serve as a means to compel conformity to church and hierarchy, then a Hussite communion where the gathered community celebrated unity with Christ in both bread and wine lent itself to shared experience and corporate identity.[52] In the apt phrase of Howard Kaminsky, the chalice was "not a quirk or an ornament," but "contained the essence of Hussitism."[53]

The Dominican John of Ragusa took the better part of two weeks to deliver the council's reply to Rokycana and the First Article.[54] Because of its length—extended by frequent interruptions from the Bohemian delegation because of the Ragusa's name-dropping and other "impertinences"—the fashion in former times was to dismiss his speech as lightweight.[55] However, since the biblical case for utraquism was difficult to refute, Ragusa had little choice but to probe more deeply and discuss at length his view of scriptural and ecclesial authority with the result that his speech, despite its wordiness, should be more fully appreciated. In addition, the Dominican later turned his reflections into a substantial work, *De ecclesia*,[56]

51. MC 1:258.

52. Miri Rubin, *Corpus Christi: The Eucharist in Late Medieval Culture* (Cambridge: Cambridge University Press, 1991), 12–13. Atwood, *Theology of the Czech Brethren*, 13.

53. Kaminsky, *The Hussite Revolution*, 98.

54. Ragusa began on January 31: MC 1:300–301, 275–84. The full speech in Mansi 29:699–868.

55. See, for example, Antony Black, *Council and Commune: The Conciliar Movement and the Fifteenth-Century Heritage* (London: Burns & Oates, 1979), 108, where he describes Ragusa as "for the most part long-winded, repetitious, and lacking in originality."

56. *Magistri Iohannis (Stojković) de Ragusio OP Tractatus de ecclesia*, Croatica Christiana, Fontes I, edited by Franjo Šanjek (Zagreb: Krscanska sadasnjost, 1983). On Rag-

a subject of particular interest in the period of the reform councils.[57]

Rokycana had laid down a formidable challenge to Ragusa. If the lay chalice was the Lord's will, by what authority can the church alter this practice or any "law of God"? Ragusa chose an interesting defense. He admitted the evidence for utraquism in the Bible and in ancient times, but argued that the church had changed other important practices, such as the observance of Sunday, infant baptism, confession, and the use of unleavened bread. Ragusa even invoked Hus against the Hussites when he correctly observed that the reformer had not initiated the lay chalice. The Dominican concluded that even if the early church had practiced utraquism, Rokycana had not proved that it was a necessity.

Ragusa advanced to a second stage of his argument on February 6 when he moved from refuting his opponent to affirming his own position. His basic assertion was that the teachings of the church are binding "in all necessary matters" since the church cannot err in whatever relates to faith. Although a distinguished conciliarist, Ragusa did not hesitate to define the church as pope and bishops who must be obeyed.[58] He drew the practical consequences of this thesis on February 11: the church has altered, and still can alter its practices, even those found in the Bible.[59] Ragusa's approach again demonstrated the interplay of ideology and exegetical method. The Dominican agreed with Rokycana that scripture is the inspired Word of God, and that while it reveals different senses under the letter of the text, all that is necessary for salvation is found in the principal literal sense. Yet this very same variety and the inherent difficulty of scripture in general create the need for a norm. The true norm, in

---

usa's ecclesiology see Krämer, *Konsens und Rezeption*, 369–83; Petar Vrankić, "Die Grundzüge der Konzilstheologie des Johannes von Ragusa," *Annuarium historiae conciliorum* 30 (1989): 287–310; Amedeo Molnar, "La Pensée hussite dans l'interprétation de Jean Stoković de Raguse," in *Misao I Djelo Ivana Stojkovića*, edited by Franjo Šanjek (Zagreb: Krscanska sadasnjost, 1986), 221–78.

57. No treatise on the subject appeared until 1300, but elicited increased attention after the outbreak of schism in 1378. Flanagin, "*Extra ecclesiam*," 339n25.

58. MC 1:301–2, 281–82.

59. MC 1:307–9, 283–84.

contrast to the Four Articles, is the reception and approval by the church. While making no reference to papal primacy or a *magisterium*, Ragusa instead proclaimed that Christ not only guarantees his presence to the church, but also gives his guiding Spirit to protect it from error in matters pertaining to faith and salvation.

The different lengths and different number of authorities cited in the two speeches further illuminate their respective methods. Ragusa adheres to the more traditional practice of building up his citations (twenty or so on February 6 alone), and even set up a table to hold his many volumes.[60] This irritated the Hussites who used their Four Articles as a kind of surgical knife, cutting away all but the most important authorities that supported their view of a biblical mandate. After Rokycana we witness a dramatic change in the tone of the next Hussite speakers as well as the audience. If utraquism could be demonstrated in early church practice, the remaining three of the Four Articles on civil dominion of the clergy, free preaching, and the suppression of public sins were fraught with radical overtones. If the First Article represents the chief sentiment of Prague, the last three were the realm of Tábor and its allies. If the one major demarcation between Rome and the Utraquists was the chalice, Táborite theology struck all along the line against the foundations of medieval church and society. In addition to the chalice for all, including children, and the belief that the New Testament was sufficient for salvation and provided a model for reform, the Táborites attacked indulgences, monasticism, and the accumulation of clerical wealth by tithes or any civil dominion. They rejected purgatory, prayers for the dead, confession to a priest, extreme unction, the intercession of the saints, and an ordered (as compared to a spiritual) episcopacy.[61] When they celebrated the Eucharist at Basel they dispensed with vestments, deleted the canon of the Mass, and shared the bread and wine around a table.[62]

60. MC 1:279.
61. Atwood, *Theology of the Czech Brethren*, 196, 111.
62. MC 1:259.

From the perspective of their reform programs, Táborites and Utraquists were leagues apart, and it was remarkable that the parties could hammer out any consensus at all. Before their agreement to the Four Articles, the Táborites had proposed twelve articles that included further reforms such as punishment for adultery and the suppression of luxurious clothing. One can now understand why Rokycana argued that he and no one else explain the article on civil dominion. The rivalry between the two sides was long-standing. Well before they arrived in Basel, Rokycana and the Táborite Bishop Nicholas of Pelhrimov had even conducted a pamphlet war expressing their differences.[63] Rokycana's suspicions proved correct. As expected, Article Two on the civil dominion of the clergy raised conciliar hackles, especially as presented from the standpoint of Tábor by his rival Bishop Nicholas. The bishop castigated the clergy for their corruption, specifically their violation of *dominium*.[64] He further maintained that they could be punished by secular authority and, failing this, by the whole body of the faithful. He supported this contention with several references to Marsilius of Padua's widely condemned treatise, *Defensor Pacis*, which Nicholas thought was written by William of Occam.[65] If this were not enough to set the members on edge, the bishop charged the council with the deaths of John Hus and Jerome of Prague. A commotion broke out, and Cesarini had to calm the speaker with the wry comment that the members were merely clearing their throats.[66] Such humor was not uncommon and may have helped to sustain the proceedings, but the Daily Journal, which recorded over three dozen instances of loud laughter, also charged that it could be disrespectful.[67]

Nevertheless, beneath the fiery Táborite rhetoric one can rec-

63. Atwood, *Theology of the Czech Brethren*, 111–12, 124–29.

64. MC 1:268–94. The full speech in Bartoš, *Orationes*, 3–32. Not all the Hussites were consistent on this point. Cesarini chided Prokop about his wealth and hearty meals: MC 1:311.

65. Kaminsky, *The Hussite Revolution*, 485.

66. MC 1:294.

67. E.g., MC 1:327, 348.

ognize an exegetical method that opposes a Spirit-filled church to a hierarchically-ordered church. The former possesses a permanent *charism* that authenticates itself in good works and contrasts sharply with Catholic abuses. In this same church the Spirit never fails to raise preachers of the Gospel and prompt Christians to hear and understand it. Nicholas's opponents, whether curial officials or conciliar advocates who resisted the pope quickly saw the dangers in such a position. It degraded the need for a regulated system of "duly appointed" clergy and shifted the emphasis to Word and deed.

The Paris scholar Giles Carlier took up the conciliar rejoinder to Bishop Nicholas and the Second Article.[68] While Carlier affirmed Ragusa's belief that the church is founded on scripture, he moved a step closer to a juridical interpretation, although he still did not invoke the papacy as the chief component of a teaching *magisterium*. Leadership in the church, Carlier argued, must always be entrusted to the hierarchy, and—with more than a passing reference to Deuteronomy 17:8–11—the hierarchy alone is charged with judging the meaning of scripture in all important matters. Like the other Hussite speakers, the Orphan Brother Ulrich of Znojmo, who addressed the Third Article on January 23, professed adherence to the Word.[69] This Word, above all, is Jesus Christ himself. Derivatively, it is the Word proclaimed through the words of the apostles, including scripture, and finally delivered by all the Lord's servants and messengers down through the ages. The marked feature of Ulrich's presentation, however, was the assertion that if priests and prelates refuse to preach the Gospel, and instead merely exercise powers of jurisdiction, they prove themselves to be of Satan, not God. Furthermore—and here is the crucial point for the plain-spoken Brother—an "evangelical life" is the measure of authentic vocation in the Spirit. Sound preaching is Spirit-effective only if it is confirmed by sound actions, an assertion

68. Charlier began on February 13: MC 1:284, 309. The full speech in Mansi 29:868–972.

69. MC 1:269, 295. The full speech in Bartoš, *Orationes*, 86–113.

that brought gasps from an audience who considered this a blatant expression of Donatism.

In his rebuttal to Ulrich, the Dominican Henry Kalteisen asserted that the license to preach is reserved for the church alone.[70] In support of this affirmation, Kalteisen made a familiar conciliarist distinction between the church as a Spirit-led community, the *congregatio fidelium,* and as a political entity. Considered as a legitimate constitutional body, the church has three primary offices: the pope who holds the vicariate of Christ, the bishops who succeed the apostles; and priests who represent the seventy-two disciples. In all cases the mark of authenticity in the spirit is obedience of lower to higher degrees.

If the assembly thought they would hear no more inflammatory speakers after Ulrich of Znojmo, they were in for a surprise. On January 26 Peter Payne gave his defense of the Fourth Article, the suppression of public sins.[71] The issue of who had the authority to interpret scripture and enact reform that had concerned Rokycana and found echoes in Nicholas and Ulrich now came to focus on whether the church could modify practices mandated by scripture and approved by the church Fathers. Not to be outdone by Ragusa, "English" literally piled up his references to establish the principle that the clergy, in imitation of the community in Acts 2:43-47, must dispense with all goods except the bare essentials.

The council had no need to guess where Payne had derived this doctrine of *dominium.* He readily admitted that it came from Wyclif, although he proffered that his fellow countryman was not alone in this conviction, alluding to the Franciscan dispute with the papacy about whether Christ himself held any property. One example of clerical luxury that he abhorred appeared all too frequently as the days passed. One can imagine the scene as Payne and his austere

70. Kalteisen began on February 18: MC 1:284, 313. The full speech in Mansi 29:971–1044.

71. MC 1:269–70, 296–97. The full speech in Bartoš, *P. Payne Anglici,* 1–40.

colleagues perceived it. A cardinal with his retinue and a train so long it must be held by servants lumbers along to the cathedral, creating a cloud of dust.[72]

In response to Payne and the case against civil dominion in the Fourth Article,[73] John of Palomar did not launch into a defense of the status quo, as his conciliar partners had done, but instead cited numerous instances in which he maintained that Payne had quoted his biblical references out of context. In support of this critique, Palomar explicitly cited his principle exegetical rule: no one should hold to the bare literal text alone, but must distinguish between the grammatical sense and the fundamentally "true" sense. Palomar, unlike the others, did not need to appeal to a teaching *magisterium*. Instead, he argued that his method would lead directly to the source and find a definitive conclusion: scripture does not command any law that requires clerical poverty. Palomar's rebuttal brought an end to the official round of debates but not an end to negotiations. Much work lay ahead—some of it tedious, some tumultuous. Yet, the Bohemian delegation had already sensed the need to return home. Their decision was prompted in part by two events. The first was a series of twenty-eight articles and six questions submitted by Cesarini at the conclusion of the formal Hussite speeches.[74] The cardinal said he wanted only to determine the extent of Wyclifite influence on the Hussite reform movement, but it was also meant to uncover, if not exacerbate, their internal differences with the hope that such self-revelation would encourage reunion with the larger whole. These questions covered the gamut: the presence of Christ in the Eucharist, their Donatist tendencies, the rumored use of chrism to oil their boots, the role of confession and prayers for the dead, and the powers of pope and council.

72. E.g. MC 1:312, 339 (referring to Cesarini).

73. Palomar began on February 23: MC 1:285, 316. Mansi 29:1105–68 gives only the text of Palomar's practice speech.

74. MC 1:271–74. Gerald Christianson, "Wyclif's Ghost: The Politics of Reunion at the Council of Basel," *Annuarium historiae conciliorum* 13 (1985): 193–208.

The second event involved a concrete proposal put forward on March 13 by Nicholas of Cusa, perhaps prompted by the council's protector, Duke William of Bavaria, who represented Emperor-elect Sigismund.[75] The proposal offered the use of the chalice to the Hussites in return for incorporation into the council where the remaining articles would be negotiated. Given the apparent differences within their delegation, it should be no surprise that the Hussites, without answering either Cesarini or Cusanus, found it necessary to return home and consult with their Diet.[76] They departed on the Tuesday after Easter, April 14, 1433.[77]

War loomed in Bohemia when agreement failed. A coalition of Utraquists and Catholic nobles routed the brotherhoods at Lipany on May 30, 1434. Prokop was killed. This paved the way for the remnant clergy to elect Rokycana as the first Hussite archbishop of Prague, although Rome never granted him consecration,[78] and to ratify an agreement with the Council of Basel, the *Compactata,* in July 1436.[79] These historic compacts ended the war, lifted the title of "heresy" from Bohemia, and agreed to the reforms of the Four Articles with some notable modifications: communion in both kinds could not be enforced on Bohemian Catholics; public sins could be punished only by those "whose office it is to do so"; free preaching must be approved by those who were duly commissioned; and the denial of civil dominion, the most problematic of all, could still allow priests to hold property if administered according to the ancient Fathers. The period of accord between Catholics and Bohemia was short-lived, however. When Aeneas Sylvius Piccolomini, once an active participant in Basel, became Pope Pius II he condemned ap-

75. MC 1:328–31. Gerald Christianson, "Cusanus, Concord, and Conflict," in *Nicholas of Cusa: A Medieval Thinker for the Modern Age,* edited by Kazuhiko Yamaki (Richmond, Surrey: Curzon Press, 2002), 206–19, here 211.

76. MC 1:324–31.

77. MC 1:354.

78. Atwood, *Theology of the Czech Brethren,* 96; Fudge, *The Magnificent Ride,* 2.

79. MC 1:495–98. Translation in Fudge, *The Crusade against Heretics in Bohemia,* No. 190.

peals to a council over a pope and in 1462 rescinded the *Compactata*.[80]

Nevertheless, a significant moment had passed. The church had tried numerous crusades, but Basel issued no interdict or excommunication to force adherence. For the first time since the age of Augustine, when the church in North Africa met with the Donatists, a group that had been branded as "heretics" entered a council and engaged in discussing Bible and reform. But with what results? The biblical foundations for reform, as in the early fifteenth century generally, were still "highly traditionalist" in their appeal to authorities.[81] The council's debaters were not alone in this appeal. It is especially evident in Rokycana's speech and the Cheb Judge that explicitly measured "evangelical truth" by a consensus of "fathers and doctors" as well as scripture. To this end, the Hussite speeches reveal a wide knowledge of theologians, jurists, and exegetes, including not only Augustine and Jerome, but Duns Scotus, Peter Lombard, the *Glossa ordinaria*, Huguccio, and Aquinas. Yet, while both sides appealed to "apostolic succession" for the preservation of truth, succession for the Táborites, and to a lesser extent the Utraquists, was of teachers and teachings rather than popes and bishops.

Furthermore, discussion of exegetical method fused with and sometimes yielded to ideology. This is frequently manifested in the highly volatile conflict over teaching authority that was bound to shape reform initiatives. The desire for certainty in the text and a means to determine how this certainty could be achieved remained the same for all three players in the drama—pope, council, and Hussites. For their part, the conciliar representatives were keen to retain traditional practices, whether or not biblical. This was not an

80. See the Introduction to *Reject Aeneas, Accept Pius: Selected Letters of Aeneas Sylvius Piccolomini (Pope Pius II)*, introduction and translated by Thomas M. Izbicki, Gerald Christianson, and Philip Krey (Washington, D.C.: The Catholic University of America Press, 2006), 3–57.

81. Froehlich, "Always to Keep the Literal Sense in Holy Scripture," 44–48.

attack on scripture but a defense of the church's *magisterium*, even though in the conciliarist view the *magisterium* derived its authority from a harmony between councils and popes rather than popes acting alone.

Despite what we might expect on the other side, the Hussites were neither "biblical literalists" nor adherents of *sola scriptura* in a modern sense. Prokop's statement to Cesarini about "conversation with the Holy Spirit" implied a more nuanced frame of reference, grounded in the *vita apostolica* that had evolved with the reshaping of Bohemian culture. The Hussites expressed this culture in their Four Articles which then guided their reading of scripture and their efforts to reform church and society. The impetus for these demands was the *lex divina* but, as Henning Graf Reventlow has observed, "evangelical law" meant the whole Bible understood in a moral sense.[82] Christ is the center of the Gospel, but the Christ found here is an example for Christian life in which two major characteristics, humility and poverty, constitute the call to discipleship in the world. The Hussites appeared radical when they applied this vision, like Wyclif before them, to the whole Catholic Church, and included the demand that clergy surrender all temporal possessions. This was a dramatic step beyond other moralizing tendencies in medieval hermeneutics.

In addition to its contributions to the formation of the Czech Brethren and the Moravians, what lasting effects this reformation had on the church remains an intriguing but open question. Perhaps we may safely say that, among other ironies, the Utraquists now appear less proto-Protestant than progressive Catholic. If any movement in the early modern period comes close to the reforming ideals of the Second Vatican Council, it may be that wing of the Hussite church that called for frequent communions, lay use of the chalice, a

82. Henning Graf Reventlow, *The Authority of the Bible and the Rise of the Modern World*, translated by John Bowden (Philadelphia: Fortress Press, 1985), 32–33. Fudge, "The 'Law of God'," 51–54.

gathered community around the table, a return to the sources, and a "national church" with a locally-elected bishop.[83]

83. Atwood, *Theology of the Czech Brethren*, 89. De Vooght, "La confrontation des thèses hussites et romaines," 98. In general, David Holeton, "The Evolution of Utraquist Liturgy: A Precursor of Western Liturgical Reform," *Studia Liturgica* 25 (1995): 51–67. The Hussite contributions to Luther are now fairly well established. When he declared "We are all Hussites," Luther was refuting John Eck's assertion at the Leipzig debate that councils and church could never err. But he was clear about how the two reformations were different. The Hussites went back to an idealized age, there to discover confirmation of their Four Articles. Luther struck out for something else, a gracious God, and followed a course that led him into St. Paul. See Scott Hendrix, "'We Are All Hussites'? Hus and Luther Revisited," *Archive for Reformation History* 65 (1974): 134–61.

9

IN SEARCH OF UNITY

Reform and Mathematical Form in the Conciliarist Arguments of Heymeric de Campo's *Disputatio de potestate ecclesiastica* (1433)

DAVID ALBERTSON

In his well-known 1433 treatise *De concordantia catholica*, Nicholas of Cusa makes arguments for conciliarism that do not yet draw upon the distinctive concepts of his later philosophical writings. He draws upon Dionysian hierarchies, yet without the Dionysian negative theology accented in *De docta ignorantia*; he seeks the unity of the church in its plurality, yet without the henological dialectics he would later borrow from Thierry of Chartres and Meister Eckhart. Indeed, the attempt to understand how Nicholas's 1433 treatise leads toward his breakthrough philosophical works of 1440 continues into the present.[1]

The research for this article was supported by an Advancing Scholarship in the Humanities and Social Sciences grant from the Office of the Provost at the University of Southern California.

1. See Jovino de Guzman Miroy, *Tracing Nicholas of Cusa's Early Development: The Relationship between* De concordantia catholica *and* De docta ignorantia (Leuven/Paris: Éditions Peeters, 2009), 35–42.

The Cusan instance is a helpful touchstone for approaching another important reformer at the Council of Basel. Like Nicholas and other learned delegates to Basel, Heymeric de Campo (Heimeric van de Velde) contributed a treatise on the relative powers of pope and council. This major work, *Disputatio de potestate ecclesiastica,* was written in the autumn or winter of 1433, just months after Cusanus composed *De concordantia catholica.*[2] Born around 1395 in Brabant, Heymeric studied at Paris from 1410 to 1420, where he learned of the third way—beyond Thomism and Scotism—of Albert the Great's approach to Aristotle through Dionysius.[3] After two years at Diest, where he began writing his first philosophical treatises, he became master at Cologne in 1422. (Cusanus lectured and studied in Cologne in 1425–26, and may have studied manuscripts of Ramon Llull in Paris in 1428 at the urging of his colleague Heymeric.)[4] By 1429 Heymeric was doctor and professor of theology, and in 1431 he rejected an offer for a theology chair in Louvain. He traveled to Basel in 1432, wrote his *Disputatio de potestate ecclesiastica* in 1433, and

2. *Disputatio de potestate ecclesiastica,* Cod. Cus. 106, fols. 89r–188r. I use Florian Hamann's partial edition in his excellent study, *Das Siegel der Ewigkeit. Universalwissenschaft und Konziliarismus bei Heymericus de Campo* (Münster: Aschendorff, 2006). Hamann explains the links between Heymeric's Llullism, his own "seal," his search for a universal science, and the Koran, and he further demonstrates similar interests in Cusanus's writings. Unfortunately, Hamann does not probe a further connection between the two men, namely their shared theological engagement of the quadrivium and their common attempt to relate number to Christology. With respect to the text of the *Disputatio,* although Hamann summarizes the conciliarist arguments corresponding to the quadrivial sciences, he overlooks the section on general mathematics altogether. On the date of the *Disputatio,* see Hamann, *Das Siegel der Ewigkeit,* 27–32; and Paul Sigmund's introduction to *The Catholic Concordance* (Cambridge: Cambridge University Press, 2003), xv–xviii.

3. On Heymeric's vita, see Hamann, *Das Siegel der Ewigkeit,* 17–64; and Maarten J. F. M. Hoenen, "Academics and Intellectual Life in the Low Countries. The University Career of Heymeric de Campo (d. 1460)," *Recherches de Théologie Ancienne et Médiévale* 61 (1994): 173–209.

4. See Rudolf Haubst, "Der junge Cusanus war im Jahre 1428 zu Handschriften-Studien in Paris" in *Mitteilungen und Forschungsbeiträge der Cusanus-Gesellschaft* 14, edited by Rudolf Haubst (Mainz: Matthias-Grünewald-Verlag, 1980), 198–205; and Eusebius Colomer, "Zu dem Aufsatz von Rudolf Haubst 'Der junge Cusanus war im Jahre 1428 zu Handschriftenstudien in Paris'" in *Mitteilungen und Forschungsbeiträge der Cusanus-Gesellschaft* 15, edited by Rudolf Haubst (Mainz: Matthias-Grünewald-Verlag, 1982), 57–70.

after another two frustrating years—not getting his reimbursements from Cologne in a timely fashion—he returned to the university. Louvain asked again; this time Heymeric agreed, and he spent the rest of his life there as professor of theology. He died in 1460, four years before Cusanus. His extant writings, which number around two dozen, are still being edited.[5] His ecclesiological treatises and philosophical works share a common desire to reinvent the Llullian art for the fifteenth century, to invest wisely his theological inheritance from Albertus Magnus, and to readily sacrifice eloquence for the sake of complexity. Antony Black has written that "if Zabarella gave conciliar theory a juristic rationale, and if d'Ailly and Gerson gave it a scriptural rationale, Heimerich was the one who gave it a philosophical basis."[6]

Heymeric and Nicholas crossed paths first in Basel, then at the University of Cologne, and perhaps also later in Louvain.[7] In 1453,

5. Several short editions have appeared in journals, but the following volume gathers the most important works: *Heymericus de Campo. Opera Selecta*, edited by Ruedi Imbach and Pascal Ladner (Freiburg: Universitätsverlag Freiburg Schweiz, 2001).

6. Antony J. Black, "The Realist Ecclesiology of Heimerich van de Velde" in *Facultas S. Theologiae Lovaniensis 1432–1797*, edited by E. J. M. van Eijl. Bibliotheca Ephemeridium Theologicarum Lovaniensium 45 (Leuven: University Press, 1977), 273–91 at 285. See also Antony J. Black, "Heimericus de Campo: The Council and History," *Annuarium Historiae Conciliorum* 2 (1970): 78–86; and Pascal Ladner, *Revolutionäre Kirchenkritik am Basler Konzil? Zum Konziliarismus des Heymericus de Campo* (Basel and Frankfurt am Main: Verlag Helbing & Lichtenhahn, 1985).

7. See Hamann, *Das Siegel der Ewigkeit*, 50–54. Heymeric's importance is only beginning to be fully appreciated. Earlier research by Cusanus scholars Haubst and Colomer identified the links between Heymeric, Nicholas and their common sources—particularly Albertus Magnus and Ramon Llull; but more recent scholarship (especially that of Maarten J. F. M. Hoenen) has not only investigated Heymeric's influence over Cusanus's theological orientation, but also emphasized the need to evaluate Heymeric's theology on its own terms. See, e.g., Rudolf Haubst, "Zum Fortleben Alberts des Grossen bei Heymerich von Kamp und Nikolaus von Kues" in *Studia Albertina*, Supplement IV. Beiträge zur Geschichte der Philosophie und Theologie des Mittelalters (1952): 420–47; Eusebius Colomer, "Nikolaus von Kues und Heimeric van den Velde" in *Das Cusanus-Jubiläum in Bernkastel-Kues vom 8. bis 12. August 1964.*, Mitteilungen und Forschungsbeiträge der Cusanus-Gesellschaft 4, edited by Rudolf Haubst (Mainz: Matthias-Grünewald-Verlag, 1964), 198–213; Colomer, "Heimeric van den Velde entre Ramón Llull y Nicolás de Cusa" in *Gesammelte Aufsätze zur Kulturgeschichte Spaniens* 21, edited by Johannes Vincke (Münster: Aschendorff, 1963), 216–32; Maarten J. F. M. Hoenen, "Tradition and Renewal:

after reading a few of his colleague's works, including *De docta ignorantia* and *De theologicis complementis*, Heymeric proposed an apt name for Nicholas's project: *theologia geometrica*.[8] In their conciliarist writings, however, it is Heymeric himself who better merits the title. More so than the future cardinal, Heymeric thoroughly integrates his own mathematical interests with his reform ideology into a stereoscopic search for unity at once numerological and ecclesiological.

In this essay I first examine the historiographical basis for relating number and church reform in the late Middle Ages by consulting Gerhart Ladner's masterly exploration of Augustinian theology in *The Idea of Reform*.[9] Then I explore how Heymeric combines mathematical and Christological arguments for conciliarism in his 1433 treatise.

LADNER ON REFORM: THE SIGNIFICANCE OF NUMBER

Ladner's study of "reform" in medieval Christianity centers on Augustine. Just as patristic images of reform culminate in those of

The Philosophical Setting of Fifteenth-Century Christology. Heymericus de Campo, Nicolaus Cusanus, and the Cologne *Quaestiones vacantiales* (1465)," in *Christ Among the Medieval Dominicans*, edited by Kent Emery, Jr., and Joseph Wawrykow (Notre Dame: Notre Dame University Press, 1998), 462–92. *Heymericus de Campo: Philosophie und Theologie im 15. Jahrhundert*, edited by Klaus Reinhardt and Harald Schwaetzer (Regensburg: S. Roderer Verlag, 2009).

8. "Heymericus compares his own geometrical-theological speculations with those of Cusanus.... However else one may interpret the relationship between the two thinkers in the 1430s, it is not at all insignificant that Heymericus judges his own geometrical speculation as comparable with that of Cusanus." Ruedi Imbach, "Das '*Centheologicon*' des Heymericus de Campo und die darin enthaltenen Cusanus-Reminiszenzen: Hinweise und Materialien," *Traditio* 39 (1983): 476 (466–477). Hamann lists five examples of comparable geometrical images in the two men's writings and then concludes that "one must therefore maintain that Nicholas of Cusa and Heymericus de Campo count as the two sole representatives of a geometrical theology in the first half of the fifteenth century and that their reflections exhibit considerable parallels, something that can scarcely be thought a coincidence" (Hamann, *Das Siegel der Ewigkeit*, 243).

9. Gerhart B. Ladner, *The Idea of Reform: Its Impact on Christian Thought and Action in the Age of the Fathers* (Cambridge, Mass.: Harvard University Press, 1959).

Augustine, subsequent reforms of liturgical practice, canon law and monastic culture flow from him. Ladner thus devotes over a third of the book and three appended excurses to the structure of Augustine's concept of reform. Reading through these passages one is reminded of the enduring importance of number not only for Augustine's early theology in such works as *De ordine*, but for his entire vision of Christian life even through *De civitate dei*.[10] Ladner's attention to what he calls the "reformative function of number" in Augustine is essential to the project of his book. In Ladner's account, number connects the major topics undergirding Augustine's theology of reform: creation, memory, time, and history.

According to Ladner, reform for Augustine is not simply a return to the perfect form enjoyed in Eden, but the promise of an improved form: creation itself introduces one into the process of continual reformation. This resistance to the symmetrical return of Greek patristic ideas of reform leads Augustine to a more complex account of creation suspended between time and eternity. All things receive their original forms, their *rationes seminales*, from the divine Word, who contains their *rationes aeternae*.[11] The discovery of seminal reasons in the world aids in the reformation of the Christian's soul because they usher her into the healing, stable order of eternal reasons. Number, as Ladner proceeds to explain, is Augustine's chief means of explaining how one accesses the formal order inherent in creation and thus becomes re-formed oneself. Hence for Augustine, "the realm of number is instrumental in man's reform."[12]

Ladner suggests that Augustine's doctrine of number underlies his more familiar accounts of time, memory, and salvation his-

10. See the classic article by Adolf Dyroff, "Über Form und Begriffsgehalt der augustinischen Schrift *De ordine*," in *Aurelius Augustinus. Die Festschrift der Görres-Gesellschaft zum 1500. Todestage des heiligen Augustinus*, edited by M. Grabmann and J. Mausbach (Köln: J. P. Bachem, 1930), 15–62; and more recently, *Augustine and the Disciplines: From Cassiciacum to* Confessions, edited by Karla Pollmann and Mark Vessey (Oxford: Oxford University Press, 2005).

11. Ladner, *The Idea of Reform*, 181.

12. Ibid., 219.

tory.[13] Augustine's theory of time as psychic distention emphasizes its inherent insecurity and instability, but Ladner points out that for Augustine time also opens the possibility of the soul's reform. The perpetual reform of the Christian is realized especially through memory, since the act of remembering one's true origin in God recalls the soul out of the flux of matter and time. Time's numerical order is a trace of divine order, and the order such numbers mediate provides a pathway for the soul to remember its eternal origin, to reclaim its true form, and thus to be reformed. Ladner writes: "For St. Augustine, number as well as time is an element of reform. Numbers belong to the realm of creation and they have a special function in leading man back to God. Yet numbers differ from time in that they are not only below the soul and in the soul, but also above it."[14]

But if time is ordered by number, then numeric awareness of that order reveals the shape of divine action in history. Ladner notes that in *City of God* one finds many examples of what he calls "the corporeal terrestrial refractions of the eternal numbers," such as the days of creation, the corresponding world epochs, and the ages of human life. The numeric structure of creation is manifested in its subsequent reformations, both corporate and individual. Augustine's *civitas Dei* is "reformed by the divine numbers of wisdom which the angelic citizens already possess forever and which are continuously transmitted to the human citizens so that they may finally share in the angelic life in heaven."[15]

With this perspective one can appreciate the attention Ladner grants to Augustinian number theory. He distinguishes mere number symbolism from Augustine's rich account of the anagogic function of a hierarchy of numeric kinds.[16] Ladner writes that number "is the very form through which creation, always prone to relapse

13. Ibid., 203.

14. Ibid., 212–13.

15. Ibid., 222.

16. Ibid., 223. Both aspects coexist in the early Platonic works in a most pronounced manner (*De ordine, De quantitate animae, De musica, De magistro, De libero arbitrio*), such that there is no evolution from one part to the other. Such themes are not confined to the early works, although Ladner draws most of his analysis from *De musica*.

through formlessness toward the nothingness from which it was drawn, can maintain itself in being. There is an ascending hierarchy of numbers in everything that is, from corporeal to spatial, to temporal numbers, and higher up to the numbers of reason and to the spiritual numbers of the angel; only when the soul turns to the highest numbers, can it be truly reformed."[17]

But what is it about numbers that grants them this "reformative function"? Following Plato in the *Philebus*, Augustine's *De musica* judges that some "certain reason" "restrains" unchecked progressions into infinity and "calls them back to some limit and form." The possibility of return to unity is secured by numerability, or as Augustine writes, the "certain articulations in numbering by which numbers return again to the one, the principle and beginning of numbers."[18] Such "articulations" break the world into "certain proportions," or numbers, which perform the crucial function of relentlessly "returning to unity" (*redeant ad unum*) all numerable things. Ladner again cites *De musica*:

> The soul ... becomes better if it lacks those numbers which it receives through the body, when it turns away from the carnal senses and is reformed by the divine numbers of wisdom [*et divinis sapientiae numeris reformatur*].... The delight in the numbers of reason is restituted and our life is converted to God thus giving to the body numbers of sanity without enjoying them for their own sake.[19]

From such passages it is clear that the "reformative function of number" lies near the center of Augustine's notion of reform and likewise of Ladner's study.[20]

17. Ibid., 455. "It is equally characteristic of Augustine's earlier and later works that he sees the world built up from numbers which are direct manifestations of divine wisdom. The realm of numbers is not instituted by man, it is rather that part of the eternal truth which acts as the all-inclusive order of spiritual as well as corporeal creation." (Ibid., 214.)

18. Translation adapted from Ladner, *The Idea of Reform*, 216; cf. *De musica* I.12.19: "... eos certa ratio coercuerit et ad quemdam modum formamque revocaverit ... articulos quosdam homines in numerando fecerint, a quibus ad unum rursus redeant, quod est principium numerorum."

19. Ladner, *The Idea of Reform*, 219; cf. *De musica* VI.11.33.

20. Ladner's careful notes on Cantor, Hilbert, and Gödel (see 454–58) underscore his interest in number.

Ladner's account of the "idea of reform" in western Christianity makes two particular claims. First, the original meaning of "reform" is the Pauline notion of return to the form of Christ, the *renovatio* of the Christian self effected by measuring it against its true image, the image of God, who is Jesus.[21] The second claim is that Augustine's version of Pauline reform permanently influences subsequent western interpretations. At the center of Ladner's book is Augustine's vision of reform, but as we have seen, at the center of Augustine's vision is the "reformative function of number." So if we seek the most lapidary denotation for Ladner's understanding of the idea of reform in western Christianity, we could do worse than to name two terms: reform by *christiformitas* and reform by numeric form.[22] Christ and number are the two Ur-Forms that ground ideologies of re-form in western medieval Christianity. The soul's anagogy to higher forms through the ordering power of number is a theme common to Plato, Aristotle, and a host of late antique Platonists, including Iamblichus, Proclus, and Boethius, not to mention Augustine. Some medieval Christian authors relate the divine Word to mathematical forms in passing, outside the context of reform, and often while in the course of evaluating how the liberal arts relate to theology generally—for example, Thierry of Chartres's *Lectiones* on Boethius, Alan of Lille's *Regulae theologicae* or *Rhythmus de Incarnatione et de septem artibus*, or Bonaventure's *De reductione artium ad theologiam*.[23] By contrast, what is remarkable about Heymeric is that he integrates, in the most explicit terms possible, both foundations of reform, precisely in order to explain his conciliarist position. In searching for ecclesial unity in his 1433 *Disputatio*, he identifies Christ as the root of mathematical unity, and he makes the fascinating suggestion that

21. See Ladner, *The Idea of Reform*, 42–62.

22. Cusanus often links *forma* and *christiformitas*, as in Sermon 280 or in his *Reformatio generalis*. See *Nicholas of Cusa: Writings on Church and Reform*, translated by Thomas M. Izbicki (Cambridge, Mass.: Harvard University Press, 2008), 506–7 and 554–57.

23. See for example G. R. Evans, *Alan of Lille: The Frontiers of Theology in the Later Twelfth Century* (Cambridge: Cambridge University Press, 1983), 61–80.

the medieval quadrivium is the first place to look for conciliarist arguments.

HEYMERIC'S ARGUMENTS FOR CONCILIARISM: NUMBER AND CHRIST

Like Nicholas of Cusa, Heymeric eventually joined the party of Eugenius IV, but unlike his colleague he wrote two further treatises on the relative powers of council and pope. The first defends his new support for the pope.[24] The second, written in June 1446,[25] is a shorter treatise that enjoins Eugenius to open a new council to resolve the lingering disputes with the Council of Basel (*Tractatus de potestate papae et concilii generalis*). As Antony Black notes, in the 1446 treatise Heymeric opposed a merely political resolution and sought to provide a philosophical justification of papal supremacy. To do so he applies Aristotelian hylemorphism to the constitution of the church, building up its structure in three moments of increasing actualization by form. (1) The "unformed or indistinct infancy of the Christian people" is dispersed internationally for the purpose of preaching the Gospel; (2) as a kind of mediation of form, namely *christiformitas,* the apostolic church of clerics is distributed in parallel structures, now for the purpose of teaching doctrine; (3) lastly, with apostolic form applied to the lay matter, the church's final end is reached by application of another level of Christiformity, namely, the ordained kingship of the papacy, producing the actual contemporary church. Thus the church can be analyzed according to its causes: catholicity (material cause), apostolicity (formal cause), and monarchical unity (final cause).[26]

This is one of Heymeric's arguments for the papacy after he decided to support Eugenius, but like Cusanus, his treatise written at

24. Black, "Heimericus de Campo: The Council and History," 78n5.

25. This is Black's date; but see dissent from Hamann, *Das Siegel der Ewigkeit,* 50.

26. Biblioteket Kungliga Universitetet, Uppsala, Cod C. 610, fol. 149v; cited in Black, "Heimericus de Campo: The Council and History," 84.

Basel expresses a confident conciliarism. In the 1433 *Disputatio* Heymeric initially presents arguments for and against the supremacy of a general council, and then in a concluding *determinatio* he resolves in favor of the council. What is particularly interesting in his treatise, beyond his conciliarist conclusions, is the kind of arguments on behalf of the council that he finds compelling.[27] In order, Heymeric proposes conciliarist arguments (1) from the principles of the various sciences, quadrivial, trivial, and others; (2) from the Llullian art; (3) from his own Llullian-inspired geometrical figure, which he names the "seal of eternity";[28] (4) and from the Koran. The first section thus uncovers Christological, and thereby pro-conciliar, analogies in individual sciences: geometry, arithmetic, music, astrology, perspective; grammar, logic, rhetoric; metaphysics, physics, medicine, moral philosophy, mathematics; law, civil and canon; and very briefly, theology. Notwithstanding a few irregularities, Heymeric's series concatenates a variety of scientific orders: the medieval quadrivium and trivium; the Aristotelian theoretical sciences; the Stoic or Hermetic sciences of a healthy soul and body; and finally the ecclesiastical authorities of law and scholastic theology.

Modern readers are probably surprised that Heymeric identifies the quadrivium—and not theology, canon law, or metaphysics—as the starting point for his conciliarist arguments, and they are not alone. Even in the early fifteenth century, its function among the sciences was already becoming awkward. On the one hand, the quadrivium must have seemed outmoded when placed alongside the new diversity of sciences flourishing in the wake of the disciplinary divorce of arts from theology after 1277. Yet precisely the multiplication of sciences provoked a search by early Renaissance philosophers for a unifying logic that could order and ground the burgeon-

27. Heymeric's arguments for the papacy are fewer and less original.

28. On Heymeric's *sigillum* in Cod. Cus. 106, see Christel Meier, "*Figura ad oculum demonstrativa*. Visuelle Symbolik und verbale Diskursivität nach Heymericus de Campo" in *Literatur—Geschichte—Literaturgeschichte. Festschrift für Volker Honemann*, edited by Nine Miedema and Rudolf Suntrup (Frankfurt am Main: Peter Lang, 2003), 755–81.

ing multiplicity of knowledge. The revival of Llullism, as Hamann notes, is a testament to this phenomenon, as are the Ramist logic, the Cartesian *mathesis universalis*, and even Cusanus's peculiar theory of a universal system of weights (*De staticis experimentis*, 1450).[29] Not a few philosophers, including Heymeric and Nicholas, returned to Boethius's account of the quadrivium.[30] His Pythagorean synopsis of arithmetic, geometry, music, and astronomy not only named the "four ways" to certain knowledge secured by divine unity, but also proposed a theory of science that dominated western European education until the thirteenth century.[31] According to Nicomachus of Gerasa, whom Boethius translated, all phenomena can be apprehended according to either multitude (number) or magnitude (quantity). Number considered absolutely is arithmetic; number considered relatively is harmonics, or *musica*; quantity considered statically is geometry, and quantity considered in motion is astronomy.[32]

Heymeric draws upon mathematics in two sections of the *Disputatio*'s pro-conciliar arguments. First, he holds that Christ, operating as the invisible authority governing a general council, makes a better principle of unity than the visible pope. As evidence he borrows examples from geometry, arithmetic, music, astrology, and perspective, so that the quadrivium confirms the superiority of Christ's uni-

29. See Stephan Meier-Oeser, *Die Präsenz des Vergessenen. Zur Rezeption der Philosophie des Nicolaus Cusanus vom 15. bis zum 18. Jahrhundert* (Münster: Aschendorff, 1989), 43–46; Timothy J. Reiss, *Knowledge, Discovery and Imagination in Early Modern Europe: The Rise of Aesthetic Rationalism* (Cambridge: Cambridge University Press, 1997), 135–54; and Neal Ward Gilbert, *Renaissance Concepts of Method* (New York: Columbia University Press, 1960).

30. Cusanus discusses the quadrivium or the Pythagorean theory of its construction by magnitude and multitude in several works, including Sermon 22, *De docta ignorantia, De coniecturis, Idiota de mente* and *De ludo globi*.

31. For an introduction, see *Boethius and the Liberal Arts*, edited by Michael Masi (Berne: Peter Lang, 1981); and Alison White, "Boethius in the Medieval Quadrivium" in *Boethius. His Life, Thought and Influence*, edited by Margaret Gibson (Oxford: Basil Blackwell, 1981), 162–205.

32. See Boethius, *Institutio Arithmetica* 1.1.1–4 in *Boèce. Institution arithmétique*, edited by Jean-Yves Guillaumin (Paris: Les Belles Lettres, 1995), 6–7.

ty.[33] Second, he provides a general account of number, recalling the Pythagorean theory of multitude and magnitude found in Boethius and Nicomachus. Number is the principle of unity, and the principle of number, says Heymeric, is the *sapientia Christi.*

QUADRIVIUM AND GENERAL COUNCIL

Heymeric not only ranks the Boethian quadrivium alongside his other major sources—the Llullian art, Heymeric's own invented "seal" figure, and the Koran[34]—but also decides to use quadrivial principles to introduce all of his conciliarist arguments. Each of the quadrivial arts manifests a *principium,* which Heymeric then interprets theologically in support of the council. The conciliarist position, he states, "can be demonstrated mathematically from the principles of geometry, arithmetic, music, astronomy and perspective."[35] Each of these five conciliar arguments therefore draws its authority from its mathematical self-evidence, such that mathematical certainty is used to resolve ecclesiological uncertainty.

Geometry

The first and perhaps prime quadrivial argument comes from geometry, to which Heymeric devotes the longest exposition.[36] The

33. Hamann (*Das Siegel der Ewigkeit,* 151n4) notes that Heymeric's decision to include perspective or optics in the quadrivium follows Boethius.

34. His introduction to the quadrivial arts is verbally the same as his introduction to these other major sections: *deinde idem potest persuaderi* (*ostendi, argui*); cf. Hamann, *Das Siegel der Ewigkeit,* 265, 275, 288, 305. By contrast, when Heymeric introduces the trivium and the several other discrete sciences (267–68), he makes a more general statement on the necessity of "figures" and images in theology, which the trivium can help to furnish.

35. "… idem potest sic persuaderi mathematice ex geometrie, arismetrice, musice, astrologie et perspective principiis." Hamann, *Das Siegel der Ewigkeit,* 265 (fol. 98v). Similar language is used by Thierry of Chartres in his commentary on Genesis: "Adsint igitur quatuor genera rationum que ducunt hominem ad cognitionem creatoris: scilicet arimethice probationes et musice et geometrice et astronomice. Quibus instrumentis in hac theologia breuiter utendum est ut et artificium creatoris in rebus appareat et quod proposuimus rationabiliter ostendatur." *Tractatus de sex dierum operibus* 30, in *Commentaries on Boethius by Thierry of Chartres and his School,* edited by Nikolaus Häring (Toronto: Pontifical Institute of Mediaeval Studies, 1971), 568.

36. Hamann, *Das Siegel der Ewigkeit,* 265 (fol. 98v).

circle has several virtues. It is the most excellent shape, superior to every polygon, the most capacious in its perfect uniformity, and immeasurable by any other shape, including squares. As curved, it is uniquely a doubled shape, simultaneously a convex and concave arc. The point that centers a circle is its beginning, middle, and end (a Llullian triad), whereas lines have only beginnings and ends, but no discrete center. Finally, the circle forms one infinite, closed obtuse angle. By contrast, however many sides a polygon has, its angles remain finite and necessarily less than 180 degrees. If one inscribed a triangle into a circle and then increased its number of sides, one would never reach the perfection of a circle.[37]

Next, Heymeric compares the council to his geometrical example: "the universal council of the church possesses a kind of union comparable to that of a circle."[38] This is achieved without much effort by reference to the image in Apocalypse 1:13 (but see also 4:4 and 11:16) where the Lamb or the Son of Man stands at the center of the circle of 24 elders. When he was writing the *Disputatio*, Heymeric was in the midst of composing his monumental commentary on the Apocalypse (over 300 manuscript pages), including an introductory *accessus* "on the philosophical interpretation of sacred scripture." Begun in Cologne, Heymeric's labors on the commentary were interrupted by his attendance at the Council of Basel, and it was not completed until May 1439.[39] His reference to Apocalypse 1 in the *Disputatio* demonstrates that even though he clearly begins his quadrivial arguments by drawing upon a preexistent tradition of theological meditations on circularity, such as those by Dionysius or Alan of Lille, he is not simply copying here but appropriating them as his own, adding the scriptural image from his own commentary in progress in order to effect the metaphorical leap from circle to

37. Similarly, Cusanus attempts to demonstrate in *De docta ignorantia* I.15 that an infinite ("maximum") triangle is equivalent to both a circle and a sphere.

38. Hamann, *Das Siegel der Ewigkeit*, 265 (fol. 98v).

39. See ibid., 56–57. While manuscripts exist in Berlin, Vienna and Bernkastel-Kues (Cod. Cus. 24), only Cusanus's version contains the 80-page philosophical introduction.

council. The image from his Apocalypse commentary bridges the quadrivial and ecclesiological reflections, as happens twice more within the quadrivial section of the *Disputatio*.[40]

Having identified Christ as the center of the conciliar circle, Heymeric transmutes the circle's perfection into an image of divine omnipresence. He alludes to Matthew 18:2 and draws from a figure common to Dionysius and the *Liber de Causis*, the infinite quantity of equivalent rays between a circle's center and its circumference. Christ is immediately present to the council just as the center of a circle is to every point on its circumference.

> Indeed the presence of Christ, which aids a general council, in terms of this image takes the position of a center with respect to its conforming circle, and for this reason all of those who may belong to the apostolic church—lower than the universal church by reason of their comparative distinction and division from one another—is likewise assimilated to the polygons variously ordered and distinguished within a given circle. For this reason the apostolic seat can only approximate very closely a general council.[41]

According to Heymeric, the hierarchical church approaches the supremacy of the universal church asymptotically, but can never reach it. Both have Christ at the center, but only the universality of the council reflects that center's unity in the infinite angle of its curve. Hence the absence of a monarch governing the general council is not a failure, but instead should be interpreted as the invisible presence of an implied Christ-center equidistant from every point gathered along the conciliar circle.

Arithmetic

Heymeric's arguments from arithmetic and music also draw upon scriptural images and may not strike modern readers as particularly mathematical. From arithmetic, says Heymeric, one knows that given any number, the cube of the number exceeds its square by a proportion equivalent to its root. This is simpler than it sounds, but

40. See ibid., 266 (fol. 98v) and 268 (fol. 99r).
41. Ibid., 265 (fol. 98v).

Heymeric seems invested in stating his quadrivial examples in sophisticated terms, even when drawn ultimately from scriptural images. Continuing with apocalyptic literature, Heymeric points out that Daniel (7:10) had 9 (viz. 3^2) angels assisting him, and their *collegio* can be compared to the general council. In Daniel two large quantities of angels are compared: one billion who "assist" and one million who "minister." Heymeric notes that these proportions exemplify the arithmetic principle, but here the mathematical argument breaks down.[42] In any case, his point is clear, as Hamann well explains. The greater number of angels are those "assisting," as Christ assists the general council. Even though there are numerous angels "ministering," as the apostolic church ministers, the proportion of those assisting is greater. Hence the general council assisted by Christ is superior to the papal ministry.[43] Even if Heymeric adverts to the scriptural image when the numbers fail to add up, his mere desire to ground conciliarism in the principles of square roots is noteworthy.

Music

The "music" that Heymeric analyzes is the sounds of water, thunder, and trumpets out of which a divine voice speaks in what he calls the *visio figurativa* of Revelation 1:15. The voices of many waters and of thunder represent the universal church collected in synods, since David heard these sounds out of a circular wheel. The voice of angelic trumpets represents the apostolic church of prelates that, because dispersed, obeys the leading trumpeter (*primus tubicen*), the pope. Thunder and waters resound with greater volume than trumpets, and therefore the "authority of the public jurisdiction of a general council" is greater than that of the well-orchestrated, but less impos-

42. 1,000,000,000 (10^9) relates to 1,000,000 (10^6) by a proportion of 1,000 (10^3). Heymerich says that the "cube of the [exponential] ratio" of the assisting angels to the ministering angels is 9, but unless I am mistaken it should be 27 (the *ratio* of 10^3 is 3, which cubed is 3^3, or 27).

43. Hamann notes: "Die höhere Rechtsgewalt ergibt sich aus der höheren Zahl ..." (*Das Siegel der Ewigkeit*, 153).

ing apostolic authority. But Heymeric draws an additional theological lesson from his musical example. The voice of the Holy Spirit fills the earth equally, *equipotenter sonans ubique,* just as the Father is "not far from any of us" (Acts 17:27). This sentiment of course echoes Heymeric's prior remarks on the equidistant presence of the divine center to every point on the conciliar circumference. The voice of the pope, by contrast, is the Gospel announced by the hierarchy of the apostolic church, a sound that originates in the church's heights and disseminates gradually to its lowest points, yet loses volume as it descends, resounding more strongly among those nearer to the papal summit, "just as something moving has stronger effects in proximity than over a distance."[44] Again Heymeric's quadrivial example relies more on the logic of the scriptural image than on the patterns of harmony found in the *De musica* of Boethius or of Augustine, but his wish to imitate them is evident.

Astronomy

Heymeric's arguments from astronomy and optics analyze observations from natural philosophy rather than scriptural images. A commonplace of Ptolemaic cosmology states that "stars" (planets) in conjunction with the "third star" (the sun) move more strongly and regularly than those farther away. As in geometry and as at least hinted in arithmetic, Heymeric again identifies the principle of astronomical order with Christ. The sun is the brightest star, the fount of all light, whose greater light is given to illuminate and thus give life to lesser lights. The planets, naturally more erratic, are invigorated by participating in the sun's universal enlivening, making them *lumina adminicula,* supporting lights. The ecclesiological meaning is clear: as the planets "formally" in conjunction with the sun stand to planets disjunct and thus declining into their own epicycles, so stands "the church synodally joined to the sun of justice residing at

44. Ibid., 266 (fol. 99r).

its center [*medio*] to the church removed from this conjunction."[45] The universal church remains more closely in conjunction with Christ when gathered in a general council. But one might ask if this is indeed an argument against papal supremacy, or on behalf of the need for pope and council alike to remain centered around the "sun of justice."[46]

Optics

Heymeric recalls that the angle of incidence of a ray of light only equals the angle of its reflection if there is no interceding material obstructing it. In fact, however, while the incident ray is "infrangible and indeflectible," the reflecting ray is not only derivative, but deviates and declines from the angle of incidence. "Therefore, just as the reflecting ray cannot equal the ray of incidence, but is generated deficiently from the same, so the apostolic jurisdiction of the pope is derived obliquely from the canonical jurisdiction of Christ presiding in a general council."[47] The incident ray is to the reflecting ray as council is to pope: "thus is the rectitude of truth and grace descending immediately from Christ into the church gathered synodally [compared] to the apostolic providence of the pope, such that the pope with his other co-apostles is a vessel of the incidence of the plenitude of grace and truth overflowing from Christ immediately and directly."[48] Heymeric is very careful here. On the one hand he states that the pope receives truth directly from Christ. On the other hand, while the council receives "straightness" itself from a vertical descent, the pope's apostolic church is a "vessel." He leaves it neatly ambiguous whether the "overflowing" from which the pope

45. Ibid., 267 (fol. 99r).

46. The image of Christ as the life-giving center of a complex planetary system also appears in the second book of Cusanus's *Dialogus de ludo globi* (see paragraphs 68–72).

47. (stet) Hamann, *Das Siegel der Ewigkeit.*, 267 (fol. 99r).

48. Ibid., "… ita se habet rectitudo veritatis et gracie immediate descendens a Christo in ecclesiam sinodaliter collectam ad providenciam apostolicam pape, ex quo ipse una cum aliis suis coapostolis est vas incidencie plenitudinis gracie et veritatis immediate et directe a Christo redundantis …", 267 (fol. 99r).

receives authority is Christ's own, or is co-mediated by the council to the pope, since strictly speaking in Heymeric's text it is not the vessel that is overflowing, but Christ's grace and truth.

Hence we can see that in each of the quadrivial sciences, Heymeric uncovers a visual figure that establishes the priority of council to pope. What is most interesting here is the way that Heymeric avoids what could have been the obvious henological priority of the papacy—papal unity reflecting divine unity and therefore securing ecclesial unity—not by avoiding the search for unity in mathematical terms, but by opening up quadrivial examples through more creative, sophisticated, and more scripturally-oriented interpretations. According to Heymeric's treatise, the oneness of Christ mediates God's unity to the world through more complex dimensions than a direct continuation of divine unity in papal unity. Christ's immanence in the structures of the world operates like a unifying principle phenomenally absent yet for that reason all the more certain—just like an implied geometrical center, an implied cubic root, an implied right angle. In other words, just as number makes its ordering presence known in the world precisely because of its absence, so too does Christ govern a universal council not through a monarchical leader, but through the absence of one. The "reformative function of number" (to use Ladner's phrase) in Heymeric's treatise issues not simply from numeric form alone, but from a strange alchemy of numeric form and *christiformitas*, a term Heymeric uses extensively in the concluding *determinatio* of his *Disputatio*.[49]

CHRIST AND NUMBER

If there are hints at an intimate connection between Christ and number in the quadrivial arguments, Heymeric makes them explicit in his general meditations on mathematics. Along with physics, medicine, law, and other sciences established outside the medieval

49. See ibid., 315–21 *passim* (fols. 159v–162v).

framework of the seven liberal arts, *mathematica* provides a further conciliarist argument. (Because of their complexity, I will translate and cite these passages at length.)

Heymeric first restates the Boethian theory of number and quantity translated from Nicomachus of Gerasa:

By considering corporeal quantity fundamentally [*principaliter*]—corporeal quantity which in physics is formally abstracted from matter—in mathematics a given thing is more certain since it is more absolute from matter of any kind. Thus it happens that the principle [*racio*] of number, which arises from the abstract simplicity of non-continuous unity, is more certain than the principle [*racio*] of magnitude, which arises from the indivisibility of a point within a continuum. From this it follows that the concrete principle of number, which is found in music, is more certain than the concrete principle of magnitude, which astrology contemplates, to which perspective is also connected.[50]

In short, the noncontinuous singularity of number is a truer reflection of divine unity than is the infinitely divisible continuity of geometric quantity. Hence the quadrivial art of music (relative number) is superior to that of astronomy (mobile quantity).

Heymeric then proceeds to elaborate the Christological analogy of this quadrivial principle:

But in the mirror of the imagination, the truth of ecclesiastical justice is reflected in a mathematical way more abstractly in the human wisdom of Christ—which works all things for humankind, arranging its measure in number, weight and measure—than in any kind of general council that continuously and materially diffuses its disseminated mystical reasons by the Holy Spirit throughout the universal limits of the world. In this way [the wisdom of Christ] is more abstract than its formal number in the apostolic keys of the pope which are constrained, as if musically, to the tempo of the evangelical and pastoral trumpet. The trumpet's sound, distribut-

50. Ibid., "In mathematica principaliter quantitatem corpoream, secundum quod est formaliter abstracta a materia phisica, considerante, est quid cercius quo ab huiusmodi materie absolucius. Unde fit, quod racio numeri, que oritur a simplicitate abstracta unitatis posicionem in continuo non habentis, est cercior quam racio magnitudinis, que oritur ab indivisibilitate puncti posicionem in continuo habentis, et ex consequenti racio concreta numeri, que invenitur in musica, est cercior ratione concreta magnitudinis, quam considerat astrologia, cui annectitur perspectiva." 272 (fol. 100v).

ed above all the sons of the Church and participated by them in particular ways, differentiates locally and regionally the earth inhabited by Christian people in the same way that stars differentiate the heavens. Therefore just as faith universally extended to the four parts of the world is more efficacious according to the vigor of the infinite goodness of the Holy Spirit than according to finite being, which obtains in one part of the world, such as the apostolic Roman Seat of the church, so its justice is necessarily more powerful and secure in the general council than in the pope.[51]

This passage is a good illustration of the Augustinian notion of number as basis of reform, as Ladner describes it. The human wisdom of Christ is more abstract than the council, which is more abstract than the papacy. Authority is derived from certainty, which mathematically is derived from degrees of abstraction, or purity of form from matter. The council works both in matter and in a continuum. The former is a sign of physics not yet abstracted in mathematics; the latter is a sign of quantity rather than number (or magnitude rather than multitude). Heymeric first compares the papacy to music, but then realizing that this would give priority to papacy (since music is higher than astronomy), he conjectures that papal music "differentiates" (*distinguere*) space in a manner akin to astronomy. With this correction made, it seems that the desired order is as follows: Christ (arithmetic; absolute number), council (music; relative number), pope (astronomy; quantity). The mind of Christ (*sapiencia humana Christi*) is the foundation of the quadrivial arts, and pope

51. Ibid., "Sed veritas iusticie ecclesiastice per modum mathematicum ad speculum ymaginacionis reflexa est abstraccior in sapiencia humana Christi, qua proficit apud homines omnia, cuius mensura in numero, pondere et mensura disponente, quam in concilio generali huiusmodi rationes misticas per spiritum sanctum materialiter distributas continuante per universos mundi terminos diffundente, et hoc modo est abstraccior quam in clavibus apostolicis pape numerum eius formalem ad motum tube ewangelice et pastoralis quasi musicaliter contrahente, cuius sonus supra filios ecclesie distributus seu particulariter participatus distinguit localiter et situaliter ipsam terram ab hominibus christianis habitatam ad instar, quo astra distinguunt celum. Sicut ergo fides universaliter expansa per quatuor partes mundi secundum vigorem infinite bonitatis spiritus sancti est efficacior quam secundum esse finitum, quod habet in una mundi parte, utputa sede apostolica ecclesie Romana, ita necesse est eius iusticiam esse pociorem atque firmiorem in concilio generali quam in papa," 272–73 (fols. 100v–101r).

and council represent different distributions of that unitary principle into the multiplicity of the world—either in the harmony of numbers (council) or the distribution of quantities (pope). Both are immediate reflections of Christ's unitive authority, but each is mediated by a different dimension of created being, namely number and quantity.

Although, as this volume's prologue points out, Ladner never fully applied his ideas about reform to late medieval texts, I would propose that Heymeric's *Disputatio* stands as a fifteenth-century confirmation of Ladner's approach. It still remains to compare the meditations on the anagogical role of number of another erstwhile Basel conciliarist who eventually became frustrated with the uncertainty he saw fomented by a general council. As Cusanus writes in *De docta ignorantia*, "all sensible things are in a continual instability because of the material possibility abounding in them. However, . . . those things, such as mathematicals, which are more abstract than sensible, are very fixed and very certain to us. . . ."[52] Nicholas grounds mystical ascent in the solid basis of mathematics. But in Heymeric's *theologia geometrica* it is not only the personal quest of the contemplative but the corporate reform of the church that can be sought in what Ladner calls the "reformative function of number."

52. *De docta ignorantia* I.11 (31), in *Nicholas of Cusa: Selected Spiritual Writings*, translated by H. Lawrence Bond (Mahwah, N.J.: Paulist Press, 1997), 100–101. Stephan Meier-Oeser comments: "For Cusanus, mathematics is not only a propadeutic bound within the canon of the lower faculty, whose validity ends precisely where the field of metaphysical and theological discussions begins, but rather represents the essential instrument of the ascent to knowledge [*Erkenntnisaufstieg*] into the highest regions of theology. Mathematics—in its specifically Cusan determination—thus becomes a universal medium of human knowledge." Meier-Oeser, *Präsenz*, 43.

10

PREMONSTRATENSIAN VOICES OF REFORM AT THE FIFTEENTH-CENTURY COUNCILS

WILLIAM P. HYLAND

It is reasonable to expect that conscientious members of particular religious orders will attempt in their own time and place to live according to the example of their founder and the spirit of the rule they profess, and when appropriate bring the perspective and insights of their order's charism or rule to deliberations affecting the wider church. The fifteenth-century general councils held at Constance (1414–1418) and Basel (1431–1449), called to deal with a variety of complex problems including church unity, heresy, and reform, certainly would qualify as *fora* for such theological discussions. The role of the Premonstratensians, or Canons Regular of Prémontré, at the councils remains an unwritten story.[1] This paper will attempt to assess the contributions of two members of the order of Canons Regular of Prémontré to theological discourse on reform at these

1. J. B. Valvekens, O. Praem., "De habitudine nonnullorum Praemonstratensium ad Concilium Basileense (a. 1431 ss.), notae quaedam," *Analecta Praemonstratensia* 55 (1979): 116–22.

councils, and examine their contributions in light of the *Rule of St. Augustine* and the wider Augustinian reform tradition.

The Premonstratensian order was founded by Norbert of Xanten in the twelfth century, and its rapid spread throughout Latin Christendom represented one of the key elements in the articulation of the Gregorian reform of clerical and regular life. The Premonstratensian charism drew its inspiration from the *Rule of St. Augustine*, and saw the mixed life of the regular canon as an ideal expression of the *vita apostolica*. This charism, expressed by twelfth-century canons by the phrase *docere verbo et exemplo*, was the basis of the involvement of the Premonstratensians in numerous apostolates, including parish life, missionary work, schools, hospice work, cathedral chapters and the episcopate, and of course the community life of their own abbeys.[2] Although there were Premonstratensian masters at the universities, most Premonstratensians who received a university education returned to their abbeys to undertake important leadership roles in the local community.[3] This primary focus on the life of the local church rather than on the debates of the university faculties was integral to Premonstratensian spirituality; indeed, studies of late medieval Premonstratensian libraries indicate a marked conservatism and decided lack of trendiness. For example, beyond practical works of canon law, the emphasis was on patristics, the Victorines, and writers such as Bonaventure, rather than on Ockham and the *via moderna*.[4] The evidence would seem to indicate that the late-medieval Premonstratensians, like the Benedictines and Cistercians described by Franz Posset, preserved a spirituality based upon *lectio divina* and couched in the rhythms of daily liturgi-

2. Caroline Walker Bynum, "The Spirituality of Regular Canons in the Twelfth Century," in *Jesus as Mother: Studies in the Spirituality of the High Middle Ages* (Berkeley: University of California Press, 1982), 22–58; Theodore J. Antry, O. Praem. and Carol Neel, *Norbert and Early Norbertine Spirituality* (Mahwah, N.J.: Paulist Press, 2007), 1–28.

3. James J. John, *A Repertoire of Students at the College of Prémontré in Medieval Paris* (M.Med.S. thesis, University of Notre Dame, 1951), 67.

4. See Joseph A. Gribbin, *The Premonstratensian Order in Late Medieval England* (Woodbridge, Suffolk, U.K.: Boydell Press, 2001), 132–73.

cal life.[5] The Premonstratensians nevertheless certainly participated in wider discussions about the life of the church, and were represented at the general councils held in the twelfth, thirteenth and fourteenth centuries. The onset of the Great Schism in 1378, with its division of Latin Christendom into rival papal obediences, had disrupted the normal functioning of the international religious orders, including the Premonstratensians. The election of Alexander V as pope by the Council of Pisa (1409), while recognized by Abbot General Peter Hermi, did not bring unity to either the church or the order.[6] This longed for harmony would be a major concern of those Premonstratensians present at Constance.

What then did Premonstratensians contribute to discussions on church reform at the fifteenth-century councils? As important representatives of the Augustinian canonical tradition, Premonstratensian intellectuals articulated the ideas of Augustine on reform and renewal, as classically set forth by Gerhart Ladner.[7] Furthermore, the Premonstratensians presented these reform ideas with a minimum of scholastic dress. Their commitment to Augustine's theology of reform was deepened and intensified by the fact that they were members of an order which lived by his rule. Augustine for them was not merely a theologian, but rather a religious and pastor whom, as living representatives of the *religio Augustini*, they personally imitated.[8] While the Premonstratensians from their very beginnings had demonstrated a keen historical interest in the life of Augustine, as evidenced by Philip of Harvengt's biography of the saint,[9] their

5. Franz Posset, *Renaissance Monks: Monastic Humanism in Six Biographical Sketches* (Leiden: Brill, 2005), 6.

6. Bernard Ardura, O. Praem., translated by Br. Edward Hagman, O.F.M. Cap. *The Order of Prémontré: History and Spirituality* (De Pere: Paisa Publishing, 1995), 147–51.

7. Gerhart B. Ladner, *The Idea of Reform: Its Impact on Christian Thought in the Age of the Fathers* (New York: Harper & Row Publishers, 1967), especially 153–283.

8. For a discussion of late medieval views of the *religio Augustini*, see Eric Leland Saak, "The Reception of Augustine in the Later Middle Ages," in *The Reception of the Church Fathers in the West*, edited by Irene Backus (Leiden: Brill, 2001), 1:367–84.

9. Carol Neel, "Philip of Harvengt's *Vita Augustini*: The Medieval Premonstratensians and the Patristic Model," *Analecta Praemonstratensia* 71 (1995): 300–311.

primary way to imitate Augustine was to live by his rule as they had received it. For it is in the rule that they found the ultimate expression and interpretation of how to live out the *vita apostolica*. And it is also to the rule that they looked as their primary model for how a Christian community should function, in other words, their primary model for the church itself. The Premonstratensians brought this model to the conciliar discussions on ecclesiastical reform. Briefly then, how does the *textus receptus* of the Rule of St. Augustine[10] present a model for Christian community? What are its particular ecclesiological emphases?

The rule presents the Christian community as described in the Acts of the Apostles, particularly 4:32–35, as the ecclesiological ideal. This Christian community's animating force, for Augustine, is *caritas*, as is evident from the preliminary sentence, "Let us love God above all things, dearest brothers, then our neighbor, for these are the chief commandments given us."[11] This is followed by an exhortation to fraternal unity, which echoes Acts 4:32, with the words *in Deum* added at the end: "The first purpose for which you have come together is to live in unity in the house and to be of one mind and one heart on the way to God" (*Rule of St. Augustine*, 1:2).[12]

A vision of community knit together by mutual love, in which members help one another along the path of eternal salvation, is the heart of the rule and an ideal for the church. The rest of the rule gives the means to this end through exhortations. The communal ownership of property is stressed, always with an eye toward the possible resentments and economic and social disparities represented by private ownership, again with a quotation of Acts 4:32–35 echoing the primitive church as model. Class differences must be put aside, "so

10. All Latin quotations from *The Rule of St. Augustine* are taken from the critical edition, L. Verheijen, *La regle de Saint Augustin, I, Tradition manuscrite* (Paris: Études Augustiniennes, 1967), 417–37. The English translation used is from the current Premonstratensian Constitutions, *The Day of Pentecost* (De Pere: St. Norbert Abbey, 1997), xiii–xx.

11. *The Day of Pentecost*, xiii.

12. Ibid., xiii.

that all live together in harmony and love. And, in each other, honor God, whose temples you have become" (*Rule of St. Augustine*, 1:8).[13] This communal spirituality is developed through exhortations on prayer, food and abstinence, care of the sick, the apportionment of clothing, etc.

From the point of view of ecclesiology, the sections on conduct and fraternal correction are especially significant. They stress a comportment that suits one's dignity as a cleric. The rule emphasizes prudence and avoiding potentially sinful situations, and for brethren to help each other in this regard. If a problematic situation does develop, the model is the process found in Mt 18:15–17, that is, admonition in private, then involving two or three others, and finally bringing the matter to the whole church. A brother who does not correct the sins of others is blameworthy and irresponsible and lacks authentic compassion.

The *Rule of St. Augustine* also has important ecclesiological passages, such as those on the primacy of the common good over individual interests and how this principle leads to charity. Seeking pardon, the need to forgive offenses, and the importance of not letting anger get in the way of charity must mark relationships in the Christian community.

The section on how superiors should behave is also relevant as a model for church leadership. After asserting how superiors must be obeyed as fathers, with due reverence, the definition of leadership, echoing Pauline pastoral exhortations, is to serve in love, with the high responsibility and accountability of those in office:

> Let your superior not deem himself happy in using his authority, but in serving you with love. In honor before you let him take the first place, but in fear before God, let him prefer the last place. Let him be for all an example of good works. Let him restrain the restless, comfort the discouraged, support the weak, with patience towards all. Let him willingly embrace regular discipline while imposing a religious fear. And although both

13. Ibid., xiv.

are necessary, let him seek to be loved by you more than feared, always remembering that he must account for you to God. Therefore, obey your superior not only for your own sake but for his also; for, the higher his position, the greater his danger.... The Lord grant that you observe all these things with love, as lovers of spiritual beauty, giving forth the good odor of Christ in the holiness of your conduct not as slaves under the law, but as free men firmly established in grace (*Rule of St. Augustine*, 7:3–8:1).[14]

Thus, the *Rule of St. Augustine* presents a view of Christian community certainly marked by obedience to superiors, but also with an emphasis on compassion, mutual responsibility, and the sacred duty of those in authority to serve with love. When the vision of community moves beyond the monastery to the church at large, these practical applications of Augustine's reform theology are the means of the church achieving its goal of moving all with one mind and heart to God. Let us see how these and other Augustinian ideas are reflected in the two conciliar orations by Premonstratensians.

THE CONSTANCE ORATION

The only known speech delivered by a Premonstratensian at Constance was on Candlemas, February 2, 1416. The text was edited by Christian Wilhelm Walch in the eighteenth century.[15] The staunchly Lutheran Walch, while acknowledging that the anonymous canon did exhibit some "vestiges of Roman errors," lauds his rare knowledge of sacred scripture and willingness to criticize the various moral problems of the day and the Roman Curia. He also notes the Premonstratensian's concern for unity with the Greek Orthodox. Walch additionally cites and quotes approvingly the earlier Protestant historian of the conciliar movement, James L'Enfant (1691–1728), who in his *Histoire du Concile de Constance* had noted the sermon is marked by a scriptural simplicity and lack of scholas-

14. Ibid., xix–xx.

15. Christian Wilhelm Walch, *Monimenta medii aevi* (Göttingen: Bibliotheca Regia Hanoverana, 1757–1764; reprinted Ridgewood: The Gregg Press Incorporated, 1966), 210–32 (henceforth Walch, *Monimenta*)

tic affectation which could even be used as a model for evangelical preachers in his own day.[16]

Although the Premonstratensian author of this well-regarded oration remains anonymous, there were several canons present at Constance who are distinct possibilities. The abbot general Peter d'Hermi (1392–1423) sent as his procurator to Constance a *bachelor formatus* named John Seneschal, who in 1418 subsequently became abbot of Dommartin in the diocese of Amiens. This John would later be part of the delegation of the Premonstratensians to the Council of Basel, and appointed as a *visitator* of the German abbeys of the order.[17] Also present at Constance was James Herries, abbot since 1411 of the Scottish abbey of Tongeland. Herries was known for his oratory and theological acumen and had studied at the University of Paris.[18] Henry Nerr was the abbot of Bellelay in the diocese of Basel from 1410–1418. He served also as vicar general of the bishop of Basel, and in 1414 was delegated as Procurator General to represent the Premonstratensian order at Constance. He also enjoyed a reputation for oratory, and is said to have won the good will of the council and Emperor Sigismund.[19] A final candidate would be Theodore van Andel, a canon of Tongerlo abbey in the diocese of Cambrai.[20] In 1410 he was the procurator of the order in Rome and in 1418 was appointed to be the Procurator General of the order at Constance. Whether he was at the council before that, specifically in 1416 when this oration was given, is unclear. Van Andel was celebrated for his learning and oratory and seems to have written a no-longer-extant history of the Council of Constance.[21] He would later serve as a prominent member of the "German" nation at the Council of Pavia-

16. Walch, *Monimenta*, lii–lv.

17. John, *A Repertoire of Students*, 53–54.

18. Ibd., 52.

19. Ibid., 101–2.

20. Ibid., 69–70.

21. André Léon Goovaerts, *Écrivains. Artistes, et Savants de l'Ordre de Prémontré:, Dictionnaire bio-bibliographique* (Bruxelles: Société Belge de Librairie, 1899–1920), 2:274; Valvekens, "De habitudine nonnullorum Praemonstratensium ad Concilium Basileense," 121–22.

Siena and was present during the first months at the Council of Basel, where he died in 1431.

In his study of reform at Constance, Phillip Stump noted this sermon during his discussion of the use of the term *status* among the conciliar participants. As Stump notes, a frequent synonym for the common good (*bonum commune*) was the *status ecclesiae*. The term *status* had a rich and complex history. Besides referring to the whole universal church, it could also refer to particular groups, for example prelates, priests, regular clergy, and the laity, who together made up the whole mystical body of the church. Discussions of the need for various groups, or "states" within the church to cooperate, each in their own appropriate way, for reform, was often found alongside the Pauline language of the church as a body whose members all needed to work together to function properly. The oration of our anonymous Premonstratensian, Stump notes, calls for love among the multiple *status*, since they are all members of the mystical body.[22] How does this emphasis on unity and charity reflect specific Augustinian ideals?

The theme for the sermon is drawn from the Sunday epistle according to the Premonstratensian rite,[23] "Owe no man anything, but to love one another" (Rom 13:8). In the prologue, which culminates in the customary Marian invocation, the speaker draws on Augustine, beginning with a citation from Book IV of *De Doctrina Christiana,* where Queen Esther is noted as an exemplar of one who prays for the temporal well being of her people. After stating how "our salvation is founded in love" and quoting John 3:16–17, he directly echoes the opening precept of the *Rule of St. Augustine,* in describing the Virgin Mary as one "who having been prevailed upon in other

22. Phillip H. Stump, *The Reforms of the Council of Constance (1414–1418)* (Leiden: Brill, 1994), 249–63, with a mention of this oration on 263, note 121.

23. This epistle is proper to the fourth Sunday after Epiphany. For the relationship of the dominical liturgy to the Feast of the Purification of the Blessed Virgin in the Premonstratensian Rite, see Pl. F. Lefevre, O. Praem., *L'Ordinaire de Prémontré d'apres des manuscrits du XIIe et du XIIIe siècle* (Louvain: Bureau de la Revue, 1941), 45.

matters is not accustomed to desert brothers loving one another with one mind and the same unanimity."[24] As the sermon progresses, the repeated emphasis, with frequent quotations of the Gospel of John, is the unmerited love and mercy of God, which demands from the Christian in return a sincere love of God and neighbor: "We are not strong enough to acquire this [eternal] life without love of God and neighbors. If you wish, says Truth, to enter upon life, keep the commandments, which, it has been shown, are grounded in the love of God and neighbors."[25]

This theme is epitomized in the very opening line of the *Rule of St. Augustine*: "Let us love God above all things, dearest brothers, then our neighbor, for these are the chief commandments given to us."[26] The Premonstratensian proceeds in the spirit of his rule to discuss the necessity and nature of reciprocal or mutual love. After quoting Augustine that "we can love unseen things, by no means unknown things," and Gregory the Great that the proof of love is in the deeds, the preacher delineates his three considerations and the human faculties to which they belong: (1) knowledge and cognition to the intellect, (2) love to the will, and (3) deeds and service to exterior effort. The canon states that in addition to the universal need to love in our capacity as an individual, everyone must also consider themselves in regard to the duties of their status, grade, and rank.[27]

The discussion of knowledge and the intellect begins, in an Augustinian vein reminiscent of *De Doctrina Christiana,* with the point that in order to love our neighbor as ourselves, we must first have a proper love of ourselves. This is developed through a discussion of Paul and Barnabas, and how they knew themselves not to be

24. "... quae nec in aliis devocata deficere solet uno animo eodemque consensu fratrem invicem diligentes," Walch, *Monimenta,* 210. *Rule of St. Augustine,* 1:2: "Primum, propter quod in unum estis congregati, ut unanimes habitetis in domo et sit vobis anima una et cor unum in Deum," Verheijen, *La regle de Saint Augustin,* 417.

25. Walch, *Monimenta,* 211.

26. "Ante omnia, fratres carissimi, diligatur Deus, deinde et proximus, quia ista sunt praecepta principaliter nobis data," Verheijen, *La regle de Saint Augustin,* 417.

27. Walch, *Monimenta,* 214.

gods, but mere human beings like their fellows. A consideration of our own weaknesses and failings and subsequent needs should lead us to the same love and empathy towards our neighbors. This self-knowledge we have as individuals should then be extended to a behavior appropriate to our status or rank within the church. This is true in the first place for prelates, whose rank obliges them to pastoral oversight:

> And if someone will have found himself a prelate or pastor, he will see that frequently, due to his office, with paternal love and not out of his own greed, he is obliged to visit his subjects or flock. Nevertheless not with harshness and force, but rather with familial love, so that he may summon his own sheep by name and lead them forth, and the sheep may follow him, knowing his voice [cf. John 10:3–4]
>
> For the Lord does not wish that pastors should visit their flock in order to consume milk, be clothed in the wool and to slaughter what is fat, with the result that they do not pasture their own flock. But rather they should diligently inquire, by means of the solicitous visitation of their jurisdiction, or through sacramental confession, if anything is infirm, sick, broken or cast down. And then they will perceive themselves obliged, by this knowledge of the flock and the needs of particular subjects, to comfort the infirm, heal the sick, bind up the broken, bring back the fallen, and search out what had been lost, according to the teaching of the Lord through the prophet Ezekiel [34:16].[28]

This portrait of ideal pastoral care strongly resonates with the above-mentioned description of the community superior from the *Rule of St. Augustine* (7:2), with the characteristic emphasis on service based in *caritas*.[29] Likewise, the following statement of the Norbertine preacher's view of the attitude a subject should have to his superior echoes the emphasis found throughout the Augustinian Rule on the mutual love that should mark relationships between subject and superior:

> Moreover, if someone considering himself should understand himself to be a subject, he should recognize that he is obliged to the one to whom

28. Ibid., 217–18.
29. *The Day of Pentecost*, xix.

he is subject to show reverence, obedience and honor, which all are based upon mutual love, and amplify and preserve that love.[30]

The first part of the sermon ends with a practical application of this idea, namely that at every level of the church, there should be a consultative process, again exercised in a spirit of mutual love, to ascertain the genuine needs and solutions needed for each status. Thus parish priests should gather in synod with their bishop, bishops with their metropolitan, and the universal church with the pope, so that solutions to problems can be found "through mutual discussion, with need and experience being understood, or indeed suitable for each status. Furthermore, let not pain be increased through envy, detraction or vengeance to the afflicted, or status wound or press down status. But rather, through mutual love, may each status be provided for more suitably."[31]

The second part of the oration discusses at some length the biblical injunction to love one's neighbor. If the participants at Constance will truly love one another, the preacher asserts, they will stand in "constancy" against those who would detract from the fruit of their labors, their work will be successful, and they will remove and condemn to oblivion many of the vices afflicting the universal church. The failure to practice mutual love, both between and within states of the church, has resulted in the present spectacle of disunity and schism rather than harmony. The council, he asserts, has made progress in this regard, reducing two of the papal obediences to one, with its ambassadors hoping to bring the third party to unity. The ministry of the council is indeed to "allow love to return and division recede into confusion." Once divisions within the Latin Church are healed through mutual love, the Premonstraten-

30. "Si quis autem se ipsum considerans se subditum intelligat cognoscet, cui ex ipsa subiectione tenetur ad reverentiam, obedientiam et honorem, quae omnia in mutua dilectione fundantur et ipsam dilectionem ampliant et conservant," Walch, *Monimenta*, 218. And for the *Rule of St Augustine*, e.g. 7:1: "praeposito tamquam patri oboediatur, honore servato," Verheijen, *La regle de Saint Augustin*, 435.

31. Walch, *Monimenta*, 219.

sian envisions for his audience that the more ancient division with the Byzantine Church will also be reconciled, followed by an even further extension of love to unbelievers:

Because with this union completed, remote will be the obstacle, than which, perhaps, none is greater, which has held the Greeks a long time in division. And easily the extension of your love, which will even include the Greeks themselves, will merit and receive a reciprocal love, through which they will be able to be joined and united with us. And thus will be removed from our midst that ancient schism, procured by the enemy of humankind, which keeps unbelievers in a certain perplexity, since they can say: "When we have dealings with the Greeks, we will be anathematized by the Latins, and vice versa." Truly, with a union of all Christians achieved through mutual love, even the Gentiles themselves will acknowledge that we are disciples of Christ, with Christ himself saying, as we said before: *In this all may recognize that you are my disciples, if you will love one another* [Jn 13:35]. And Christ speaking to the father about his own, said: *they have been gathered into one*, and it follows, *so that the world may know that you have sent me* [Jn 17:23].

Therefore, let the fervent love of your most reverend paternities take action, while you have time, toward the good of complete union, not restricting love to one's own person, nor to one's household, nor a town, nor a city, nor a province, nor a kingdom, nor to one nation, nor finally even to all Christendom. But rather you should be solicitous to extend love itself effectually to the people who do not believe, even if they seem to be enemies.[32]

The final part of the sermon deals with the necessity of action. Love must be exercised in the twofold aspects of person to person and status to status. All members of the church in their capacity as baptized individuals are called to be solicitous to the wants and needs of their neighbors. The need to practice oversight, and if necessary, correction, with regard to the behavior of one's neighbor is discussed in conjunction with the injunctions of Mt 18:15–17. Significantly, this same text also forms the heart of the teaching of the *Rule of St. Augustine* (4:9) on the necessity of fraternal correction, including the danger that recalcitrant sinners can pose to the harmony of

32. Ibid., 223–24.

the community.[33] The canon regrets the fact that this ideal of fraternal correction is not always put into play at the council, where certain individuals under the guise of zeal do nothing but foment further divisions:

> Wherefore, it must be noted, that there is found within certain men a certain diligence for continually maligning and contriving sects and divisions, just as we have learned most clearly about the partisans of ecclesial schism. Such men are pinned down in discord, and love is not for them; rather division is their whole glory. Let the sacred synod beware, I implore, lest through such abettors the spirit of discord mixes itself among us, and drives away mutual love.[34]

What the speaker calls this "honest and commendable exercise of love" must ultimately be the mark of relations between each status, as well as relations between pastors and their flocks. The preacher criticizes pastors who do not imitate Christ the good shepherd, but rather extort and fraudulently use and squander for their own sinful purposes funds meant for the sustenance of the people in their care, causing resentment and despair. Rather, they should inspire love and respect among the people by their good actions. Here he develops, like several other speakers at Constance, the language of Rom 12:4–5, and 1 Corinthians 12 on the mystical body of Christ and the relationships between the members. [35] This emphasis on mutual solicitude also calls for the subjects to respect the place of the head, despite the fact that in recent memory the head "from its own state is pressed down and sunk into the mire, indeed is trampled underfoot by men."[36] He warns against subverting the authority of the Apostolic See and asserts the due reverence and indeed love which must be shown to its role as head. The Premonstratensian stresses that important matters of the faith must be referred to the pope or the universal council and does not set the two up in opposition to

33. *The Day of Pentecost*, xvi.

34. Walch, *Monimenta*, 226.

35. Stump, *The Reforms of the Council of Constance (1414–1418)*, 232.

36. Walch, *Monimenta*, 228.

one another. Yet for him this papal authority must be exercised, like all pastoral power, for the edification and not for the destruction of the church, and in a spirit of genuine humility, with the pope "recognizing himself to be 'servant of the servants' not just in charters patent, but continually in the secret recesses of his own heart."[37]

As noted above, this description of pastoral authority as service in charity closely echoes the descriptions of the superior in the Augustinian Rule. Fittingly then, the Premonstratensian concludes his sermon and the discussion of the mutual love between members of the church with an explicit reference to his order's rule, encapsulating its teachings on fraternal correction in a Christian community and their applications for the wider church:

> Let them [i.e., all Christians] exercise their duties faithfully and with fervent love of persons, bearing burdens mutually, just as members of the same body. Member should not put down member, nor status depress status. But what in these will have to be corrected, let the abuse be taken away and the status preserved, with love of the people and hatred of the vices, according to Augustine's teaching in the Rule, which will happen wholesomely if according to the saying of the apostle, there is among you love without pretense [Rom 12:9].[38]

JOHANNES WIFFLET, O. PRAEM., AT THE COUNCIL OF BASEL

The opening of the Council of Basel in late 1431 had seen an almost immediate rise in tensions between the council fathers and the absent and hostile Pope Eugenius IV, tensions that escalated in the early months of 1432. As this fissure deepened between pope and council, the council also awaited the possible visit of a Bohemian delegation to debate the controversial theological issues dividing the Catholics and Hussites. Into this tumultuous atmosphere the Premonstratensian Johannes Wifflet, canon of Tongerlo abbey and

37. Ibid., 231.

38. Walch, *Monimenta*, 231. See *Rule of St. Augustine*, 4:10, *The Day of Pentecost*, xvii, for the reference.

master of theology at the University of Paris, arrived at the beginning of March. Within a few weeks, Wifflet preached before the council on the feast of the Annunciation, March 25, 1432. About two weeks later on April 11, Wifflet was among those members of the council added to the deputation *pro fide,* but his death in late July cut short his work with the council.[39]

Wifflet's sermon for the Feast of the Annunciation is essentially a commentary on a scriptural verse taken from the Gospel of the day: "the power of the Most High shall overshadow you" (Luke 1:34). These words spoken by the angel to Mary signify the moment of the Incarnation, and the sermon is a reflection on the meaning and implications of this doctrine for personal and ecclesial reform. The main thesis is that the power of God is demonstrated through the Incarnation, a miracle intended to empower human beings to be reborn as children of God. Wifflet frequently cites sacred scripture. His only direct quotation of Augustine is from *On Holy Virginity,* where he makes the point that the miraculous birth of Christ from a virgin signifies the church about to be born from the action of the Holy Spirit. Wifflet has two points to make about how the power of God is manifested in the Incarnation. Firstly, the Incarnation itself is an act of divine power which points to the reformation of that deformity which had followed the Fall of Adam. Secondly, the divine power in the Incarnation allows the faithful to be born from the church through the Holy Spirit, and, through this same Spirit's power, the inherited spiritual deformity of human beings is repaired.

Wifflet proceeds to discuss the original prelapsarian state of Adam, his endowments and perfections in paradise. In this state Adam's body was in perfect subjection to the higher powers of his soul. All this changed by Adam's disastrous withdrawal of his will

39. For Wifflet's life and work and an edition of the sermon given at Basel, see William P. Hyland, "The Incarnation, Reform and the Unity of the Church: a Sermon of Master Johannes Wifflet O. Praem. For the Feast of the Annunciation at the Council of Basel (1432)," *Analecta Praemonstratensia* 83 (2007): 156–71 (henceforth "Wifflet").

from its principal good, and the result was the flow of infinite evils which have since plagued humanity. Only God's own son, the second Adam, could satisfy and repair the infinite punishment (*infinita pena*) owed for human sin. As from Adam all human beings are descended by a natural propagation, so now from Christ all are reborn from a spiritual regeneration.

After laying the groundwork for the theological foundations of reform, Wifflet turns his attention to the state of the church, and parallels its development with that of humanity in general. Thus, after describing the church's original state and how its members, particularly prelates, should ideally act, Wifflet proceeds to describe current problems. Following in the footsteps of Jean Gerson and Pierre D'Ailly, his predecessors at the Council of Constance and indeed the University of Paris,[40] Wifflet argues that too many recent human laws and dispensations are compromising the integrity of the church, and need to be reformed:

> And as long as this state of governance (*regimen*) stood in the church, which was according to the said laws which immediately and indirectly proceed from principles of the faith clearly known in supernatural light, this rule of governance was correct, and if in the meantime it could be returned to that state, would be well reformed. And those new additions should be dismissed from the divine and human laws set up by Christ and our fathers, and holy laws would be offered to be put into practice, and dispensations from them would not be admitted.[41]

According to Wifflet, the reign of sensuality in the church has generated a long list of vices shared by both prelates and princes, namely negligence, ambition, greed, and cruelty. These vices, so prevalent among those who bear the responsibility for the well-being of the members of the church, corrupt the whole mystical body. Wifflet, directly echoing his Premonstratensian predecessor at Constance, discusses the respective duties of bishops, priests, and deacons, and laments how they are happy to receive tithes from

40. Stump, *The Reforms of the Council of Constance (1414–1418)*, 216–18.
41. "Wifflet," 169.

the faithful while committing a host of abuses instead of discharging their responsibilities. These abuses have led to a deformity of the church, and are, Wifflet believes, why both the Greek Orthodox and Bohemian Hussites criticize the church and distance themselves from it: "And who could say the cause is and was any other why the Greeks withdrew (*recesserunt*) from the church than that? And I believe that it was the reason why the Bohemians as we speak attempt to destroy the ordinances of the church."[42]

The Premonstratensian canon does not spare those religious who neglect their vows and forsake the *vita apostolica* to which they are bound, and the misbehavior of the clergy is matched by that of the princes, whose horrible and irresponsible wars demoralize clergy and people and create conditions extremely hostile to reform.

> And who can excuse the princes, who ought to exert themselves to govern their subjects with civil laws (*legibus civilibus*) and lead them to virtues and even the salvation of their souls. Instead they involve themselves in wars so abominable that out of them arise demoralization of the whole clerical state and spring forth the reproaches of the whole Christian people: robberies, theft, betrayals.[43]

Wifflet ends the sermon with the assertion that the council fathers must first reform themselves if they hope to accomplish any of the tasks at hand. If the leaders of Christendom would make peace, and come together in unity to address their own personal reform, they would have nothing to fear from their opponents. A Latin Church reformed and at peace would be the best argument for the Bohemians and Greeks to return to unity, as he says by ironically using a military metaphor:

> I believe if we were reformed in the church, and peace would exist among the princes, this would be the most powerful argument which could lead to the return (*reductionem*) of the Bohemians and Greeks. For indeed if they would see us drawn together and equipped with virtues, and by peace united as an ordered line on the field of battle, *they* would fear *us*.[44]

42. Ibid., 169.
43. Ibid., 170.
44. Ibid., 170 [emphasis in text added].

Wifflet stresses that now is the time for personal reform, to let the Incarnate Christ renew the whole church, the whole mystical body consisting of the pope and other members of the church. He concludes by asking the council fathers to trust in the promise of the Lord to St. Peter that prayers offered in sincerity will lead to perseverance.

Throughout this sermon, Wifflet's approach seems to fit the Premonstratensian style noted above, namely a minimum of scholastic citations. The only medieval writer he quotes directly is the fourteenth-century Franciscan turned Benedictine Pierre Bersuire.[45] Wifflet's only direct quotation of a patristic source is from the *De Sancta Virginitate* of St. Augustine,[46] and his description of the results of the Fall and the subsequent changes in Adam's state follow Augustine's teachings in many works, for example Book 14 of *De Civitate Dei*. One may thus ask, how does Wifflet fit in with the categories of reform in the Augustinian tradition, as well as his recent predecessors at the Council of Constance?

Wifflet's vocabulary of reform in this early stage of Basel in the first place fits well with the conclusions of Christopher Bellitto and Phillip Stump about reform at Constance, namely that there was a convergence of several streams of thought and imagery that have deep roots in patristic thought.[47] Throughout the sermon, Wifflet frequently uses the terms *reformatio*, with explicit reference to the reformation of the deformity which resulted from the Fall of Adam.[48] Likewise, the Virgin Mary is referred to as the "mother of our reformation and redemption" (*mater nostrae redemptionis et reformationis*).[49] But by far the most prevalent and striking imagery in

45. Ibid., 170.

46. Ibid., 166.

47. Phillip H. Stump, "The Influence of Gerhart Ladner's *The Idea of Reform*," in *Reform and Renewal in the Middle Ages and the Renaissance Studies in Honor of Louis Pascoe, S.J.*, edited by Thomas M. Izbicki and Christopher M. Bellitto (Leiden: Brill, 2000), 16; Christopher M. Bellitto, *Nicolas de Clamanges: Spirituality, Personal Reform, and Pastoral Renewal on the Eve of the Reformations* (Washington, D.C.: The Catholic University of America Press, 2001), 127–34.

48. "Wifflet," 170.

49. Ibid., 168.

the sermon are those terms which express reform in terms of newness, birth, and regeneration, which would place Wifflet in the company of a small but notable category of reformers from Constance.[50]

This emphasis is manifested early in the sermon as he introduces the customary *Ave Maria* prayer, where in one short sentence referring to the Incarnation he uses the words *nasci*, *renovaret*, *innovare*, and *ad novitatem reducere*, followed by a second sentence referring to the mission of the archangel Gabriel as *nova legacione* and *novo modo*.[51] Wifflet goes on to assert that the Incarnation represents a *novus ordo* from heaven, which will destroy the power of the old.[52] He then proceeds to link this idea of newness to spiritual rebirth through the power of the Holy Spirit, stressing how "the faithful are born from mother church through the spirit, through which spirit also the deformity which by men was committed is reformed."[53] Wifflet also uses the language of spiritual regeneration to describe the nature of our spiritual rebirth from Christ, the second Adam, and our common spiritual destiny as part of the mystical body.[54] Strikingly, this language of newness, rebirth and regeneration is linked to the work of the council itself, whose fathers are exhorted to share in this task of the Spirit: "Let us therefore make all things new. For now is at hand the time in which all things according to nature are renewed. Christ, the one who today took on flesh that he might renew all things, he teaches us, he instructs us."[55]

CONCLUSION

The two conciliar orations delivered by Premonstratensians considered in this article demonstrate a strong adherence to aspects of the spiritual heritage of St. Augustine. The anonymous Constance oration exhibits an eloquent and nuanced attempt, both implicit and

50. Stump, *The Reforms of the Council of Constance (1414–1418)*, 218–21.
51. "Wifflet," 165.
52. Ibid., 166.
53. Ibid., 166.
54. Ibid., 167.
55. Ibid., 171.

explicit, to apply to the reform and renewal of the whole church ideals of community found in the *Rule of St. Augustine,* including leadership style, obedience, fraternal correction, and most striking of all, a deep mutual love uniting all of the members of a community as they move in one mind and heart on the way to God. Indeed, he extends this concern for unity to Greek Christians and even nonbelievers. This is a deliberate attempt to apply the lived reality of a Premonstratensian understanding of the *religio Augustini* to questions of universal import. The sermon given by Johannes Wifflet at Basel is an excellent example of the application of theological ideas of reform and renewal to individual and institutional reform, so deeply rooted in the Latin and specifically Augustinian patristic heritage. Like his confrère at Constance, Wifflet extends this concern beyond the bounds of the Latin Church, although in Wifflet's case with perhaps more of an emphasis on bringing (*reductio*) alienated outsiders back to their proper order under Latin Christendom. This is not to deny that the ideas of the bishop of Hippo were part of the general mindset and vocabulary of many Latin Christian thinkers. What it does show, however, is that when members of a large and venerable religious order, the Canons Regular of Prémontré, known more for their pastoral and administrative rather than academic pursuits, were called upon to contribute to an international forum on church reform, they were able to bring to bear the insights of their particular Augustinian outlook in a nuanced and indeed eloquent manner.

11

"MEMORIAM FECIT"

The Eucharist, Memory, Reform, and Regeneration in Hildegard of Bingen's *Scivias* and Nicholas of Cusa's Sermons

ANN W. ASTELL

Two Christian sacraments—Baptism and the Eucharist—figure prominently in the argument of Gerhart Ladner's classic 1959 work, *The Idea of Reform*. Ladner notices a shift in emphasis in Christian spiritual formation from prebaptismal conversion (during the times of Roman persecution) to postbaptismal conversion (beginning in the fourth century), the latter, whether monastic or "secular," having to do with penitential practice and Eucharistic reception.[1] In an important passage early in the book, Ladner distinguishes sharply between baptismal regeneration, which is "instantaneous" in its effect and "nonrepeatable,"[2] and the idea of reform, which "on the contrary contains as an essential element of multiplicity involving

1. Gerhart B. Ladner, *The Idea of Reform: Its Impact on Christian Thought and Action in the Age of the Fathers* (Cambridge, Mass.: Harvard University Press, 1959; New York: Harper and Row, 1967), 319.

2. Ibid., 32.

prolongation and *repetition*."[3] Ladner goes on to say: "The ceaselessly repeated sacrifice of Christ in the sacrament of the altar may perhaps be seen as the exemplary cause and the vivifying center of Christian reform, even though in the age of the Fathers this meaning was not yet very often formulated explicitly, except in the liturgy itself."[4]

Despite the acknowledged centrality of the Eucharist, Ladner actually devotes only a few pages to the sacrament in *The Idea of Reform*, presumably because of this early lack of explicit doctrinal formulation. These few pages include the following: a mention in a footnote of Gregory of Nyssa's *Oratio catechetica* 37, which, Ladner writes, "fits the Eucharistic sacrament into the doctrine of spiritual image-likeness, assimilation, vision, and deification";[5] a mention, also in a footnote, of the Eucharist understood as a medicine;[6] a short passage linking the purity of the host to penitential purification;[7] and a discussion of a single chapter from Book X of *The City of God*, where St. Augustine "explains how the City of God adheres to Him, because it truly offers the Corpus Christi in its two-fold sense of the Eucharistic sacrament and of the community of the faithful."[8]

The Eucharistic *memoria Christi* is arguably the missing link for Ladner in St. Augustine's strong association of memory with reform in *De Trinitate* and the *Confessions*. "Already in his *Confessions*," writes Ladner, "the concept of memory ... had become a psychological focus through which conversion is initiated, reformation gained out of time and multiplicity. Memory of sin and of God, memory as distraction and as consciousness, is the bridge [to reform]."[9] In *De Trinitate*, according to Ladner, "*Memoria* ... stands for the mind in so far as it is conscious of the external world, of itself, and of God."[10] In neither *De Trinitate* nor the *Confessions*, however, does Augustine (in Ladner's analysis) explicitly link memory *per se* to the Eucha-

3. Ibid.
4. Ibid.
5. Ibid., 98n59.
6. Ibid., 311n32.
7. Ibid., 294.
8. Ibid., 281.
9. Ibid., 202.
10. Ibid., 199.

rist,[11] celebrated at Christ's command: "Do this in remembrance of me" (Luke 22:19; cf. 1 Cor 11:24–25).[12]

Explicit doctrinal formulations that confirm Ladner's characterization of the Eucharist as "the exemplary cause and vivifying center of Christian reform" can be found, however, in high- and late-medieval texts which link Eucharistic celebration and reception to memory. In this essay I take up Ladner's suggestion to extend his study of the idea of reform beyond the "age of the Fathers" through a comparison of the Eucharistic writings of two mystics of the German Rhineland, Hildegard of Bingen (1098–1179) and Nicholas of Cusa (1401–1464).[13] Although no direct evidence survives to link Cusanus to the legacy of the twelfth-century abbess, it is hard to imagine that her name—so famous in her own time—would have been unknown to him.[14] Born in Kues between Koblenz and Trier, Cusanus was notably active in 1438–1439 in Koblenz, not far from

11. In an important, highly original, and revisionary paper, "Eucharistic Exegesis in Augustine's *Confessions*," given at the Reconsiderations Conference III, hosted by the Augustinian Institute at Villanova University, September 17–19, 2009, John Cavadini has argued that the Eucharist appears in Augustine's recollections "at the intersection of memory and hope." I thank him for sharing the text of his paper with me.

12. I use *The Holy Bible*, Revised Standard Version, Catholic Edition (San Francisco: Ignatius Press, 1966).

13. Ladner himself encourages the extension of his study, which is limited in scope to the patristic period, to considerations of the idea of reform in later periods, from the Middle Ages through the sixteenth and seventeenth centuries, when even the Reformation itself came to be seen as needing reform. See *The Idea of Reform*, 34.

14. Hildegard's fame and ecclesiastical influence during her own time are unquestionable. As Barbara Newman, in *Sister of Wisdom: St. Hildegard's Theology of the Feminine* (Berkeley: University of California Press, 1989), 11, notes, "Hildegard's correspondence spans the three decades from 1147 to her death and ranges over all sectors of society, from popes, emperors, and prelates to abbots and abbesses, priests, monks, and laypeople. By the mid-1150s her fame was such that Frederick Barbarossa invited her to meet with him at his palace in Ingelheim.... Between 1158 and 1161, ... Hildegard undertook the first of four extended preaching journeys [in the Rhineland]." Newman attributes Hildegard's enduring reputation in the late Middle Ages to the work of Guibert of Gembloux, who composed her *Vita*, and Gebeno of Eberbach, whose *Pentachronon* "kept an important, if thematically limited, selection of her writings in wide circulation." See Barbara Newman, "Hildegard and Her Hagiographers: The Remaking of Female Sanctity," in *Gendered Voices: Medieval Saints and Their Interpreters*, edited by Catherine M. Mooney (Philadelphia: University of Pennsylvania Press, 1999), 16–34 and 195–202, quoted at 33.

Bingen, as a papal advocate during the conciliarist movement associated especially with the Council of Basel.[15] My point is not to argue for any direct influence of Hildegard upon Cusanus, however, but rather simply to compare the Eucharistic thought of these two medieval reformers.

Separated in time by three centuries, their very different writings about the sacrament of the altar provide benchmarks for the development of Eucharistic thought and devotion in relation to the idea of reform. For Hildegard, the eschatological church in its relationship to Christ is the bridal model for the priestly celebrant and the communicant alike, whereas for Cusanus the Eucharist itself is the priestly model, the Bridegroom who offers himself for the Bride, the church. Hildegard sees the priest primarily (but not exclusively) *in persona Ecclesiae,* that is, as representing the church in her endless worship of God and self-surrender to him through Christ. Cusanus, by contrast, places more emphasis on the priest's acting *in persona Christi* both to accept and transform through consecration the church's bridal offering and to woo the church through Christ's gifts. These two different emphases are not contradictory, however, because Hildegard and Cusanus both take seriously the bridging function of the sacramental priesthood and the dynamic spousal relationship between Christ and his Church—a relationship that makes the two mysteriously one, the church participating in Christ's action, and Christ in that of the church. Both of their remembered Eucharistic "visions"—Hildegard's vision experiential in an extraordinary way, Cusanus's in the ordinary way of faith—call the church on earth to reform and seek to enable it, in union with Christ, to be fruitful in regeneration.

15. On the historical question of Cusanus's activity in Koblenz, see H. Lawrence Bond, "Nicholas of Cusa from Constantinople to 'Learned Ignorance': The Historical Matrix for the Formation of the *De docta ignorantia,*" in *Nicholas of Cusa on Christ and the Church: Essays in Memory of Chandler McCuskey Brooks for the American Cusanus Society,* edited by Gerald Christianson and Thomas M. Izbicki (Leiden: Brill, 1996), 135–63, esp. 146–49, 151, and 156.

Both Hildegard and Cusanus see Eucharistic reform as intrinsically related to regeneration, understanding that term, as they do, in a way that differs from the "vitalistic renewal" idea of cyclical, repeated regeneration from which Ladner sharply distinguishes both Christian regeneration (which is, by definition, "nonrepeatable") and reform.[16] They again differ from one another in their complementary emphases. Hildegard's ecclesial orientation leads her to stress Mother Church's life-giving activity of sacramental regeneration, whereas Cusanus places emphasis on the individual Christian's passive experience of ardently accepted rebirth in Christ through membership in the church.

Hildegard, writing partly in response to the (anti-sacramental) Cathars,[17] envisions the reforming power of the Eucharist as oriented toward spiritual procreation and regeneration through the church's spousal union with Christ in the sacrament. For Hildegard, the church, predestined in and through Mary to be Christ's virginal bride, is always already conformed to her Bridegroom through His grace and stands beside Him on a transcendent plane as the exemplar for the individual Christian, who is called into a fruitful communion with Christ in Eucharistic self-giving. Thus understood, Barbara Newman explains, "the [personified] Church not only represents the mystical body of Christ, but as a corporate person she is also the bride of Christ," in whose ideal brideship and maternal fecundity her members participate, imperfectly on earth, perfectly in Heaven.[18] Joined with Christ, the church—and, in the church, the individual soul—draws life from him and becomes through him an agent, a giver, of new life.

16. Ladner, *The Idea of Reform*, 16–26.

17. On the Cathars' dualist theology and rejection of the material universe as evil, see Joseph L. Baird and Radd Ehrman, "Introduction," *The Letters of Hildegard of Bingen*, translated by Joseph L. Baird and Radd Ehrman, 3 vols. (New York: Oxford University Press, 1994–2004), 1:1–26, esp. 13–14. See also Hildegard of Bingen, Letter 15r, *Letters*, 1:54–65.

18. Barbara Newman, *God and the Goddesses: Vision, Poetry, and Belief in the Middle Ages* (Philadelphia: University of Pennsylvania Press, 2003), 41.

Cusanus, writing in the midst of the doctrinal discussions surrounding transubstantiation, places much more emphasis than Hildegard does on the soul's participation in Eucharistic change, on its transformation through that of the host.[19] In so doing, he develops the traditional language of reformist thought—*reformatio, renovatio, restauratio*—to include a theo-aesthetic vocabulary of christiformity. As sacramental participant in Christ's death and resurrection, the communicant is changed, reformed, morally and ethically, but also transformed ontologically, and ultimately reborn, regenerated, in the glorified life to come. One with Christ, the soul is and remains for Cusanus an object, a recipient, of Christ's new life, given in the sacraments.

For both Hildegard and Cusanus, the liturgical actions through which communal and personal remembrance is expressed, caused, and safeguarded, play a crucial role in the experience of Eucharistic grace. Memory must, in their common understanding, be made through memorial gestures, words, and images, which support the recollection of revealed truths. Mindful of God's presence and consciously present to Him, the soul, receptive to grace, is able to recognize the marvelous divine manifestations (*sacramenta*) of salvation history, to participate in those saving mysteries, and to receive grace ever anew through the sacramental signs Christ instituted, bequeathed to the church, and commanded. The memory that is consciously made, crafted, manufactured through the Eucharistic liturgy is by definition a work of art, an imitation of God's own artistic memory-making.[20]

19. On this point, see Donald F. Duclow, "Eckhart and Nicholas of Cusa: Eucharist and Mystical Transformation," *Eckhart Review* 17 (2008): 44–61. I thank Professor Duclow for calling my attention to this study of his.

20. On memory in Eucharistic theo-aesthetics, see Ann W. Astell, *Eating Beauty: The Eucharist and the Spiritual Arts of the Middle Ages* (Ithaca: Cornell University Press, 2007), especially 21, 64–65, 72–74, 89.

NICHOLAS OF CUSA'S EUCHARISTIC MEMORIAL: PROCESSION, PROTHEME, THEME

"Memoriam fecit" is the theme of Nicholas of Cusa's 1446 sermon, preached at Mainz on the Feast of Corpus Christi. Arguably the most artistic of Cusanus's ten extant Eucharistic sermons,[21] it draws its inspiration from Psalm 110:4–5: "He has caused his wonderful works (*mirabilium*) to be remembered; the Lord is merciful (*misericors*) and compassionate (*miserator*); he has given food to those who fear him."[22] Cusanus plays upon the literal meaning of the phrase "memoriam fecit mirabilium suorum," "he has made a memory of his marvels," marvels being both the object of an active memory and the active subject of a passive memory formed by the experience of God's marvels. Cusanus's choice of these verses from the psalmist characterizes the Eucharist as a memorial center formed at the powerful conjunction of strong emotions: human misery and divine compassion, on the one hand, and human marveling at God's miracles, on the other.

21. In addition to Sermo LXII, "Memoriam Fecit" (cited below), I count the following sermons: Nicolai de Cusa, Sermo III, "Hoc facite," *Sermones I (1430–1441), Opera omnia iussu et auctoritate academiae litterarum Heidelbergensis ad codicum fidem edita*, 16, Fasc. 1–2, edited by Rudolf Haubst, Martin Bodewig, Werner Krämer, and Heinrich Pauli (Hamburg: Felix Meiner, 1991), 41–55; Nicolai de Cusa, Sermo LXIII, "Qui manducat hunc panem," *Sermones II (1443–1452), Opera Omnia* 17, Fasc. 5, edited by Marc-Aeilko Aris, Heidi Hein, and Hermann Schnarr (Hamburg: Felix Meiner, 2006), 354–55; Nicolai de Cusa, Sermo LXIV, "Qui manducat hunc panem," *Opera Omnia* 17, Fasc. 5, 356–59; Sermo CLXXVIII, "Accepit ergo Jesus panes," *Sermones III (1452–1455), Opera omnia* 18, Fasc. 4, edited by Silvia Donati, Harald Schwaetzer, Franz-Bernhard Stammkötter (Hamburg: Felix Meiner, 2004), 285–88; Sermo CLXXXIII, "Una oblatione consummavit in sempiternum sanctificatos," *Opera omnia* 18, Fasc. 4, 314–21; Sermo CLXXXIX, "Qui manducat hunc panem," *Opera omnia* 18, Fasc. 4, 357–69; Sermo CCVIII, "Unde ememus panes," *Sermones IV (1455–1463), Opera omnia* 19, Fasc. 1, edited by Klaus Reinhardt and Walter Andreas Euler (Hamburg: Felix Meiner, 1996), 13–18; Sermo CCXXXV, "Hoc facite," *Opera omnia* 19, Fasc. 3, edited by Walter Andreas Euler and Harald Schwaetzer (Hamburg: Felix Meiner, 2002), 193–200; Sermo CCLXXXVI, "Pange, lingua, gloriosi corporis mysterium," *Opera omnia* 19, Fasc. 7, edited by Silvia Donati and Heide Dorothea Riemann (Hamburg: Felix Meiner, 2005), 638–40. Other sermons have, of course, Eucharistic passages. The indices to the four volumes of sermons list a total of seventeen sermons in which the word "eucharistia" appears.

22. Nicolai de Cusa, Sermo LXII, "Memoriam Fecit," *Opera omnia*, 17, Fasc. 5, 343–53, at 343. All translations from Cusanus's sermons are my own.

As Mary Carruthers's magisterial work on medieval arts of memory has taught us, memorial images were understood to be formed, retained, and stored in the mind partly on the basis of the strong emotions associated with their visualization.[23] Among the books of the Bible, the Psalter especially abounds, Carruthers notes, in its injunctions to "remember," to "be mindful of."[24] In selecting as his Eucharistic theme verses from Psalm 110 about God's making of memories out of marvelous works, Cusanus suggests something of tremendous import about human art: namely, that "all crafted things are made in the first instance for human remembering—both directly, to attract attention and thus to be remembered . . . and then [indirectly] *through the work of memory* for knowing, cognition."[25]

Skillfully repeating words and sounds (and thus participating in the making of his listeners' memories), Cusanus declares: "The marvelous God has accomplished marvelous works, and many are the marvelous testimonies of his works. But that he might leave us a memory, a memorial, of all his marvels, he gave himself as food to those fearing him": "<Deus mirabilis> (mirabilia opera) operatus est et multa sunt <testimonia mirabilia> operum eius. Sed ut omnium <mirabilium suorum> nobis memoriam relinqueret, se <dedit escam timentibus eum>."[26] Cusanus goes on to remind his auditors that "feasts are memorials of things that have happened"—for example, the feasts of Tabernacles and of Passover—and that the Feast of Corpus Christi is no exception to this rule, gratefully recalling, as it does, "the institution of the sacrament by which we are nourished through life in the life of our spirit."[27] The Latin phrase "*res gesta,*"

23. See Mary J. Carruthers, *The Book of Memory: A Study of Memory in Medieval Culture*, Cambridge Studies in Medieval Literature (Cambridge: Cambridge University Press, 1990); Mary J. Carruthers, *The Craft of Thought: Meditation, Rhetoric, and the Making of Images, 400–1200*, Cambridge Studies in Medieval Literature 34 (Cambridge: Cambridge University Press, 2000).

24. Carruthers, *Craft of Thought*, 67.

25. Ibid. Emphasis added.

26. Nicolai de Cusa, Sermo LXII, "Memoriam Fecit," *Opera omnia* 17, Fasc. 5, 343.

27. Ibid., 343: "Festa enim memoriae sunt gestarum rerum: ut festa tabernaculorum,

by which Cusanus refers to the historical event of the institution of the sacrament, means of course "something that has been carried or borne out" (from the verb *gerere*), but that very verb choice already links the Eucharist to gestation, pregnancy, child-bearing, and (re)generation.

In a self-reflexive protheme, Cusanus considers the role of the preacher, whose inspired word from the pulpit can accomplish a marvel similar to that produced by the words of consecration, spoken by the priest at the altar. When the preacher "renews in memory the deed accomplished," he "incites the mind to the apprehension of what is figured, inflames the desire, and provokes longing."[28] Thus, declares Cusanus, he "does what the offering of the great sacrifice effects, and carries across through the word of the Lord the members of Satan, so that they might be 'members of Christ,' even as, through the word spoken *in altari*, the bread of bodily material is translated [*transfertur*] into the bread of eternal life."[29] Likening the preacher to a priest of the Old Testament who offers a preparatory sin offering, Cusanus explains that he reminds people of their sins so that he might induce them to confession and lead them to cast their sins into the fire, as it were, as an immolation from which a sweet odor pleasing to God might arise. Thus Cusanus links the work of penitential reform (so emphasized by Ladner) to Eucharistic reception.[30]

Part 1 of the carefully constructed sermon builds upon this idea. "Let us all go up to the altar," he invites his listeners, to offer our-

---

quia in deserto fuerunt absque domibus filii Israelis in illis, et Paschae, quia transiverunt mare rubrum, etc. Oremus pro gratia, ut digne memoriam recolamus institutionis sacramenti, quo reficimur per vitam in vita spiritus nostri, etc."

28. Ibid., 344: "quia praedicator renovat in memoria rem gestam, incitat intellectum ad apprehensionem figurati, inflammat desiderium et provocat suspiria."

29. Ibid., 344: "Unde facit, quod facit oblationem magni sacrificii, et transfert per verbum Domini membra Satanae, ut sint <membra Christi>, sicut per verbum in altari transfertur panis materialis corporalis in panem vitae aeternae."

30. Ladner observes: "In the liturgy, the idea of purity is, of course, intimately connected with penance and with the subsequent reception of the Eucharistic sacrament.... [P]rayer for a pure heart after reception of the *hostia pura* sums up the celebration of the purest sacrifice": *The Idea of Reform*, 294.

selves there in communion with Christ, so that we might be nourished by the Eucharistic sacrament.[31] He envisions this spiritual action as a realization of the deeper significance of the joyful liturgical action the people have just performed, singing hymns and following the sacrament, surrounded by incense, in a candle-lit procession from the street into the church. "There [at the altar]," he indicates, "we are about to offer to God the Father Christ, who is in us, and ourselves in him."[32] Rhetorically speaking, the altar and, even more precisely, the sacrificial sacrament upon it, is the *skopos*, the "target" at which Cusanus directs the thoughts of his listeners and the movement of their bodies.[33] Literally bearing Christ in the host and spiritually being borne by him, Cusanus invites his listeners to imagine that they have not only entered the church from the city street, but have been transported from this world to a heavenly realm, to God's tabernacle on high, bearing aloft an ornamented world, beautiful, glowing with light, and redolent with the fragrance of the prayers of the saints. The people's Corpus Christi commemoration, in short, is meant to bring them into God's presence and His eternal present.

In her studies of medieval processional paths, Carruthers emphasizes their mnemonic value as people passed from station to station, each marked by an image or images that served to give the mind access to other, associated memories, located through the image.[34] I do not know the historical path of the Corpus Christi procession in Mainz to which Cusanus refers, but it may well have included such stations commemorating God's miracles in salvation history and linked them via the processional *ductus* (literally, its leading, drawing, or flow of movement) to Eucharistic remembrance, the sacrament itself making out of the many images one single, consummate sign of God's abiding presence, even as the procession manifested

31. Nicolai de Cusa, *Opera omnia* 17, Fasc. 5, 345: "Accessimus omnes usque ad altare."

32. Nicolai de Cusa, *Opera omnia* 17, Fasc. 5, 346: "usque ad altare … et ibi nos oblaturos Deo Patri Christum, qui in nobis est, et nos ipsos in illo."

33. See Carruthers, *Craft of Thought*, 79.

34. Ibid., 266–69.

the "unity-in-diversity" of the members of the Church.[35] For Cusanus, the physical and mental movement of the people, the colorful procession in which they have just participated, is the source of energy—in rhetorical terms, *enargeia*; literally, the "bringing-before-the-eyes"—upon which he draws to further the train of thought, to develop the tri-partite argument of his sermon on the sacrament.[36]

HILDEGARD OF BINGEN'S REMEMBERED EUCHARISTIC VISION

The sixth section of Book II of Hildegard's multi-volume *Scivias,* composed over a period of ten years (1141–1151), similarly begins by evoking a vivid, experiential memory—a vision recounted in words and represented in illustrations—that reveals the spiritual significance of a repeated, reforming sacramental action.[37] As Barbara Newman observes, this section of the *Scivias,* the longest in the work, "deals with subjects of burning interest to twelfth-century theologians: the nature of the eucharist and of the priesthood."[38] The text records a vision—a mystical Mass that Hildegard "saw"—followed by an explanation of its significance, which Hildegard claims to have "heard."

The vision itself is represented in two different illuminations, the images of which do not combine in quite the same sequence found in the visionary narrative.[39] The very use of two illuminations artificially creates in retrospect a two-part structure within the vision

35. Ibid., 55. Carruthers refers here specifically to the liturgies around the stational churches in Rome.

36. On *enargeia,* see ibid., 118, 130–33, 134, 135, 139, 168, 172, 328, note 2.

37. For the Latin text, I use *Hildegardis Scivias,* edited by Adelgundis Führkötter, O.S.B., with the help of Angela Carlevaris, O.S.B., *Corpus Christianorum Continuatio Medievalis* [*CCCM*], Vols. 43 and 43A (Turnhout: Brepols, 1978). For an English translation, I use Hildegard of Bingen, *Scivias,* translated by Mother Columba Hart and Jane Bishop (Mahwah, N.J.: Paulist Press, 1990).

38. Barbara Newman, "Introduction," in Hildegard of Bingen, *Scivias,* 33.

39. I reprint here (on pages 202 and 206) the figures that appear in *Hildegardis Scivias,* edited by Führkötter, with the help of Carlevaris, cited in note 37. That critical edition reprints in color the figures as they appear in Adelgundis Führkötter, *The Miniatures from the Book Scivias—Know the Ways—of St. Hildegard of Bingen from the Illuminated Rupertsberg*

itself, which is described as a continuous action, by highlighting (in the second illumination) the appearance of the priest, who combines symbolically in himself features both of Christ and of the church (whose spousal union at the cross is depicted in the first illumination).[40] The artwork has, in that sense, its own memorial logic, reflective of the mind's associative patterns and means of recall. Art historian Madeline Caviness has argued convincingly that the illuminator of the Rupertsberg *Scivias* worked under the direction of Hildegard herself, who first sketched the visions she had seen and wrote color notations, using a wax tablet for jotting down her memories.[41]

In the top half of the first image we see what Hildegard first saw: "the Son of God hanging on the cross."[42] At his side stands a crowned woman, whom Hildegard identifies as the church, holding in her hands a chalice, into which flows the blood from Christ's pierced side. In contrast to this static visualization, Hildegard's actual vision, as she recalls and narrates it, is filled with movement: the woman comes "forth like a bright radiance" from the "ancient counsel" of God; she is "led" to Christ and raises herself upward in order to be "sprinkled by the blood from his side," and thus she is "joined with him in happy betrothal and richly dowered with His body and blood."[43] This marriage, which unites Christ with his church, shows the church in her

---

Codex (Turnhout: Brepols, 1977). Reprinted with the kind permission of the copyright holders, Brepols Publisher, Turnhout, Belgium.

40. In the Latin critical edition by Führkötter and Carlevaris (*CCCM* 43 *and* 43a, cited above), the two illuminations appear between pages 228 and 229 and between pages 272 and 273, respectively. The second illumination thus appears approximately half-way through the text (pp. 225–306), which first reports and then interprets the sixth vision. The widely separated placement of the illuminations thus also artificially creates a two-part structure within the vision.

41. Madeline H. Caviness, "Hildegard as Designer of the Illustrations to her Works," in *Hildegard of Bingen: The Context of Her Thought and Art* (London: Warburg Institute, School of Advanced Study, University of London, 1998), 29–62.

42. Hildegard of Bingen, *Scivias,* II.6, 237: "Et post haec uidi cum Filius Dei in cruce pependit" (*CCCM,* 43:229).

43. Ibid., 237: "praedicta muliebris uelut lucida splendor ex antique consilio propere progrediens per diuinam potentiam ad ipsum adducta est, et sanguine qui de latere eius fluxit se sursum eleuante perfusa ipsi per uoluntatem superni Patris felici desponsatione associata est atque carne et sanguine eius nobiliter dotata" (*CCCM,* 43:229–30).

lxxxvi. Quod nemo propter pondus peccatorum suorum desperet.

lxxxvii. Euangelium de eodem.

lxxxviii. Quod peccata et per elemosinam et per corporalem satisfactionem deleri debent.

lxxxviiii. De libro sapientie.

xc. Quod elemosina lac uoluptatum [illegible]

xci. Qui elemosinam dant. et qui suscipiunt. eam suscipiunt. hoc in uanum non faci[unt].

xcii. Quod pauperes et diuites. et honores [illegible] potestatis appetentes. unusquisque secundum intentionem suam remuneratur.

xciii. Quod sacerdotes exorando et cohercendo moneant populum de confessione.

xciiii. Quod sacerdotes auctoritate [illegible] ueritatem magisterii populo non ostendentes. non sacerdotes sed lupi uo[cantur].

xcv. Quod elemosina coram deo [illegible] ululant super iniquitate sacerdotum. et celi iniquitatem eorum suscipiunt.

xcvi. Quod sacerdotes habent potestatem ligandi et soluendi.

xcvii. Verba euangelii de eodem.

xcviii. Quod nullus absque culpabili culpa ligandus est.

xcviiii. Quod si aliquis innocens constrictus fuerit. propter honorem dei solutionem querere debet.

c. Quod rebelles ad Christum reuerti nolentes. et obdurati nullam misericordiam querentes. antiquum serpentem imitantur.

ci. Verba diaboli.

cii. Quod homines de tenebrositate infidelitatis per incarnationem filii dei educti sunt.

predestined conformity to Christ as His spotless bride. The heavenly voice which Hildegard then hears explicitly orientates this unitive, spousal love to the procreation of spiritual children: "May she, O Son, be your Bride for the restoration of My people; may she be a mother to them, regenerating souls through the salvation of the Spirit and water."[44] The scroll in the illumination similarly identifies Jesus and his *sponsa*. Hildegard's vision thus confirms Gerhart Ladner's general observation: "Both in Mary, the virginal mother of Jesus, and in the Church, the bride of Christ and the mother of Christians, virginity and motherhood are indeed identical."[45]

In the lower half of the illumination, the crowned woman appears again, this time in the lower corner with her hands and eyes upraised. A priestly figure, the heavenly archetype of the celebrant of the Mass, the church is pictured as womanly in accord with the Pauline theology of Ephesians 5:21–33, which names her the bride of Christ; with grammatical logic (*Ecclesia* being a feminine noun); and with Hildegard's personal sense of identification with her. A feminine visionary in Hildegard's vision, the church beholds the host and chalice on the altar, at the foot of the extended trunk of the cross. The cross's extension in the visualization reflects Hildegard's verbal testimony that the "image [she first saw] grew in strength."[46] Once again the necessarily static rendering in the illumination contrasts with the dynamic temporality of the vision itself, wherein the bride is said to approach the altar "frequently," "each time" beholding the Eucharist as her dowry and showing it to the Father and his angels.[47] Hildegard's own gaze coincides with that of the Bride as she sees what the *sponsa* sees.

The four circled scenes—two at each side of the extended cross—

44. Ibid., 237: "'Haec, Fili, sit tibi sponsa in restaurationem populi mei, cui ipsa mater sit, animas per saluationem spiritus et aquae regenerans'" (*CCCM*, 43:230).

45. Ladner, *The Idea of Reform*, 324.

46. Hildegard of Bingen, *Scivias*, II.6, 237: "cum eadem imago iam hoc modo in uiribus suis proficeret" (*CCCM*, 43:230).

47. Ibid., 237: "ipsa frequenter accedebat et ibi dotem suam deuote reuisens, eam superno Patri et angelis eius humiliter ostendebat" (*CCCM*, 43:230).

depict what Hildegard sees much later in her vision, when "suddenly there appeared before [her] eyes as if in a mirror the symbols of the Nativity, Passion and burial, Resurrection, and Ascension of our Savior."[48] The illuminator has transferred these scenes from the second part of Hildegard's vision (that is, after the appearance of the priest, depicted in the second illumination) to the first, presumably because they serve both to highlight Hildegard's identification with the church as visionary and also to make explicit the Real Presence of Christ in the Eucharistic species on the altar. Surrounding the chalice and the host, the four scenes point to the Eucharist itself as a memorial center, generative of remembrance of the Gospel as a whole, of the whole Christ (*totus Christus*).

Concerning medieval, monastic visions, Carruthers emphasizes that the "orthopraxis of prayerful meditation" regularly included cognitive visualizations and assumed a dynamic interaction between human picture-making and divine inspiration—so much so that "the result of this assumption was a weak distinction (from our standpoint) between meditative reading and visionary experience."[49] Because "human thinking ... was considered to be *embodied*,"[50] medieval visionaries understood that what they saw before them was also, at least partially, a living mirror of their own minds and a reflection of its store of remembered and interpreted images. Hence Hildegard speaks of seeing "as if in a mirror the symbols" (*signa ... uelut in speculo*) of mysteries in the life of Christ, mysteries that were the frequent object of her disciplined meditation.

In the second illumination of Hildegard's vision, at the top, there appears a priest in vestments, his hands outstretched in prayer

48. Ibid., 237: "Cumque haec aspicerem, statim etiam signa natiuitatis, passionis et sepulturae necnon resurrectionis et ascensionis saluatoris nostri ... uelut in speculo ibi apparent" (*CCCM*, 43:231).

49. Carruthers, *Craft of Thought*, 184. On this topic, see Barbara Newman, "What Did It Mean to Say 'I Saw'?: The Clash between Theory and Practice in Medieval Visionary Culture," *Speculum* 80.1 (2005): 1–43.

50. *Carruthers, Craft of Thought*, 187. Emphasis original.

(similar to the outstretched hands of the *sponsa* in the lower half of the earlier picture and to the hands of Christ stretched upon the cross), his face turned toward the host upon the altar, over which angels hover. In Hildegard's narrative of her vision, when the priest approaches the altar to celebrate the Mass, it is surrounded by a heavenly light. At the singing of the *sanctus,* this light suddenly intensifies. Hildegard's memory of her vision—which is, at the same time, a remembrance of the mystical meaning of the Mass, which is itself a memorial of Christ's Passion, death, and resurrection—describes the moment of consecration as an instantaneous change. The offering is taken up to heaven and replaced on the altar in a moment, "as a person draws in a breath and lets it out again," with the result that "the offering was made true flesh and true blood, although in human sight it looked like bread and wine."[51]

During the time between the consecration and the singing of the *Agnus Dei* Hildegard sees the four scenes described earlier, as if the elevated host functions as a trigger for the memory of Christ's entire life.[52] After the *Agnus Dei,* Hildegard again hears a heavenly voice, this time calling the faithful to eat the body and drink the blood of God's Son "to wipe out Eve's transgression, so that [they might] be restored to the noble inheritance."[53] In this way, Hildegard invokes the idea of Eucharistic restoration and reform. In the bottom half of the second illumination are depicted in differing colors the five spiritual states in which people receive communion, some to their glorification, others to their purification, some to their condemnation.

The lengthy interpretation of this two-part vision in the *Scivias* emphasizes both regeneration and reform. The same unitive love

51. Hildegard of Bingen, *Scivias,* II.6, 237: "uelut homo halitum sum introrsum trahit et iterum eum extrorsum emittit, ita eam ueram carnem et uerum sanguinem effectam, quamuis in conspectu hominum uelut uinum apparerent" (*CCCM,* 43:230–31).

52. One might compare Hildegard's Eucharistic vision in this regard to those of another German visionary, Gertrude of Helfta (ca. 1256–1301). See Astell, *Eating Beauty,* 21, 85–98.

53. Hildegard of Bingen, *Scivias,* II.6, 237: "ad abolendum praeuaricationem Euae, quatenus in rectam hereditatem restauremini" (*CCCM,* 43:231).

Et post hec vidi cum filius Dei in cruce pependit quod predicta muliebris imago velut lucidus splendor ex antiquo consilio prodiens per divinam potentiam ad ipsum adducta est, et sanguine qui de latere eius fluxit se sursum elevante perfusa, ipsique per voluntatem superni patris felici desponsatione associata est, atque carne et sanguine eius nobiliter dotata. Et audivi vocem de celo illi dicentem: Hec fili sit tibi sponsa in restaurationem populi mei, cui ipsa mater sit, animas per salvationem spiritus et aque regenerans. Et cum eadem imago iam hoc modo in virtutibus suis proficeret, vidi quasi quoddam altare ad quod ipsa frequenter accedebat, et ibi dotem suam devote revisens eam superno patri et angelis eius humiliter ostendebat. Unde etiam cum sacerdos sacris vestibus indutus ad celebranda divina sacramenta ad idem altare accederet, vidi quod subito magna serenitas lucis cum obsequio

that unites the church as bride to Christ the bridegroom empowers the church both to give new life to souls through "the regeneration of the Spirit" in Baptism and to restore sinful souls, strengthening them in virtue, in and through the Eucharist that nourishes them.[54] "As long as you need help," Hildegard's God assures humanity, "My Son's … body and blood will be consecrated on the altar to be received by believers for their salvation and the purgation of their crimes."[55] Since the sacramental bread is, in fact, the Virgin-born flesh of God's Son, "which is obscured by no shadow of sin and clouded by no stain of iniquity," those who receive it worthily "are bathed in heavenly light in body and soul and cleansed by faith from their inner uncleanness."[56]

Seeing the Virgin Mary as the earthly figure for the bridal church,[57] Hildegard emphasizes that Mary literally stood beneath the cross, sharing in Christ's Passion through her maternal compassion, and that the body of Christ, offered up on the cross, was uniquely Mary's gift to God as well, her virginity yielding its fruit in a spotless victim, human and divine, and a pure sacramental bread. The sinful past and lost time of the faithful, who have "forgotten" their "necessary food" (*escam necessitatis*), can be restored "in another form" (*in alium modum*) through a new time of salvation, their

54. Ibid., 239: "regenerationem spiritus et aquae" (*CCCM,* 43: 233).

55. Ibid., 247: "quia quamdiu tibi subueniendum est … tamdiu etiam caro et sanguis eius in altari consecrabitur ad percipiendum credulis hominibus ad saluationem et ad purgationem criminum eorum" (*CCCM,* 43: 246).

56. Ibid., II.6, 252: "Panis autem iste caro Filii mei quam nulla obscuritas in peccatis offuscat nec ulla macula in iniquitatibus obnubilat, ita ut qui eam digne susceperint in anima et corpore caelesti lumine perfundantur et a maculis interioris sordis suae fideliter emundentur" (*CCCM,* 43:253).

57. In the third vision of Book II, Hildegard sees the virginity of Mary glowing in the hearts of the faithful and hears the words: "All believers should join with their whole wills in celebrating the virginity of that spotless Virgin in the Church" (*Scivias,* II.3, 172): "ut intellectui tuo infunditur, uirginitatem eiusdem illibatae Virginis tota intentione in ecclesia amplecti debet" (*CCCM,* 43: 140). For a suggestive survey of such references, see Sharon Elkins, "The Virgin Mary in the Visions of Hildegard of Bingen (1098–1179)," in *Women Christian Mystics Speak to Our Times,* edited by David B. Perrin (Franklin, Wis.: Sheed and Ward, 2001), 143–55.

hunger satisfied through penitence and Eucharistic reception.[58] They can be transformed, as it were, into other Marys, giving their lives to God through the offering of bread and wine, being changed (in a manner similar to Mary's own virginal conception) at the moment of consecration, and bearing Christ within themselves through communion. "As Divinity displayed its wonders in the womb of the Virgin," writes Hildegard, "it shows its secrets also in this oblation."[59]

Nicholas of Cusa makes a similar Marian interpretation of Eucharistic change in his 1457 sermon, "In die sacramenti," which takes as its theme the text of the Eucharistic hymn attributed to Thomas Aquinas: "Pange, lingua, gloriosi corporis mysterium." Writes Cusanus: "Even as a virginal substance is transformed through divine power into the Son, so too the substance of bread by divine power is transubstantiated into the Son."[60] In a 1455 sermon on Holy Thursday, Cusanus explains that Christ had to be born of an immaculate Virgin, incorporating mention of the dogma of Christ's Virgin birth from a sinless mother into his defense of Eucharistic transubstantiation. "Christ therefore is the repairer of an obfuscated image, who teaches us by what means the image is able to be renewed from obfuscation, and he begins to effect and to teach [that transformation], so that by a visible example [*visibili experimento*] we might stretch out toward renascence."[61]

In a remarkable passage in that same sermon, Cusanus suggests

58. Hildegard of Bingen, *Scivias*, II.6, 242; *CCCM*, 43:238.

59. Hildegard of Bingen, *Scivias*, II.6, 244: "ut diuinitas mirabilia sua in utero Virginis ostendit, ita etiam in hac oblatione secreta sua demonstrat" (*CCCM*, 43:242).

60. Nicholas of Cusa, Sermo CCLXXXVI, "Pange, lingua, gloriosi corporis mysterium," *Opera omnia* 19, Fasc. 7, 640: "Sicut enim ex virtute divina virginea substantia in Filium est transformata, ita et substantia panis divina virtute transsubstantiatur in Filium."

61. Ibid., CLXXXIII, "Una oblatione consummavit in sempiternum sanctificatos," in *Opera omnia* 18, Fasc. 4, 316: "Christus igitur reparator est imaginis offuscatae, qui docet nos quo modo imago possit de offuscatione denuo renasci, et coepit facere et docere, ut visibili experimento pertingeremus ad renascentiam." Sentences like these confirm Donald F. Duclow's general observation: "Within the Christian tradition, it may be hard to find a better symbol for mystical transformation than the Eucharist. For in its liturgical reality and symbolic resonance, this sacrament is all about transformation" ("Eckhart and Nicholas of Cusa: Eucharist and Mystical Transformation," 58). For the Eucharistic

that the Eucharist, instituted as a sacrifice of thanksgiving "in memory of [Christ's] liberation from everlasting death" ("in memoriam illius liberationis a morte perpetua"), is a Passover memorial that transforms memory itself, purifying it, allowing it to understand the sensory appearances of things in an illumined, sacramental way, until the church and its members resemble Mary herself as a virginal Bride, a sealed chamber:

> Consider memory to be like a place or womb or dwelling, in which the soul collects and reposes all the things that come from the world to itself through the means of the senses. And it has a door of entry, through which the impressions [*species*] of things come into itself. This door ought to be closed to night, its lintels and doorposts sealed with the blood of the spotless Lamb. And the angel-destroyer of life, who is "the prince of this world" and of its shadows or works, prowling around in the darkness, finding the blood on the lintel of the door of memory, passes by, seeking elsewhere the soul it slays. But to day or light this door ought to be open.[62]

Like Mary, who "kept all these things [concerning Jesus], pondering them in her heart" (Luke 2:10, 51), the Christian who keeps the Eucharistic *memoria Christi* remembers all things differently, seeing them as marvelous signs (*sacramenta*) of God's love.

CUSANUS'S SPOUSAL CHURCH AND EUCHARISTIC FOOD

Cusanus's 1446 sermon, "Memoriam Fecit," makes no explicit reference to Mary, but it does invoke the theme of bridal union in

---

context in which Cusanus makes these remarks on reform and rebirth, see also *Opera omnia* 18, Fasc.4, 317 and 320, where Cusanus refers to the Virgin Birth and discusses Eucharistic transubstantiation.

62. Ibid., CLXXXIII, "Una oblatione consummavit in sempiternum sanctificatos," in *Opera omnia* 18, Fasc. 4, 318: "Attende memoriam esse quasi locum seu ventrem sive domum, in quam anima colligit et reponit omnia, quae veniunt de hoc mundo ad ipsam per vias sensuum, et habet ostium introitus, per quod rerum species in ipsam intrant. Hoc ostium debet esse nocti clausum et signatum, in super liminari et postibus sanguine immaculati agni signatum, et angelus devastor vitae, qui est <<princeps huius mundi>> et tenebrarum seu negotium perambulans in tenebris, reperiens sanguine ostium memoriae linitum, praeterit, alibi quaerens animam quam mactet. Et diei sive luci debet hoc ostium esse apertum."

a Eucharistic context. In that sermon, to which we paid close attention at the start of this paper, Cusanus considers the sacramental food that God gives to those who fear him under a triple aspect, calling it the admirable food of faith, the more admirable food of hope, and the most admirable food of charity. The three-part movement of his argument can be seen to correspond to the sequential parts of the Mass: the food of faith emphasized in the entrance rite and the liturgy of the Word, the food of hope stressed in the offering of gifts to be consecrated, and the food of charity mirrored in the consecration itself and in the communion that follows. Part 3 abounds in marital imagery, but already in Part 1 Cusanus calls attention to the festive attire of his auditors, who have just participated in the Corpus Christi procession, and leads them to understand its deeper significance as a sign of espousal: "Taking off our soiled clothes, we have prepared ourselves like a bride, we who want to appear peacefully at ease and gracious in the sight of the bridegroom."[63] The Eucharist itself, he reminds them, demands that "we are led by signs from exterior to interior things and from sensible to intellectual things, from signs to what is signified."[64]

In Part 2, Cusanus emphasizes that our hope is nourished when we consider that there is something marvelous to be discovered in everything. "Even as our God is hidden," he writes, "so he has made all things occult."[65] Giving a litany of assorted natural marvels in the macrocosm, but also in the microcosm, Cusanus concludes with the greatest marvel of all, that of Eucharistic transubstantiation, which is accessible to faith alone.[66] God feeds us with this food that

63. Ibid., LXII;Nicolai de Cusa, "Memoriam fecit," 345: "Deferentes lautas vestes praeparavimus nos ut sponsa, quae volunt in conspectus sponsi placidae et gratae videri."

64. Nicolai de Cusa, "Memoriam fecit," 345: "et signis duceremur de exterioribus ad interiora et de sensibilibus ad intellectualia, de signis ad signata."

65. Ibid., 346: "Sicut Deus noster occultus est, ita fecit omnia et omnium entitatem occultam."

66. Ibid., 347. Cusanus has an extensive list of natural and mythological marvels, whereas Hildegard in the *Scivias* mentions as natural analogies for Eucharistic change only the appearance of chicks from eggs and of butterflies from cocoons. See Hildegard of Bingen, *Scivias,* II.6, 246.

we may "dare to hope that our corruptible substance is able to be transferred through Christ" into what Cusanus calls *christiformitas*, "so that in union with him we may obtain eternal life."[67] Using the vocabulary of transference, transformation, and transumption, Cusanus discovers the ground for hope in the memory of this sacrament precisely as *mirabilis*: "And in this way I find the nourishment of my hope in the memory of this marvelous sacrament."[68]

Part 3 of "Memoriam Fecit" returns to and develops the theme of the church as Christ's spouse, joined to Him in communion, the most marvelous food of love. In the Eucharist, Cusanus writes, Christ has given "a memory of His love, by which He has given us life through His own death"; by this food, we "are reminded of the marvelous works of the greatest love."[69] Listing God's gifts of love in a crescendo that begins with God's physical creation—earth, water, air, and fire—and continues with His acts of spiritual recreation, His gifts of grace, Cusanus presents the Eucharist within the context of God's wooing love, which seeks to win the love of His bride, the Church. God does not love us, however, that He might be loved in return—as if He needed our love, which he does not, since He himself is *Caritas*; rather, He loves us for our sake, Cusanus teaches, in order to convert us into his own spirit of love. God loves universally—the sick and the healthy, the rich and the poor, the wise and the untaught, the kings of this earth and the lowliest of servants—and unconditionally; God does not cease to love us, Cusanus observes, when we are needy on account of senility, infirmity, poverty, stinkiness, leprosy, or disease (no matter how horrible).

Shifting from the first-person plural pronoun—we, our, us—Cusanus speaks more intimately at the end of the sermon, address-

67. Nicolai de Cusa, Sermo LXII, Nicolai de Cusa, "Memoriam Fecit," 348: "Ut sperare valeamus substantiam nostrum corruptibilem per Christum posse transferri ad christiformitatem, ut sic in unitate cum ipso aeternam vitam assequamur."

68. Nicolai de Cusa, "Memoriam Fecit," 348: "Et hoc modo escam spei meae reperio in memoria mirabilis huius sacramenti."

69. Ibid., 349: "memoriam reliquit dilectionis suae, qua nos morte sua vivificavit. . . .esca amoris, scilicet memorari mirabilium operum amoris maximi."

ing each one with the second-person singular—*tu, tibi, te*—to paint vividly the extreme marvel of Christ's love: "He who out of pure goodness alone created you, out of pure love alone, that He might raise you up, 'was humiliated to' the point of incarnation and 'death'; moreover, he who determined for the sake of heavenly delights to be with you 'to the very consummation,' ascended, that he might fulfill the promise of salvation in glorious beatitude."[70] Finding the entire Paschal mystery in the Eucharist, Cusanus exhorts his listeners in conclusion, "Let us feast therefore on this food of life, so that we might be transformed into the life that never ends, where life without death reigns in eternity! Amen."[71]

In another of his Eucharistic sermons, given during the octave of Corpus Christi in 1456, Cusanus identifies this change, whereby the soul and ultimately the body are glorified by feasting on Christ's resurrected body, with regeneration, a birth to new life: "Therefore this sacrament of the memory of death prefigures the resurrection of life.... And if you attend rightly, this sacrament is the sacrament of his regeneration, concerning which it is said: 'when the son of man in regeneration' will sit, etc., indeed, [a foretaste of the day when] he will then raise us to new life, and conform us to himself."[72] Cusanus thus confirms Ladner's view that regeneration, as understood by Christians, "means that each individual Christian must die with Christ, be reborn in Him, and begin a new life following Him,"[73] both in this world and in the "new heavens and ... new earth" to

70. Ibid., 351: "ipse, qui sola pura bonitate te creavit, solo puro amore, ut te exaltaret, 'humiliatus est usque ad' incarnationem et 'mortem'; etiam, qui constituit pro summis deliciis esse tecum 'usque ad consummationem', ascendit, ut promissum ad impleret quoad salvationem, in beatitudine gloriosa."

71. Nicolai de Cusa, *Opera omnia* 17, Fasc.5, 353: "Pascamur igitur hoc cibo vitae, ut in vitam perennem transformemur, ubi regnat vita sine morte in aeternitate! Amen."

72. Nicolai de Cusa, Sermo CCXXXV, "Hoc facite," *Opera omnia* 19, Fasc. 3, 200: "Hoc igitur sacramentum memoriae mortis praefigurat resurrectionem vitae.... Et si recte attendis, istud sacramentum est sacramentum illius regenerationis, de qua dicitur: <cum sederit Filius hominis in regeneratione> etc., scilicet quod convivificabit tunc nos, et conformabit nos sibi."

73. Ladner, *The Idea of Reform*, 51.

come (Isa. 65:17). For Cusanus, the suddenness of Eucharistic transubstantiation, which both follows a penitential reform and lends it energy for future works, is not unlike the suddenness of death and its changing of human life.

EUCHARISTIC MEMORY: *MEMORIA CHRISTI* FROM HILDEGARD TO CUSANUS

With what general comparisons between Hildegard's Eucharistic visions and Cusanus's Corpus Christi sermons may we then conclude? At first sight the differences in genre, gender, setting, liturgical occasion, and historical situation are so obvious as to discourage any attempt at comparison, even between two mystics who lived within the same geographical region, albeit three centuries apart. What is striking in the end, however, are the similarities in their Eucharistic memories, grounded in the Church's own *memoria Christi,* but heightened through the conscious practice of memorial techniques, the arts of memory, which render their compositions beautiful and secure for them a place in our remembrance even today. Although Hildegard foregrounds the celestial church as a visionary and visual model for the earthly communicant and Cusanus foregrounds the transubstantiated host as the agent of change, both see Christ and the church as existing in a dynamic, spousal relationship with each other that is generative of new life. The church's Eucharistic memory is and remains for them the memory of Christ, which recalls and effects moral reform and spiritual transformation in the souls of the faithful through liturgy and sacrament. Imitating God's own practice, Hildegard and Cusanus alike have "made a memory," a Eucharistic memorial, for us: "Memoriam fecit."

12

VISIONS OF REFORM

Lay Piety as a Form of Thinking in Nicholas of Cusa

INIGO BOCKEN

One of the leading ideas in Gerhart Ladner's work is the observation that the idea of reform belongs to the very center of Christian experience and thinking from its earliest beginnings. The idea of reform is a genuine Christian idea, enabling us to understand the proper significance of Christian thinking in comparison with the Greek ideal of cyclical renewal or of the modern "institutional" conception of reform.[1] In the view of Ladner, the Christian idea of reform is indissolubly connected with the notion of man being the image of God. The idea of reform necessarily contains the attempt of the human being to *return* to his original essence, which, in one way or another, has been blurred through the finite and material interests of the world in which we live. Or, in the words of Ladner himself, the idea of reform may be defined "as the idea of free, intentional

1. Gerhart B. Ladner, *The Idea of Reform. Its Impact on Christian Thought and Action in the Age of the Fathers* (Cambridge, Mass.: Harvard University Press, 1959), 2–3 and passim.

and ever perfectible, multiple, prolonged and ever repeated efforts by man to reassert and augment values pre-existent in the spiritual-material compound of the world."[2] The Christian idea of reform therefore refers primarily to the personal and individual conversion of the faithful towards the religious path on earth, leading to the rediscovery of his or her ultimate goal and essence, that is, being the image of God. All attempts to realize institutional or cultural reforms since early Christianity are in one way or another related to the *personal* search for the reparation of the original bond between the human soul and its divine source, in order for the believer to see God face to face.

One of the most fascinating insights of Ladner's book is that the need for reform in early Christianity circles around the question of who is the agent of the reform. Is it the human being, specifically the human soul? Or is it God who is the only one with the necessary power to establish the human being's return to the divine? It is interesting to note that Ladner finds the first position in the works of the Greek fathers, whereas the second position can be identified with Augustine, both main sources for Christian thought in the Middle Ages and modernity.

In this contribution I want to discuss the ideas of reform in Nicholas of Cusa (1401–1464) as they can be found in his more speculative writings against the background of these two questions—the relation between personal and institutional reform on the one hand and the agency of reform on the other. I hope to show that the obvious relation between Cusanus and the reform movement of the Devotio Moderna—the *Brethren of the Common Life*—can offer a fruitful perspective in order to better understand Cusanus's idea of reform.

2. Ibid., 35.

VISION OF REFORM. POLITICS AND THE VISION OF GOD

It is quite well known that the idea of reform plays an important role in the life and work of Nicholas of Cusa. As a young lawyer he was a main actor in the discussion of ecclesial reforms during the Council of Basel, which resulted in his book *De concordantia catholica*, one of the major books on political thinking in the late Middle Ages. Cusanus discussed the need for reform of the papal institutions against the background of the history of the councils since the beginning of Christianity. He did so with an eye on the historical and changeable character of institutions and human laws. With the failure of the conciliar movement, however, the idea of reform seemed to disappear for a time in the writings of Cusanus. He turned towards a more speculative way of spiritual thinking, stressing the personal relation to the Divine and investigating the role of the cognitive powers in this process. The idea of reform only returns in his later book, the *Reformatio generalis,* written in 1460 on behalf of the pope. There he argues that ecclesiological reform presupposes personal reform, the ability of the soul to ascend toward its divine origin, in line with Ladner's observation about the concept of reform in early Christianity.[3] In this essay, I want to develop the idea that Cusanus, after the dramatic events in Basel, became convinced that every *vision of reform,* as he developed in *De concordantia catholica,* required primarily a *reform of vision*: a new way of seeing and observing, in which the ultimate vision of God becomes real al-

3. Nicholas of Cusa, *Writings on Church and Reform,* edited and translated by Thomas M. Izbicki (Aldershot, Vt.: Ashgate 2008), ch 6: "Nos igitur, qui cunctos Christianos reformare cupimus, utique aliam nullam possumus eis formam, quam imitentur proponere, quam Christi, a quo nomen receperunt. Illa est lex viva et forma perfecta, in qua fit iudicium vitae et mortis aeternae. Conformes ei sunt filii vitae benedicti, qui vocantur ad possessionem regni Dei. Difformes vero, quia filii mortis, maledicti in gehennam abiicientur. Esse igitur debet omne studium nostrum, ut abluamur poenitentia et reinduamus formam innocentiae, quam in lavacro Christi recepimus; tunc enim, quando Christus in gloria Dei Patris apparuerit, similes ei erimus, eiusdem scilicet formae, quae solum in regno Dei, ad quod tendimus, reperitur." *Reformatio generalis.*

ready in this world and is able to work through the earthly seeing. I hope to show that this *reform of vision* is an essential characteristic of Cusanus's way of thinking. It is in my view not by accident that most of the philosophical and theological works of the cardinal can be read as manuals, helping the reader in his or her attempt to reform their ways of seeing the world from the perspective of God. Again and again Cusanus refers to his proper attempts to understand the meaning of the vision of God as a *manuductio*. His are not definite and completed theories about the divine or of the process of divinization of the human being, but rather paradigmatic practices of searching and finding the divine within human life, of which the ecclesial life is a part. As I will show, his works are of a high mystagogic character, offering different ways of turning the perspective of actual human perception and vision.[4]

REFORM OF VISION

In his marvellous study on the gaze of Nicholas of Cusa, the French Jesuit Michel de Certeau refers to the remarkable fascination of the cardinal for the momentary glance within human vision and perception, interrupting the directive gaze or orientation of the viewer.[5] Even the superficial reader of *De visione Dei* recognizes immediately de Certeau's observation. For already in the riddle, hidden in the title of the book, where Cusanus plays with the subjective and objective genitive, one understands how the author directs the attention of the reader towards an oppositive perspective, which irritates the narrow understanding of the words. The ambiguity of the language leaves open whose vision is exactly the theme of the book. The scenery of the *De visione Dei* may be well known. The book is written on behalf of the Benedictine monks of the Abbey of Tegern-

4. Johannes Hoff, *Kontingenz, Berührung, Überschreitung. Zur philosophischen Propädeutik christlicher Mystik nach Nikolaus von Kues* (Freiburg/München: Verlag Karl Alber, 2007), 80 ff., 416 ff.

5. Michel de Certeau, "The Gaze of Nicholas of Cusa," *Diacritics* 17/3 (1987): 2–38.

see, who asked the cardinal for help in their spiritual search. They receive a painting, an omnivoyant portrait, whose look follows the viewer of the painting. It is interesting that Cusanus refers here in the text to a self-portrait of the Flemish painter Rogier van der Weyden, which was in the town hall of Brussels in the time of Cusanus.[6] This reference not only attests to the awareness of Cusanus of the newest developments in the visual arts of his time, but also shows how he is of the opinion that the *vision of God*—or *theoria*—can be found within actual cultural and human practices. In classical tradition since Plato, the ideal of *theoria* was reserved only for those who were free from earthly duties and cares.[7] Human action was in a way an obstacle for the action of God, leading the soul to its original state.[8] The reference to a work of art made by human hands—not an *acheiropoieton*—as the context in which the vision of God can be realized, is significant for a tendency present in the whole of Cusanus's work. Cusanus expresses this tendency himself in *Idiota de sapientia* and *De apice theoriae,* where he describes how in an earlier time he was searching for the divine truth and wisdom in dark and remote rooms. But "now" he realizes that, with the psalmist's words, "wisdom is proclaiming everywhere in the streets" (*clamat in plateis*).[9] Cusanus seems to be convinced that the monks of Tegernsee

6. Nicholas of Cusa, *De visione Dei* C II, H 81. "Harum etsi multae reperiantur optime pictae,—uti illa sagittarii in foro Nurembergensi, et Bruxellis Rogeri maximi pictoris in pretiosissima tabula, quae in praetorio habetur, et Confluentiae in capella mea Veronicae, et Brixinae in Castro angeli arma ecclesiae tenentis, et multae aliae undique—, ne tamen deficiatis in praxi, quae sensibilem talem exigit figuram, quam habere potui, caritati vestrae mitto tabellam, figuram cuncta videntis tenentem, quam eiconam Dei appello."

7. Andrea Wilson Nightingale, *Spectacles of Truth in Classical Greek Philosophy. Theoria in its Cultural Context* (Cambridge: Cambridge University Press, 2004).

8. Hannelore Rausch, *Theoria. Von ihrer sakralen zur philosophischen Bedeutung* (München: Wilhelm Fink Verlag, 1982).

9. "Ego autem tibi dico, quod 'sapientia foris' clamat 'in plateis,' et est clamor eius, quoniam ipsa habitat 'in altissimis.'" *Idiota de sapientia* I, 3; "Putabam ego aliquando ipsam in obscuro melius reperiri. Magnae potentiae veritas est, in qua posse ipsum valde lucet. Clamitat enim in plateis, sicut in libello De idiota legisti. Valde certe se undique facilem repertu ostendit" Nicolai de Cusa, Opera omnia, Hamburg 1940–2002, *De apice theoriae,* n 5.

are able to reach *theoria*, the vision of God, within the time of this earthly life, that is, within the universe of daily experience.

Cusanus develops a scene of theatre, to which the monks are invited to participate. It is a kind of experiment, which only makes sense if the reader, as the viewer, really becomes part of it in an active way. The experiment is a *practice* (*praxis*), in which—in the words of de Certeau—the *act* enables the words.[10] The vision of God cannot be achieved through theoretical efforts, but only inasmuch as the reader or viewer of the painting himself follows the path which is shown by Cusanus. Whoever enters this scenic space understands how he will be able to see the invisible divine light. The monk has to move from the right to the left and vice versa around the portrait, getting the impression that it has been made only for him and that he is in the center of the attention of the gaze. The more the viewer explores this way of seeing, the more he feels he is confirmed in his impression that he is at the center.

The amazement of the viewer on the circle around the portrait is intensified further when his brother in faith, performing the same experiment, reports the same experience. The fact that the second monk coming from the opposite direction has the same experience is incomprehensible for the first one. He cannot understand this, unless he believes what his colleague on the circle around the portrait is telling him—that he is in the center of the attention as well. "And so, through the disclosure of the respondent he will come to know that that face does not desert anyone who is moving—not even those who are moving in opposite directions."[11] He discovers that what he sees is only his way of seeing, from a concrete, determined point of view. He is not at the center at all; his way of seeing is only one of many ways of seeing. The point of the experiment, however, is that Cusanus does not see any reason to deny the truth of this concrete way of seeing—this perspective. Both perspectives

10. De Certeau, "The Gaze of Nicholas of Cusa," 15.

11. Nicholas of Cusa, *De visione Dei*, I, 4.

are true. It is only within his concrete way of seeing that the viewer understands that it is impossible to see perfectly and fully what he sees. Furthermore, he understands why he is not able to see it as it is in itself. For it is impossible to take a point of view other than his own. In *De docta ignorantia* Cusanus stresses that even if we would try another thousand years to imitate the position of the other, we never will achieve it.[12] We may be tied to our own perspective, but we are not its prisoners. The fact of being bound to our own concrete way of seeing and experiencing is, in the view of Cusanus, not the expression of a tragic situation at all. For it is only from within this perspective that we are able to understand that there are other ways of seeing and understanding. There always will be perspectives that we do not immediately grasp. However, this knowledge opens the possibility of seeing other perspectives. A human being is able to move in several directions in order to collect more points of view, though he only is able to integrate these within his own way of seeing. Therefore, Cusanus is able to quote in the sixth chapter of *De visione Dei* the critical argument of the Greek philosopher Xenophanes. There he says that God is for the lion a lion, for the ox an ox, for the young man he appears as a young man, for the old man like an older man.[13] It is interesting and also important that Cusanus quotes here Xenophanes—a citation that, as far as I know, is not found in any other medieval text.[14] For Cusanus, the argument gets a new meaning: it does not demonstrate the anthropomorphic way of religious thinking, as was the case in Xenophanes. Rather, it stresses the unavoidable character of human practices, in this case

12. "Etiam si mille annnis unus aliam imitari studeret in quocumque, numquam tamen praecisionem attingeret, licet differentia sensibilis aliquando non percipiatur." Nicolai de Cusa, Opera omnia, Hamburg 1940–2002, *De docta ignorantia* II, 1.

13. "Sic, si leo faciem tibi attribueret, non nisi leoninam iudicaret, et bos bovinam et aquila aquilinam. O Domine, quam admirabilis est facies tua, quam si iuvenis concipere vellet, iuvenilem fingeret, et vir virilem et senex senilem," Nicholas of Cusa, *De visione Dei* VI, H 191.

14. Pauline Moffit Watts, *Nicolau Cusanus. A Fifteenth Century Vision of Man* (Leiden: Brill, 1982), 115.

the practice of making images (which is one of the themes of the book, as the reference to van der Weyden may have shown already). In the view of Cusanus, the unavoidable character of images gives reason to take seriously concrete human practices. Even the most abstract metaphysical insights and ideas are bound to the practical human imagination. Therefore, the vision of God necessarily takes place within the context of human acting and practice. It is here that the reform can be achieved; it is here that every concrete image can become the image of God.

The divine truth remains invisible, but it is an invisibility working within the visible. Divine truth would become visible if human beings could see all perspectives at once, which is impossible. The invisible divine truth in the view of *De visione Dei* appears within the seeing of the senses already, as we become conscious of the paradoxes of visual experience itself. The meeting with the other monk on the line—the other viewer—shows us that we can see what we see only if we could see all possible ways of seeing. We only see what we see, if we were able to see it from all possible perspectives. Therefore, we see in fact something we cannot see. The point of this argument is that this "invisible" truth is not separated from the process of visual seeing. Far more, it is a constitutive part of it.

In everything we see, we are able to realize that there are always more ways of seeing than we can grasp. Again and again, Cusanus gives examples of these kinds of vanishing points within visual perception.[15] What is interesting here is the phenomenological way Cusanus is arguing when he shows that our direct way of seeing—our perspective—has been interrupted "suddenly." The act of perceiving itself confronts us with the limits of our perception. The confrontation with these limits is interpreted by Cusanus as an appeal to see in a new way. In *De visione Dei,* the viewer sees "suddenly" that he is the one who is viewed himself. In his perspec-

15. E.g. in his *De beryllo* from the year 1458 where Cusanus sees in the *coincidentia oppositorum* a vanishing point of our perception of reality.

tive there appears a vanishing point, which shows him the gaze of the other. In order to make clear what he wants to show Cusanus further sketches in another example. In chapter 10 of *De visione Dei,* Cusanus describes his own experience while he is preaching. Holding his sermon, he sees the men and women in the church listening to his words and realizes that every one of his listeners hears the sermon in his way, with his particular background, intelligence, and presuppositions. The meaning of his words is not exhausted at all by his own understanding of them. He becomes conscious of the fact that the real meaning of his words only can be understood through the totality of interpretations of the listeners in the church. To use a central category of *De concordantia catholica*: the meaning of the word can only be explained and developed through the *consent* of the hearers. The consent of the hearer is not some attitude *outside* the word, but is part of it. The same is true for the divine, which only can be imagined and seen through human images, as the reference to Xenophanes has already shown clearly. In other words, we have to imagine before it is possible to interrupt the direct perception of the image we are making. The need for consent shows that if we want to see what we see, we have to find another direction of seeing—a reform of vision.[16] It is not by accident that Cusanus refers to the painting practices of his time. Van der Weyden is named explicitly, but one also can think on the painting of Jan Van Eyck, who in all his works is playing with this kind of riddle—interrupting and interrupted perspectives—in order to open space for the real light, the light of God.[17] The perspectives are broken up so that they can become themselves images of God.

However, the art of painting is only one of the practices Cusanus is referring to when he aims at a "reform of vision." In fact, Cusanus

16. Recently, the famous German art historian Hans Belting referred to this characteristic of Cusanus's writings in his history of the gaze: Hans Belting, *Florenz und Bagdad. Eine westöstliche Geschichte des Blicks* (München: Beck Verlag, 2008), 135.

17. Craig Harbison, *Jan Van Eyck. The Play of Realism* (London: Reaktion Books, 1991)

seems to discover in the pictorial innovations of his time expressions of the need for inner reform felt at the time. He is convinced of the fact that institutional reform is not enough, and that there is a need of inner conversion. This inner conversion consists in the discovery of new ways of seeing the real. Cusanus is very well aware of the developments in the optics of his time, as is shown in recent research.[18]

There are a lot of places in his work where one can find this sudden interruption or disruption, this turning of perspective. In *De docta ignorantia,* one can see how this interruption is even constitutive for human knowledge in general. As is well known, knowledge for Cusanus is a question of measuring—*mensurari.* Whoever tries to know something he did not know before is comparing something which is uncertain with what is certain. To search for knowledge is to realize a proportion between what is known and what is still unknown. There is, however, at least one concept which limits this process of comparing. It is the concept of *maximum,* the greatest, which was well known to Cusanus from the work of Anselm. *Maximum* escapes necessarily the process of comparing, which is characterized by a difference between measure and measured reality. However, it is impossible to think of a measure outside the maximum. Then, it would be not the superlative *maximum* anymore. If we try to understand the meaning of *maximum,* the concept teaches us that it is incomparable, and in this sense it is also unknowable. Nevertheless, we know that it is unknowable, and we also know why. The concept of *maximum* confronts us not only with the limits of our knowing, but reveals to us within our practice of knowing what it means to know something. We learn that knowing something unknown is in fact the exploration of the measure we know already, the

18. Belting, *Florenz und Bagdad. Eine Westöstliche Geschichte des Blicks,* 125–40; Inigo Bocken, "Sehen und Gesehen Werden. Unendlichkeit und Sinnlichkeit im 15. Jahrhundert," in *Kann das Denken malen? Philosophie und Malerei in der Renaissance,* edited by Tilman Borsche and Inigo Bocken (München: Wilhelm Fink Verlag, 2010), 83–97.

measure we are using already when we are confronted with something we do not know yet. As such, the measure we know already appears as something unknown. If we are searching for the right, adequate measure in order to know, we have to investigate the measure we thought we knew already. Again, we see here in the midst of the practice of knowledge, the "sudden" turn of perspectives, which we only can see and not grasp by reason. Suddenly we discover that the measure we thought we knew is not so well known, but is unknown in itself. It presupposes another measure, unifying the known and the unknown, for example *maximum*. The sudden discovery shows us that, as is indicated in *De docta ignorantia*, it is the greatest possible measure (*maximum*) which is presupposed and intended, although never reachable. In other words: the epistemological arguments of Cusanus show that one can find already in the process of knowledge the need for "reform," though he did not use the word as such here. Real knowledge requires an attitude, the attitude of *docta ignorantia*. This attitude consists not only in the virtue of humility, but also in the awareness that our actual knowledge is always part of a more comprehensive process, in which perspectives differing from our first concrete starting perspective play a decisive role.[19] However, Cusanus is very well aware of the fact that we are never to able to understand this process outside of our own actual knowledge. Our actual knowing is required in order to think about the immeasurable truth. We have to do something, to act in the way we are, before we are able to see that a measure bigger than ours is acting within us.[20] In this sense, the *reformative* act always requires a *performative* act.

Another example, very close to the epistemological consider-

19. The proper role of humility in the attitude of *docta ignorantia* in contrast to the Augustinian version of it, is analyzed by the German philosopher Tilman Borsche, when he speaks of Cusanus understanding the stratagem of humility: Tilman Borsche, *Was Etwas ist. Fragen nach der Wahrheit der Bedeutung bei Platon, Augustin, Nikolaus von Kues und Nietzsche* (München: Wilhelm Fink Verlag, 1989), 173 ff.

20. "Ait enim Veritas: Non vos estis qui loquimin, sed spiritus patris vestri qui loquitur in verbis." Nicolai de Cusa, Opera omnia, Hamburg 1940–2002, *De docta ignorantia* II, 10, h I, p. 98n153.

ations in *De docta ignorantia,* is the reference in the third chapter of the same book to the relation between a polygon and a circumscribed circle.[21] Cusanus compares the relation between human mind and truth with the relation between a polygon and a circle. Although the circle is an infinite polygon, the latter will never reach the circle.[22] Enlarging the number of angles, we are able to see "suddenly" in a moment that the polygon is oriented towards a circle. Suddenly we see the circle by enlarging the angles. This seeing, however, cannot be achieved by logical argumentation. One has to see it; then one will understand. Some see it earlier; other mathematicians will need some more time.[23] We are, however, able to know the measure only in the endless process of measuring. Reform requires some exercise; it is situated within the creative, measuring act of men. A reformative act is always a performative act.

REFORM AND THE JUSTICE OF GOVERNMENT

The idea of reform, however not explicitly named as such, in this sense of the reciprocity of perspectives, and as such a reform of vision, can be found in *De coniecturis* (1441–1445). Cusanus discusses here the justice of government and the relation between the king and his subjects. In *De coniecturis* II.13 Cusanus describes how the obedience of the people can only be warranted inasmuch as the king understands his own actions in the light of his concern for the well-

21. Recently, Donald Duclow showed the central meaning of this image in his book *Masters of Learned Ignorance. Eriugena, Eckhart, Cusanus* (Aldershot, Vt.: Ashgate, 2006).

22. "Intellectus igitur, qui non est veritas, numquam veritatem adeo praecise comprehendit, quin per infinitum praecisius comprehendi possit, habens se ad veritatem sicut polygonia ad circulum, quae quanto inscripta plurium angulorum fuerit, tanto similior circulo, numquam tamen efficitur aequalis, etiam si angulos in infinitum multiplicaverit, nisi in identitatem cum circulo se resolvat." Nicolai de Cusa, Opera omnia, Hamburg 1940–2002, *De docta ignorantia* I, 3, h I, p. 9, nr. 10.

23. The same is true, as one can read in *De visione Dei,* for the reading of a book. Some will understand the content of a book immediately after a quick look at the book as a whole; some will never really understand the intention of the author even after a comprehensive reading of all its sentences. See Nicholas of Cusa, *De visione Dei* c. 8, h VI n 29.

being of the people (*salus populi*).[24] The power of the king is limited by the way the people expect this cure from him. A just government can only be achieved inasmuch as both of these perspectives can become identical, so that the governor sees the *salus populi* as his own well being. In fact, the structure of the argument is the same as that in *De visione Dei*. There is a rupture between the perspective of the people and that of the king, whose perspective represents the whole of all perspectives. As in *De visione Dei*, where the vision of God can only be achieved in a human way, as the reinterpretation of the Xenophaneian argument shows us, the perspective of the governor can only be explained and developed within the several perspectives of the people. The reform of the individual citizen consists in his awareness of the common good, represented in the image of the king. The reform of governance consists in the awareness of the "autonomy"—to use this somewhat modern concept—of the perspective of the citizen, namely the viewers. There is no way to find a synthesis in a rational way. Only in the practice of governing can this justice of government be achieved. In Cusanus's political considerations about the conjectural character of just government, we find the same reciprocity of perspectives as in his theological considerations in *De visione Dei*. At least here, it becomes clear that the reform of vision is not excluding a vision of reform. Far more, Cusanus seems to understand that the criteria of reform have to be found again and again, in every practice anew and in a different way.

24. "Dum enim regnicolis quibusdam regalem curam propter eos esse videtur, rex non minus ipsam in se reflectendo se suae curae et salutis populi finem constituit. Nec esset voluntaria populi oboedientia et principis diligentia, si et populus se subiectionis et rector se etiam laborum suorum non conicerent praemia hinc inde suscepturos. Quapropter rector naturalis in veritatis legibus incedens causas ipsas, quantum potest, in unum nectit, ut in populi salute suam quoque arbitretur. Haec summatim, quantum hoc loco datum est, de intellectualium spirituum natura dicta sufficiant." Nicolai de Cusa, Opera omnia, Hamburg 1940–2002, *De coniecturis* II, 13, n 139.

This chapter started with a reference to the layman, who plays a crucial role in several of Cusanus's works. In his three dialogues with the *idiota,* Cusanus presents the layman as a kind of phenomenologist who is observing his own occupations without being hindered by learned judgments. In this case, the layman reflects on what is going on while making a spoon.[25] The spoon-maker claims to possess a creative ability which does not need any real object which his art imitates: "The spoon has no other exemplar except our mind's idea of the spoon.... In my work I do not imitate the visible form of any natural object, for such forms of spoons, dishes and jars are perfected by human artistry alone."[26]

The layman describes the process of the production of the spoon, whose exemplar is invented by the mind and which is realized in wood. However, the spoon is not realized in a perfect way. The spoon maker describes his experience that the idea of the spoon which he has in mind is never fully realized by the one he makes. This, in fact, is the experience of every artist: the real and concrete work of art is still not able to fully and exhaustively express the artist's idea. There can still be alternative expressions, and although it is the artist's own idea, he is able to understand that it is still not the ultimate, divine idea. The artist discovers in his practice of making the measure which determines his act of making. In his own idea he is confronted with a measure which is not fully known by himself.

There is no doubt that Cusanus was well aware that the idea of the *idiota* refers to the reform movement of the Devotio Moderna,

25. This example has been made famous by Hans Blumenberg's analysis of modernity in his *Legitimität der Neuzeit* (Frankfurt a.M. 1966), 20; see Elizabeth Brient, *The Immanence of the Infinite: Hans Blumenberg and the Threshold of Modernity* (Washington, D.C.: The Catholic University of America Press, 2002), 184 and passim.

26. "Coclear extra mentis nostrae ideam aliud non habet exemplar. Nam etsi statuarius aut pictor trahat exemplaria a rebus, quas figurare satagit, non tamen ego, qui ex lignis cocleana et scutellas et ollas ex luto educo. Non enim in hoc imitor figuram cuiuscumque rei naturalis." Nicolai de Cusa, Opera omnia, Hamburg 1940–2002, *Idiota de mente* II, h V n 62.

which was founded in Deventer and spread very successfully in the Netherlands, Germany, and Switzerland in the time of Cusanus. Several studies in recent years showed that the relation between Cusanus and the Devotio Moderna was quite complicated.[27] Being papal legate in Germany and the Netherlands, the canon lawyer Nicholas of Cusa seemed to be anxious about the unity of the church, which was threatened by the large number of the independent houses of brothers and sisters in this movement. His policy towards its development was characterized by a critical distance. In regard to their spirituality, however, Cusanus's attitude towards the brothers and sisters of the common life was far more positive. It is well known that the legate Cusanus attempted to establish the rule of Windesheim in several monasteries and orders.

One of the main reasons for the success of the Devotio Moderna was certainly the development of cities in the Netherlands and Flanders in fifteenth century.[28] The movement can be seen as a kind of monastic life for the citizen.[29] The urban character of this reform movement initiated by Geert Groote had implications for the attitude toward a hierarchical interpretation of reality. For in the view of its main spiritual authors, like Thomas à Kempis, the divine hierarchy never can be articulated by human ideas. It is in the practice of daily life that inner reform has to take place. The brothers and sisters of common life had to discover the image of God within themselves—*imitatio Christi*—by living their humble active life and performing their reform towards Christ in daily duties and work.[30] Geert Groote and Thomas à Kempis were very well aware of the

27. Nikolas Staubach, "Cusanus und die devotio moderna," in *Conflict and Reconciliation. Perspectives on Nicholas of Cusa*, edited by Inigo Bocken (Leiden: Brill, 2004), 31–56; Inigo Bocken, "The Language of the Layman. The Meaning of the *imitatio Christi* for a Theory of Spirituality," *Studies in Spirituality* 15 (2005): 217–49.

28. John Van Engen, *Sisters and Brothers of the Common Life. The Devotio Moderna and the World of the Late Middle Ages* (Philadelphia: University of Pennsylvania Press, 2008).

29. Berndt Hamm, *Bürgertum und Glaube. Konturen der städtischen Reformation*, (Göttingen: Königshausen und Neumann, 1996).

30. Van Engen, *Sisters and Brothers of the Common Life*, 15.

fact that human beings never can leave the domain of human action, which is the field in which God's action becomes apparent.[31] Inspired by nominalist theology, the faithful had in this view the task to discover the active power of God within the human order of action.

There is a clear relationship between this paradigm of theory and action and the figure of the *idiota* in Cusanus. Cusanus never ceases to stress that the human being has the ability to think for himself. The *idiota* is the one who is able to liberate himself from every form of outer knowledge of tradition and to understand that wisdom proclaims itself openly in the streets. The whole process of truth and reality starts all over again with every individual. As is stressed in the main writings of the Devotio Moderna, every human being has to follow the path of Christ over and over again. The philosophy of Cusanus seems to deliver the ontological background of this way of thinking. Referring to the infinity of the universe, as is the case in the second book of *De docta ignorantia*, Cusanus attempts to demonstrate that in an infinite circle, the center is everywhere and necessarily identical with its periphery.[32] In other words, every place in the universe is center. We are able to know *that* the center is everywhere; however, it is not possible for human beings to understand all the centers at the same time. This ability is reserved for God, who is the real center that never can be reached by rational arguments. In this tension between the concrete and the divine center, man can be understood in the view of Cusanus as microcosm in which the whole of reality is present, though in the way of his concrete being.

It is precisely here that we meet a further meaning of the idea of the layman, namely the concrete character of the reform. Given the task to start all over again in each individual, the vision of God can

31. See Heiko Obermann, *Zwei Reformationen. Luther und Calvin* (München: Siedler Verlag, 2002), 36–40.

32. "Centrum igitur mundi coincidit cum circumferentia." Nicolai de Cusa, Opera omnia, Hamburg 1940–2002, *De docta ignorantia* II, 11, h I, p. 100, n 154.

only be reached within practice—within the context of several attempts to achieve this vision. The disruptive and interruptive break between the human perspective and the divine can only be repaired in a personal practice, in becoming the image of God yourself.

This dimension opens new perspectives on the relation between theory and practice in the fifteenth century, as I mentioned already with regard to the developments in the visual arts. For becoming the image of God can only be practiced in concrete, finite enterprises. This means that one can achieve this reform in every human action—in painting as well as in spoon making (as is the case in *Idiota de mente*).

The idea of reform in the speculative thinking of Cusanus can be defined as the attempt to integrate perspectives, which are breaking up the actual existing perspective. In this sense, Cusanus's attempts to reform are not absent after *De concordantia catholica*. The intuition of this book goes further—for example, in the idea of consent—which is decisive for the way man can become the image of God.

The discovery of the need of inner reform in the concrete practice of seeing the world, as can be found in *De visione Dei*, is connected with the spiritual developments in the reform movement of the Devotio Moderna. Also one can find here, as is the case in the *De imitatione Christi*, the need of seeing in a different way. We have to discover the interruptions in our daily seeing of the world. The relation between the Devotio Moderna and the innovations in the practices of seeing and painting has been well discussed in the last few years.[33] Until recently many scholars believed that both developments—the innovations in painting and the spiritual reform within the Devotio Moderna—had nothing to do with each other, or had

33. Kees Veelenturf, *Geen povere schoonheid. Laatmiddeleeuwse kunst in verband met de Moderne Devotie*, (Nijmegen: Valkhof Pers, 2000), 85–112 and passim; Heiko A. Oberman, *The Two Reformations. The Journey from the Last Days to the New World* (New Haven: Yale University Press, 2003), 45–60.

even to be seen as opposite cultural developments. In Cusa's way of understanding *reform,* however, it can become clear that there is an intrinsic relation between the new ways of seeing in concrete pictorial practices and in the devotion of everyday life, as it can be found in the tradition of the Devotio Moderna.[34] The interruptions of earthly seeing in the view of Cusanus refer to the presence of the divine vision we are able to discover in our everyday life experience.

CONCLUSION: THE IDEA OF REFORM AT THE THRESHOLD OF MODERNITY

In this chapter I have analyzed the idea of reform in the work and practice of Nicholas of Cusa, against the background of the pious movement of the *devotio moderna*. The case of Nicholas of Cusa may be a convincing illustration of Ladner's intuition that "reform" is one of the most fundamental principles of Christianity. Both in an institutional and in a spiritual way, the return to the original "form"—in the sense of *christiformitas*—can be seen as one of the central intuitions of Cusan theories and political practice. At the same time, Cusanus is confronted with one of the main problems at the base of the modern idea of progressive evolution. It is the awareness of the inaccessibility of the ultimate divine measure that is crucial for Cusanus. This inaccessibility was one of the motives of the modern idea of progression, differing from the Christian idea of reform. However, Cusanus's theories can be understood as attempts to tackle this problem of the unknowable measure by referring to human practice as the concrete scene on which the divine becomes manifest, a lesson he learned without any doubt from the Devotio Moderna.

34. Bocken, "The Language of the Layman," 217–49.

13

CARTHUSIANS AS PUBLIC INTELLECTUALS

Cloistered Religious as Advisors to Lay Elites on the Eve of the Protestant Reformation

DENNIS D. MARTIN

Recent scholarship has begun to reinvigorate our understanding of reform along Ladnerian lines in the century before the Protestant Reformation. Scholars of the German Protestant Reformation from Bernd Moeller to Berndt Hamm have, over a period of nearly fifty years, pointed to the rise of educated administrative elites in the cities and at princely courts as central carriers of the reform impulse. Where once the Reformation was explained against the background of sets of ideas, for example late scholastic theology and Renaissance humanism, for the past several decades we have focused on those who applied these ideas in public chanceries and public squares.[1]

1. Berndt Hamm, *Frömmigkeitstheologie am Anfang des 16. Jahrhunderts: Studien zu Johannes von Paltz und seinem Umkreis*, Beiträge zur historischen Theologie, 65 (Tübingen: J. C. B. Mohr, 1982). See also Berndt Hamm, *Lazarus Spengler (1479–1534): Der Nürnberger Ratsschreiber im Spannungsfeld von Humanismus und Reformation, Politik und Glaube*, Spätmittelalter und Reformation. Neue Reihe, 25 (Tübingen: Mohr Siebeck, 2004). Some

Daniel Hobbins's well-known article on Jean Gerson as an "author" and "public intellectual" helped shift the context for Gerson away from the university milieu and from "scholastic theology" as a set of ideas to the broader stage of public life and to theology as applied to public moral questions.[2] Less well known, however, is Dieter Mertens's anticipation of parts of Hobbins's thesis in an effort to grapple with the post-Gersonian writings of the Carthusian reformer James the Carthusian (Iacobus Cartusiensis, Jacob Kunike de Paradiso, d. 1465).[3] In many ways, Berndt Hamm's *Frömmigkeitstheologie,*

---

of his essays are available in English in *The Reformation of Faith in the Context of Late Medieval Theology and Piety,* edited by Robert J. Bast (Leiden: Brill, 2004). Berndt Hamm, *Bürgertum und Glaube: Konturen der städtischen Reformation* (Göttingen : Vandenhoeck & Ruprecht, 1996); Rudolf Suntrup and Jan R. Veenstra, editors, *Stadt, Kanzlei und Kultur im Übergang zur Frühen Neuzeit/City Culture and Urban Chanceries in an Era of Change,* Kultureller Wandel vom Mittelalter zur Frühen Neuzeit/Medieval to Early Modern Culture, vol. 4 (Frankfurt a. M. and New York: Peter Lang, 2004); Robert Gramsch, *Erfurter Juristen im Spätmittelalter: Die Karrieremuster und Tätigkeitsfelder einer gelehrten Elite des 14. und 15. Jahrhunderts,* Education and Society in the Middle Ages and Renaissance, 17 (Leiden: Brill, 2003) are representative of a vast literature, including a variety of typically massive essays by Klaus Schreiner in volumes of conference proceedings. A starting point is "Laienfrömmigkeit—Frömmigkeit von Eliten oder Frömmigkeit des Volkes," in *Laienfrömmigkeit im späten Mittelalter: Formen, Funktionen, politisch-soziale Zusammenhänge,* edited by Klaus Schreiner and Elisabeth Müller-Luckner, Schriften des Historischen Kollegs: Kolloquien, 20 (Munich: Oldenbourg, 1992), 1–78.

2. Daniel Hobbins, "The Schoolman as Public Intellectual: Jean Gerson and the Late Medieval Tract," *American Historical Review* 108.5 (December 2003), 1308–37. A revised form of the article appears as chapter 5 in *Authorship and Publicity before Print: Jean Gerson and the Transformation of Late Medieval Learning* (Philadelphia: University of Pennsylvania Press, 2009).

3. *Iacobus Cartusiensis: Untersuchungen zur Rezeption der Werke des Kartäusers Jakob von Paradies (1381–1465),* Veröffentlichungen des Max-Planck Instituts für Geschichte, 50; Beiträge zur Germania Sacra, 13 (Göttingen: Vandenhoeck und Ruprecht, 1976), 136: "In the writings of the *eximius doctor Iacobus Carthusiensis* both professor and monk speak ... not about scholarly themes but about the monastic life and its reform, as well as the reform of other 'states of life.' His writings carry relevance because they deal with [*behandeln,* i.e., *tractare*]—independently of the requirements of university instruction—the problems of contemporary reform movements, by seeking to make *scientia* and *sapientia* bear fruit in solving current problems. They construct neither doctrinal systems (where they do this, they find no dissemination) nor guide directly to contemplation more by *affectus* than *intellectus.* Instead they use scholarly means to work through practical problems, that is, right and serviceable behavior (*prudentissime hominum saluti providet*). Because and to the degree that they provide this they become useful (*utilis*) to their recipients.... A comparison of James's literary production with that of the professors teaching at the same time at

published a few years later, grappled with the same problem: how to understand literature that fully fits neither scholastic theological categories nor monastic devotional writing.[4]

Monastic reform was once viewed as a matter of structural renewal and practice of spirituality largely within monasteries, while "popular religiosity" was similarly studied for its own sake. In recent decades, however, Eamon Duffy on lay religious practice in England, Augustine Thompson on Italian cities, and John Van Engen on the Devotio Moderna in Germanic regions have helped revitalize our understanding of how religious practice could flourish in the day in, day out life of relatively ordinary people. They have thus turned our attention away from the spectacular practices of the "unquiet souls" studied by Richard Kieckhefer and the "high culture" of Renaissance humanists or late scholastic speculative theologians and philosophers to the less obvious sources of information embedded in parish church design, wills and testaments, and annotations in the margins of daily prayer books soiled by the pious fingers of middling, educated lay folk.[5]

---

the university [in Erfurt] shows that the themes taken up by James find no specific treatment among the academics, not even among the members of religious orders teaching at the university. The demand for a literature that was theologically grounded (*autenticus*) but which dealt with the problems of religious life in outsider's [*exoterisch*] language (*stilo non tamen difficili et inusitato*) is demonstrated above all by the enormous reception of the works of Gerson in the fifteenth century.... The writings of James were often transmitted together with those of Gerson, since they, like his, were—as *libri autentici* and *libri devoti*—immediately useful to their readers."

Hobbins is aware of some of the earlier efforts to define and describe the "common" and public theology he has studied in Jean Gerson. On p. 125 of *Authorship and Publicity* he cites Berndt Hamm's *Frömmigkeitstheologie*, including a reference to Johann of Hagen's description of his goal of writing in "a simple and intelligible style." At p. 191, after summarizing the distribution of Denys the Carthusian's writings, he briefly describes that of James the Carthusian, based on Dieter Mertens's monograph. But only Denys appears on Hobbins's chart of tractate writers, pp. 137–139. Ironically, Denys the Carthusian was not formally a university master, whereas James the Carthusian did have a brief teaching career at Kraków and thus would have fit better in the chart than Denys.

4. See also Sven Grosse, *Heilsungewissheit und Scrupulositas im späten Mittelalter: Studien zu Johannes Gerson und Gattungen der Frömmigkeitstheologie seiner Zeit*, Beiträge zur historischen Theologie, 85 (Tübingen: J. C. B. Mohr, 1994).

5. Eamon Duffy, *The Stripping of the Altars: Traditional Religion in England, c. 1400–*

The present paper seeks to extend the range of this re-visioning to the manner in which the educated bourgeois and petty aristocratic administrators of the fifteenth century turned to cloistered monks for theological, church-law, and moral advice about how to exercise their mundane obligations. The Erfurt Carthusian monk, James the Carthusian—a former teacher at the University of Kraków and staunch conciliarist—and the Fleming Denys the Carthusian have received considerable attention. In the present study we shall focus specifically on the Erfurt Carthusian Johann Brewer of Hagen (d. 1476),[6] a younger contemporary of James the Carthusian. Johann had a carefully thought-out justification for the seeming anomaly of a cloistered Carthusian giving advice to a narrow but well-placed public, based on his own theology of the holiness of ordinary life in the world. His tractate on the spirituality of medicine will serve to illustrate. A further example, by an anonymous Carthusian (probably Johann of Hagen), offers particularly visible Ladnerian reform credentials. In this instance, an expert opinion occasioned by the visions granted to Denys the Carthusian after the Fall of Constantinople single-mindedly employs the Turkish invasions to exhort its readers to personal salvific reform along the lines of Gerhart Ladner's *The Idea of Reform*.[7]

---

c. 1580 (New Haven: Yale University Press, 1992); Eamon Duffy, *Marking the Hours: English People and Their Prayers 1240–1570* (New Haven: Yale University Press, 2006); Augustine Thompson, *Cities of God: The Religion of the Italian Communes, 1125–1325* (University Park, Pa.: Pennsylvania State University Press, 2005); John H. Van Engen, *Sisters and Brothers of the Common Life: The Devotio Moderna and the World of the Later Middle Ages* (Philadelphia: University of Pennsylvania Press, 2008).

6. The fundamental study is Joseph Klapper, *Der Erfurter Kartäuser Johannes Hagen: Ein Reformtheolog des 15. Jahrhunderts*, 2 vols., Erfurter Theologische Studien, 9–10 (Leipzig: St. Benno Verlag, 1960/61). Stephen M. Metzger has published a thorough census of surviving manuscripts of Johann of Hagen's corpus of writings: "The Manuscripts of Writings by Ioannes Hagen de Indagine, O. Cart.," *Bulletin de philosophie médiévale*, 50 (2008), 175–256. The immense Erfurt Charterhouse library catalogue found in Erfurt Domarchiv Hist. 6 was published by Paul J. G. Lehmann as *Mittelalterliche Bibliothekskatalogue Deutschland und der Schweiz*, vol. 2: *Bistum Mainz: Erfurt* (Munich: C. H. Beck, 1928). The catalogue of the Karthause Salvatorberg occupies pp. 232–593, while 581–93 contain comments by the librarian, Conrad Volradi about John von Hagen and a listing of his writings with their shelfmarks.

7. *Sentimentum cuiusdam Cartusiensis super Infestationem Thorcorum* found in Brixen,

Disillusioned after the Council of Basel, James the Carthusian, a university professor and Cistercian from the monastery of Paradies east of Frankfurt on the Oder joined the Carthusians at Erfurt in 1442. As Dieter Mertens, supplemented more recently by Christoph Fasbender,[8] has shown in great detail, his Carthusian *confratres* intentionally disseminated his writings throughout German-speaking Europe. Though his popularity did not reach the level of Jean Gerson, his most widely transmitted work, on ghostly apparitions, survives in nearly eighty manuscripts and fourteen printed editions. Two more titles, on the art of dying and on the "evils of this age," survive in more than fifty manuscripts each; three more—on monastic reform, ecclesiastical offices, and the jubilee year—are known in more than forty copies each. Eleven other works, including many on social and economic issues, are each extant in more than thirty manuscripts. All together, fifty of his writings survive in at least ten copies each, disseminated through a network of Carthusians, Benedictines, Austin Canons, and former Erfurt teachers and students.[9] Missing almost entirely from his corpus are commentaries on Scripture, but he wrote on annuity contracts, Masses for the dead, the vice of dancing, and whether one legitimately might mill grain on Sundays, as well as such typical spiritual and devotional themes as how to live more se-

Neustift [Augustinian Canons], Ms. 754, fol. 13r–18r; Vienna, Österreichische Nationalbibliothek, cvp 4067, 176v–186v.

8. Christoph Fasbender, "Die deutsche Philologie und das Erbe der Kartäuser," in *Das Erbe der Kartäuser*, edited by Jürg Ganz and Margrit Früh, Analecta Cartusiana, 160 (Salzburg: Institut für Anglistik und Amerikanistik, 2000), 134–44; Christoph Fasbender, *Von der Wiederkehr der Seelen Verstorbener: Untersuchungen zu Überlieferung und Rezeption eines Erfolgstextes Jakobs von Paradies; mit einem Abdruck des Autographs*, Jenaer Germanistische Forschungen, Neue Folge 12 (Heidelberg: C. Winter, 2001).

9. In addition to Mertens's 1976 study, see Ludger Meier, *Die Werke des Erfurter Kartäusers Jakob von Jüterbog in ihrer Handschriftlichen Überlieferung*, Beiträge zur Geschichte der Philosophie und Theologie des Mittelalters, 37, Heft 5 (Münster: Aschendorff, 1955); Dieter Mertens, *Iacobus Cartusiensis*, 277–85; *Jakub z Paradyża, Opuscula inedita*, edited by Stanisław Andrzej Porębski, Textus et studia historiam theologiae in Polonia excultae spectantia, 5 (Warsaw: Akademia Teologii Katolickiej, 1978).

curely (that is, rightly, in religious life) (*De statu securiore incedendi in hac vita*) and "the little flame of devotion." His *De habitibus acquisitis et infusis ac de caritate*, a nuanced summary of the various positions of the scholastic doctors on justification, grace, free will, and predestination,[10] offers a sort of "soteriology for dummies" exercise in public theology that merits attention in light of the debates over these issues that would roil early sixteenth-century Christendom.

In contrast, Denys the Carthusian also wrote on a wide range of topics, including commentaries on each book of the Bible, but with considerably more limited distribution.[11] He never intended to write for a broader audience. The public transmission of his writings began ten years after that of James the Carthusian and arose from encouragement given him by activist preachers and reformers, most notably Nicholas of Cusa during his reform legation of 1451–1452. Some of Denys's writings—for instance, his *Sentences* commentaries or his compendium of Aquinas's theology (*Summa fidei orthodoxae*)—survive only in printed form from the *Opera Omnia* editions of the sixteenth and nineteenth centuries. His most widely circulated work is the account of his visions regarding the Fall of Constantinople, which has survived in seventeen copies. His Scripture commentaries are known in at best one or two manuscripts each. Today, Denys the Carthusian is routinely employed as a benchmark for pre-Protestant Reformation Catholic theology, but only because his collected writings were published in the sixteenth and nineteenth centuries.[12] Scholars have employed them readily without realizing that

10. Meier, no. 47; dated in 1449 by Mertens; edited by Porębski from Breslau University Library, I Fol. 321, found in autograph in a Dresden manuscript FN1Landesbibliothek cod. P 42, dated 1449; Mertens, *Iacobus Cartusiensis*, 38.

11. See Kent Emery, Jr., *Dionysii Cartusiensis Opera Selecta: Prolegomena: Bibliotheca Manuscripta*, 1B: *Studia Bibliographica*, Corpus Christianorum Continuatio Mediaevalis, 121A (Turnhout: Brepols, 1991), esp. the "Novus Elenchus" of Denys's writings found on 445–540.

12. *Doctoris ecstatici D. Dionyisii Cartusiensis Opera Omnia* (Montreuil, Tournai, Parkminster: Typis Cartusiae S.M. de Pratis [Charterhouse of Notre-Dame-de-Pres], 1896–1913), 42 vols. bound in 44.

Denys's corpus of writings was less typical of Carthusian "public theology," in many ways, than that of either James the Carthusian or Johann Brewer of Hagen.

Johann, the second of our two Erfurt Carthusians, was the one with the most deliberate tractate-writing program of all three Carthusians and the one who carefully catalogued all his writings and recorded a *diarium* of his life as a public intellectual, though his "public" was the smallest and most idiosyncratic of the three. Indeed, he seems to have been mostly a private consultant to public figures at princely courts and in the urban chanceries, in business and the civic community. Many of his tracts survive only in crabbed autographs.

Born about 1415, Johann Brewer appears to have studied arts and perhaps some law at Cologne in the 1430s, arriving at Erfurt in 1439 to study law but entering the Charterhouse a few months later, in January 1440.[13] He tells us that he spent his first ten years as a Carthusian in massive systematic reading, prayer, and much excerpting. After fourteen years he began serving as head of Carthusian houses, first at Eisenach (the location of the court of a collateral branch of the Saxon-Thüringian dukes), then at Erfurt itself (1457–1460), followed by Frankfurt on the Oder (1460/61–1464), where the margraves of Brandenburg held court, and finally at Stettin near the mouth of the Oder River (1464–1467), before returning for what proved to be nine years as a simple monk at Erfurt.

From two distinct catalogue-diaries of his life and writings,[14] we

13. Klapper gives Johann's remarkable autobiographical account, in which he explained that after pondering the "short duration and misery of human life, especially since at that time (it was the year 1440) pestilence reigned in Erfurt," he decided to enter the Charterhouse before finishing his degree because he thought that without a degree he might be able to avoid being importuned to become head of a charterhouse. He noted the irony that he wrote these autobiographical notes after having become prior. Klapper, 1:14–15.

14. The first was compiled 1456–57 at Eisenach-Erfurt (Erfurt Domarchiv Hs. Hist. 1, fol. 335r–348r); the second begun at Frankfurt-Oder and finished ca. 1468 in Erfurt (ibid., fol. 251r–274r). Both have been systematized and excerpted liberally in Klapper 2:145–53, 128–39.

learn that, after ten years of silent reading and study, he began to respond to urgent requests from lay people and fellow religious to employ his knowledge of Scripture, law, theology, and civic life to their benefit. His was not a broad public but a well-placed one. Because he in many cases was responding ad hoc to specific requests, many extern copies have been lost and we are largely dependent today on the copies he kept for his own records.[15]

At first his works were mostly derivative of the body of writings by James the Carthusian,[16] but he soon found his own voice.[17] He describes in detail how and when he began. "In 1451 I was induced by various people and especially by my superior to write some things useful to others, so that not only I but others would profit from my reading. Although at first I was unwilling, nevertheless I acquiesced to their desire."[18] He seems to have met Nicholas of Cusa when the latter visited Erfurt in June 1451 on his reform legation,[19] and it is not farfetched to assume that Nicholas was among those who urged him to write "for the utility of others," just as Nicholas had urged Denys the Carthusian. At the same time, however, one ought not forget that by 1451 the Carthusians at Erfurt, including, presumably, Johann of Hagen, had been engaged in deliberate "publishing" of James the Carthusian's tracts for the better part of

15. Stipulating in his detailed catalogues that each monastery he served should become owner of those treatises written during his time spent at that house. The preponderance of autographs is now clearly established by Metzger's manuscript census (see note 6 above).

16. This according to a comment in Paderborn Erzbischöfliche Akademische Bibliothek, cod. 118 (formerly Erfurt Charterhouse library H 101), fol. 133v, as transcribed by Klapper 2:37, cf. 1:31–32.

17. See Dieter Mertens, "Hagen, Johannes (von Hagen)" in *Die deutsche Literatur des Mittelalters: Verfasserlexikon*, 2nd ed., edited by Kurt Ruh, Franz Josef Worstbrock, Burghart Wachinger, and others (Berlin: Walter de Gruyter, 1977–2006), vol. 3 (1981), col. 390 (hereafter cited as VL).

18. From the second register of his writings (the one that covers only the period up to 1457); Klapper 2:145–46, fol. 336v.

19. See Klapper 1:35, 59–60, 72, 84, 96–99, 115–17, 124 and Erich Meuthen, with Hermann Hallauer, *Acta Cusana: Quellen zur Lebensgeschichte des Nikolaus von Kues*, 4 vols. in 5 (Hamburg : Meiner, 1976–2000), index, particularly # 1367; cf. Klapper, 1:117.

a decade. Furthermore, both authors understood the need to adjust their style and content to a broader audience. For James the Carthusian the tractate genre aimed at a "not difficult and unaccustomed style" while Johann of Hagen tells us he sought to express "simple doctrine in a common and easily understandable style."[20]

Thus Johann of Hagen did not stumble into tractate writing. Indeed he worked out a theoretical grounding for this activity, employing the principle of allegory.[21] Activity in the world had, in itself, spiritual meaning. In Johann's view, one need not be a cleric or monk to be spiritually engaged, rather, the monastic life itself serves the *aedificatio aliorum*,[22] a point on which he and James the Carthusian disagreed.[23] Temporal activity signifies beyond its temporality, if done *sub specie aeternitatis*. Laymen need not, therefore, devalue their activity in the world in deference to supposedly "higher" spiritual callings, rather, their lives signify spiritually when lived in light of their creaturely relationship to the Creator. Since God alone is the End worthy of true enjoyment and all created things (therefore all temporal activity) are means toward that End, *cupiditas* falsely treats this life and temporal activity as an end in itself, but Christian *caritas* truly values created, temporal things and activity as means to the End, namely, enjoyment of God. The "universal call to holiness"—often considered an innovation at the Second Vatican Council—was alive and well in the mind of a fifteenth-century Carthusian in Erfurt.[24]

20. *"stilo non tamen difficili et inusitato"*; *"facilem doctrinam in stilo communi et facili omnibus intelligibilem."* Klapper 2:132; cited Mertens VL 3:390.

21. Mertens in VL 3:397; Heinrich Rüthing, "Jean Hagen," in *Dictionnaire de Spiritualité ascetique et mystique*, edited by Marcel Viller and others (Paris: Beauchesne, 1932–1995), vol. 8 (1974), 543–52, at 543.

22. Rüthing, DSAM 8:543; Mertens in VL 3:397.

23. Examined in some detail by Mertens, *Iacobus Cartusiensis*, 203–35

24. Nor was this unique to Johann among Carthusians. More than two and a half centuries earlier, Adam of Eynsham, secretary and biographer to the Carthusian saint, Hugh of Lincoln (d. 1200) wrote: "To lay persons who praised this angelic way of life and lamented the hindrances of life in the world, and whom he knew had neither the intention nor the capacity to follow a better way of life, he gave the following advice, 'The kingdom

In pursuit of this goal, Johann wrote approximately four hundred works, many of them very short. Before looking at a specific example, we shall survey the larger picture. Johann's writings ranged from several treatises on contracts (really, a general theory of business ethics)[25] and other utterly down-to-earth business matters (which mattered greatly to monasteries living from investments) to contemplative spirituality to such grubby details of church reform as whether requiring entrance endowments of new monks and nuns constituted simony. Like Denys the Carthusian, he wrote commentaries on each book of the Bible, commenting on some books as many as six or ten times (the Song of Songs and the Apocalypse). He also wrote on Marian topics, integrating all the leading female figures from the Old Testament (for example, Esther and Judith) with Marian theology.[26]

Thus, while Johann produced conventional works on the full range of contemplative, mystical, ascetic, and moral theology topics, he also wrote on a variety of economic and political topics: for example, on droughts and rain-imploring Masses[27] and, at the request of Landgrave Wilhelm of Thüringia's master of agriculture, on the spirituality of farming (*De agricultura corporali et spirituali et de*

of God is not confined only to monks, hermits and anchorites. When at the last, the Lord shall judge every individual, he will not hold it against him that he has not been a hermit or a monk, but will reject each of the damned because he had not been a real Christian. A Christian is expected to possess three virtues, and if, on the day of judgment he lacks any of them, the name of *Christian* will be useless to him.' The man of God ... taught that even married people, who never rose above the natural obligations of their state, should not be considered to be devoid of the virtue of chastity but equally with virgins and celibates would be admitted to the glory of the heavenly kingdom." See Adam of Eynsham, *Magna Vita Sancti Hugonis*, edited and translated by Decima L. Douie and Hugh Farmer (London: Nelson, 1961; Oxford, 1985), IV.9 (vol. 2, 43–48, at 46–47).

25. Extant in Paderborn Erzbischöfliche Akademische Bibliothek cod. 118, 176r–ca. 185r. See Klapper 2:150–51, 129.

26. The Erfurt catalogue edited by Lehmann (note 6 above) lists *Expositio libri Judith de beata Virgine* (C 11; extant in Parkminster cc. 9 [D 170]; *Expositio libri Esther de beata Virgine* in C 14, item 11, not extant, though possibly it could be Jena U-LB MS Elect. f. 41. See Klapper 2:11.

27. Klapper 2:135, Hist. 1, fol. 262r: *De causa siccitatis et de remediis ac officiis misse pro pluvia*.

agricolis),[28] as well as whether monasteries may licitly supply cartage services in military campaigns as part of their feudal obligations (*An licitum sit religiosis concedere currus ad bella*).[29] He wrote a series of tractates for the landgraves of Thüringia, the duke of Saxony, the prince elector of Brandenburg and their various noble cousins, as well as their administrators[30] on how to govern, including soldiering and chancery work,[31] but also on management of comital fishponds.[32] He even found time to write about how to collect taxes.[33] For a prince's chief cook he wrote a work, *De rege et sacerdote*;[34] for the Marquise of Brandenburg and her daughters, a manual of Christian comportment.[35] He wrote on the perils of debased coinage for Landgrave Wilhelm of Thüringia[36] but also on "spiritual numismat-

28. Description in Klapper 2:131, Hist. 1, fol. 254r; extant in Oxford Hamilton cod. 54; Wolfenbüttel Herzog August Bibliothek nov. 684; parts of the original codex, which was H 66 in the Erfurt library, have been lost, at the beginning and end.

29. Listed in the medieval Erfurt Carthusian catalogue edited by Lehmann (note 6 above) as found in codex H 61, possibly extant in Oxford Hamilton 54.

30. See Klapper 1:121–25 for an overview, with cross references to the details and excerpts from Erfurt Domarchiv Hist. 1 in volume 2.

31. *De regimini principis* was rewritten, at the request of the duke's chancellor emeritus, in German. Klapper, 1:122; 2:149, Hist. 1, fol. 342v.

32. "Item scripsi alium tractatum ad magistrum piscium in Wissensee, qui est advocatus eiusdem principis. Dicitur magister piscium eo, quod est provisor istius stagni prope dictam civitatem et de piscatoribus eiusdem stagni accipit racionem." Inc: Venite post me et faciam vos fieri piscatores hominum (Klapper 2:149, Hist. 1, fol. 343r). The work may actually have more to do with how to live a Christian life as a government official in general—the work was written for an *advocatus* of Landgrave Wilhelm of Thüringia, the Vogt of Weißensee, who, among his other duties, had charge of the landgrave's fishponds. In the Erfurt Carthusian library catalogue, the description of codex H 74, mentions a *Tractatus de confessione et absolucione et de regimine boni advocati et de aliis annexis* (which the Erfurt librarian noted was also found in F 21 and H 61). See also Klapper 2:149, Hist. 1, fol. 343. For H 74, see Lehmann (note 6 above), p. 408.

33. Klapper 1:123; 2:131, 149; Hist. 1, fol. 256r and 342v: "Item alium tractatum ad exactorem eiusdem principis in Salcza, et pertractat ista verba Apokalipsis: 'Christus dilexit nos et lavit nos a peccatis nostris in sanguine suo et fecit nos reges et sacerdotes.'"

34. Klapper 2:233, Hist. 1, fol. 259r: "Item ad magnum coquinarium de rege et sacerdote." This cryptic entry is followed immediately [259v] by the entry about the marquise and her daughters cited in note 35 below.

35. Klapper 2:133, Hist. 1, fol. 259v: "Item ad peticionem marchionisse Brandenburgensis et filiarum eius scripsi tractatus tres scilicet: qualiter se debeant habere ad deum et eterna et sanctos eius, sowie gegen sich selbst und gegen anderen Menschen."

36. *De moneta* Paderborn Erzbischöfliche Akademische Bibliothek cod. 118, fol. 185vb–187vb. See Mertens in VL 3 and Klapper 1:122; 2:130, 150, Hist. 1, fol. 347.

ics" and, for the *Bürgermeister* of Eisenach, on the spirituality of business.[37] He also dealt with marriage, marital sexuality (requested by a physician in Erfurt), the permissibility of dancing, prodigies of nature, epidemiology,[38] and the use of torture in witchcraft cases.[39]

In between the conventional spiritual and the socio-political, we find a variety of treatises on church life and on the life of the mind, from canon law to church and monastic reform, popular superstition, magic,[40] the art of dying and Masses for the dead, Trinitarian theology, spiritual direction, psychology, the Immaculate Conception, Carthusian history and Carthusian liturgy, all the offices and roles within the Order from infirmarian to tailor to bookbinder to vicar, cantor, sacristan, procurator, and prior. He covered monastic formation, fraternal correction, visitations, conciliar theory, Hussites, interdicts, tyrannical superiors in monasteries, bishops, indulgences, eschatology, how to keep peace between peasants and their monastic landlords, the art of memory, the various arts and sciences, university life in general, historical chronicles, grace and free will, soteriology, and the fate of unbaptized children.

But did these treatises have any depth? Were they inconsequential ephemera? We do not yet know the answer, at least in most instances. As noted above, most of them survive only in difficult-to-decipher autographs. To be sure, Johann's *De perfectione et exerciciis sacri ordinis Cartusiensis* was published for Carthusian internal use three times in the seventeenth century. One work was published shortly after his death, at Zwolle, about 1481–1483: a *Tractatus de diversis gravaminibus religiosorum* (also known as *De regimine religio-*

37. Titled *De moneta temporali* in the Erfurt Charterhouse library catalogue, under the ancient shelfmark H 101. Inc. Ostendite michi numisma census (Klapper 2:130, no. 88, Hist. 1, fol. 254r), extant in Paderborn 118. *De spirituali negotiatione/De mercatore* is found in the same codex, fol. 130va–134va).

38. *Tractatus contra pestilentiam,* copied off in Erfurt Domarchiv Hist 1, fol. 10v–11r (see Klapper 2:7, 46); cf. Weimar Herzogin Anna Amalia Bibliothek, quarto. 22, fol. 154r–165r.

39. Klapper 1:65, discusses this in relation to the accused witch of Blomberg, with excerpts from Johann's own account, 2:92–99.

40. *De arte magica* in Erfurt Domarchiv Theol. 15. See Mertens in VL 3: 397.

sorum). Fortunately, his treatise on the spirituality of medicine (*De regimine sanitatis maxime spiritualium virorum*), apparently written at Eisenach, has been edited as part of a dissertation, though its editor, Manfred Peter Koch, did not know that the author was Johann of Hagen.[41] This modern edition permits us to glimpse Johann's method.

After an introduction (par. 1–57), the treatise on spirituality of medicine consists of a commentary (par. 58–90) on one of the basic medieval medical textbooks, the *Regimen sanitatis*, followed by Johann's own recommendations for a healthy way of life. We learn that God created things good and that sin introduces disease and death (par. 2–10), that all science or human knowledge gained by study is a gift of God (par. 25–31), with medical knowledge the noblest science (par. 32). The anatomy of the body is summarized based on the dignity of the various members (par. 36–47). From Galen's *Ars medica* Johann then summarizes the division into healthy body, sick body, neutral body (par. 48–57). He knows not only the Salerno tradition but also standard medical literature in general, including Avicenna and Arnold of Montpellier. Beside recommending fresh air, moderate exercise, and rare bathing, Johann offers advice on food (for example, do not eat bread hot out of the oven), on wine and beer, on the superiority of asses' milk to cows' milk, and of lighter meats to "*carnes grossas*." Indeed, he declares that eating too much wild game, especially of the great carnivores, can turn one into a beast. He cov-

41. This Bonn dissertation from 1969 was published in 1999 as *"Das Erfurter Kartäuserregimen": Studien zur diätetischen Literatur des Mittelaters*, Analecta Cartusiana, 141 (Salzburg: Institut für Anglistik und Amerikanistik, 1997). Mertens does not mention the *De regimine sanitatis* in VL; Rüthing mentions it under "miscellaneous" at the end of his article, with no reference, though it is followed by a reference to the *Tractatus contra pestilentiam*, as cited in note 38. Johann of Hagen mentions it as having been written at Eisenach as "*Tractatus de regimine sanitatis virorum spiritualium, quomodo se regere se debeant in vera sanitate et deo placendo serviant*," with its incipit ('Altissimus de terra creavit medicinam'), permitting us to verify that the work published by Koch is indeed Johann's *De regimine*. Johann further describes his tract: "Et ponuntur ibi multa de rebus naturalibus et de his, que sunt contra naturam. Ponuntur eciam aliqua experimenta rusticorum medicine, que tamen experiencia docente sepius profuerunt." See Klapper 2:151, Hist. 1, fol. 345r.

ers psychology of moods and passions, a Christian's obligation to take care of his health, and offers a basic pharmacology.

In short, the treatise presents a down-to-earth, concise, practical integration of the mundane and the spiritual. Manfred Koch concludes that Johann did not simply draw from standard medieval textbooks, but also possessed solid knowledge of practical "home remedy" medicine of his day, which he valued highly. He did not follow his sources slavishly even from a technical medical perspective. He sought above all to integrate means of spiritual health with means of physical health, for the practical use of monks and nuns and friars.

We turn now to the expert opinion on the "infestation of the Turks," a commentary on Denys the Carthusian's visions relating to the parlous state of Christendom after the Fall of Constantinople.[42] Until now known in three copies[43] this *Opinion* [*Sentimentum*] *of a certain Carthusian regarding the Infestation of the Turks* is also found, dated 1459, in an Austrian *vademecum* codex[44] that might best be called a Ladnerian "conversion" collection, concerned above all with how to live, how to face death, how to turn one's life around, and how to train one's affections toward God.

The author of the *Sentimentum* tells us he had met Denys the Carthusian in Mainz and quotes his assertion that "reformation of the Church will only come through the sword."[45] The author's in-

42. *Epistola ad principes catholicos* in *Opera Omnia*, vol. 36 (Tournai, 1908) (= Opera Minora, vol 4), 503–24: articulus XIII: "Confirmatio praedictorum ex verbis et revelationibus Sanctorum et Catholicorum," 516–17; articulus ultimus (= art. 14), 517–24.

43. Mainz Stadbibliothek I. 175; Wolfenbüttel Herzog August Bibliothek Helm 366; Augustinian Canons library at Neustift near Brixen in the South Tyrol, cod. 754. See Kent Emery, *Opera Selecta: Prolegomena*, vol. 1, 188–89, 206–7.

44. Vienna, National Library cvp 4067, which corresponds to the codex G-7 in the medieval Aggsbach catalogue. Emery knew, from the fifteenth-century Aggsbach catalogue that such a copy had existed but did not realize that cvp 4067 represents Aggsbach G-7. See Emery, *Opera Selecta: Prolegomena*, vol. 1, 336–37; cf. Theodor Gottlieb, *Mittelalterliche Bibliothekskataloge Österreichs*, 1: *Niederösterreich* (Vienna: A. Holzhausen, 1929), 590–91, reprinted in Spiritualität Heute und Gestern, vol. 7, Analecta Cartusiana, 35.7 (Salzburg: Institut für Anglistik und Amerikanistik, 1990), 79–80.

45. ÖNB cvp 4067, fol. 181v, line 22 to 182r, line 12: "Reverendus iam prefatus pater

terest in the purportedly prophetic work, *De novem rupibus/Das Neunfelsenbuch*, attributed to Rulmen Merswin (d. 1382)[46] intersects with a strong interest at the Erfurt Charterhouse in this and similar texts.[47] Linking it to the Erfurt Charterhouse, of course, still leaves James the Carthusian as a possible author, and this is not the place for an extended argument in favor of Johann of Hagen as author.[48] One of the four copies is from Brixen, which points to a likely con-

---

noster Carthusiensis dixit me audiente in domo Maguntinensi quod ecclesiam contingit nunquam reformari nisi per gladium. Prelati inquit magni et presidentes consilio volunt alios pauperes religiosos compellere ad reformacionem et ipsi volunt in suis dignitatibus et dominiis permanere et beneficia sua plurima retinere vel forte augere Videant utrum concordant cum primis sancte ecclesie prelatis Si ut Christus in asello aliquis eorum sedet Si ut appostoli singuli singulis contenti tunicis Si ministrare magis parati sunt quam ministrari Si verbo et exemplo alios docent et instruunt secundum quod primitive ecclesie rectores sancti fecerunt." Emended slightly from Brixen Neustift 754, fol. 15v, lines 26–35.

46. Translated in augmented form into Latin by Johann of Schaftholzheim (fl. 1356–1381). See Adolar Zumkeller in DSAM 8 (1974): 722–23 and Georg Steer in VL 6 (1987): 419–42.

47. E.g., Erfurt Charterhouse catalogue codex D-4 (edited by Lehmann, note 6 above), 307–8.

48. See Klapper 1:78–79, who uses the term "mystic" loosely to include visionaries and overinterprets his evidence. The *De novem rupibus* was present in the Erfurt Carthusian library in codex D-4, which included other mystics and visionaries. We do know that John of Hagen wrote a concordance of the women visionaries, a *De concordia*, in which he shows how the women visionaries' revelations correspond to Scripture but he also insists that these visions are not of the same authority as Scripture (see Klapper 2:126–27, Hist. 1, no. 85, fol. 241r: "Item scripsi alium tractatum de concordia, scilicet qualiter tales visiones prefatarum possunt concordare, cum in multis videntur dissonare et contraria ponere." But Denys the Carthusian and James the Carthusian and many other Carthusians also placed high value on the women visionaries. See Dennis D. Martin, "Carthusians as Advocates of Women Visionary Reformers" in *Studies in Carthusian Monasticism in the Later Middle Ages*, edited by Julian M. Luxford, Medieval Church Studies 14 (Turnhout: Brepols, 2008), 127–53, for additional discussion and literature. Klapper pointed out that Johann of Hagen wrote a whole series on enduring persecution, beginning with a *Vademecum in adversitate* (Erfurt Charterhouse catalogue [edited by Lehmann, see note 6 above] H 10, item 16) and *De paucitate justorum* (H 101, no. 10, extant in Paderborn 118 [note 16 above]). The additional titles he cites from codices of the Erfurt library catalogue (*De persecucione toleranda* [D 93, no. 27], *De preparacione ad martirium subeundum* [H 93, no. 33], *De causis persecucionum et malorum* [H 93, no. 30]) are not mentioned in Johann of Hagen's own registers of his writings but they are attributed to him, together with others on the virtue of patience and fortitude, in the list of Johann of Hagen's writings compiled after his death by Konrad Volradi, the librarian of the Erfurt Charterhouse. Volradi's list is found in Lehmann, (note 6, above), 581–93, here at 588; cf. Klapper 1:60, 2:25, referring to in H 10, item 16.

nection to Nicholas of Cusa, who was bishop there precisely during the years after the fall of Constantinople and who asked Denys the Carthusian to write a treatise "Against the Perfidy of Muhammed." All signs point to this anonymous treatise as having originated at Erfurt and probably at the request of Nicholas of Cusa. Its "public" is, admittedly, a narrow one, namely, whoever requested the "expert opinion." But if indeed Nicholas of Cusa requested it of Johann of Hagen, then it enjoyed a "public" that mattered a good deal in the 1450s, since Nicholas was the point man for general church reform under popes Nicholas V and Pius II.

And indeed, the *Sentimentum* actually has as much to do with church reform as with the Turks. It reflects a theology of "meek" submission to God *in caritate*: we ought rather to be willing to suffer for a time materially in this life than to suffer eternally in hell.[49] Until head and members in the church learn detachment from power and dignities, reform is doomed.[50] Affliction from God can rouse Christians from torpor and indifference.[51] But the *Sentimentum* offers no doloristic apocalyptic hopelessness. Since God rules history and Christ himself counseled to pluck out one's eye rather than go to hell with both eyes intact, in the end, the *reformatio* that counts is personal conversion from sin. The rulers of Christendom have failed so badly that severe suffering may be the only way God can recall malfeasant prelates to their senses. *Fiat*, let it be so. In this way, the *Sentimentum* fits well within a longstanding Carthusian tradition

49. Dennis D. Martin, *Fifteenth-Century Carthusian Reform: The World of Nicholas Kempf*, Studies in the History of Christian Thought, 49 (Leiden: Brill, 1992), esp. Introduction, ch. 3, and Epilogue.

50. See the quotation from ÖNB 4067, fol. 181v–182r, in a previous note.

51. ÖNB cvp 4067, fol. 181v, line 11–22: "Et eligibilius utique est sustinere brevem tribulacionem quamque gravem, ut fiat ecclesie purgacio et felix sequatur ubique renovacio et emendacio, quam si dominus quasi diucius miserendo et corporibus parcendo periculum semper augmentetur, animarum tamen nulla sequitur emendacio voluntaria diu iam satis expectata. Dominus enim in ista revelacione pie [scil. to Denys the Carthusian] sue intencione propositum dignatus est exprimere ubi dicit quod per huiusmodi persecucionem vult ecclesiam erigere et ad pristinum bonum reducere, quia ut dictum est supra, aliomodo difficulter fieri potest."

of refusing to place one's hope in institutional or political machinations. Instead, the Carthusians, by the very lives of penitence they lead, call all Christians to live up to the faith they profess.

CONCLUSION

One might, at this point, legitimately ask, given the limited dissemination of Johann of Hagen's tractates, may one label him a "public intellectual"? So what if he wrote on such a surprising range of topics? Did he have any significant impact or does he represent a quirk of late medieval history? Why hasn't he left a mark on our mental landscape of the pre-Reformation era alongside Gabriel Biel or Nicholas of Cusa or even Denys the Carthusian? Johann of Hagen represents a public intellectual in the sense that his advice was sought by members of governing circles, from ducal and comital courts as well as from the civic leadership of the towns of central Europe. How much impact did he have on them? Even to hope to answer that question would require detailed prosopographical research into the courts and towns of Thuringia, Saxony, Brandenburg, and Pomerania, not to mention the immense labor of producing even provisional transcriptions of a representative sampling of his writings.

But why have we not heard about Johann of Hagen when we have heard a lot about Gabriel Biel, Johann von Paltz, Johann von Staupitz, and others? A full monograph outlining his life's work based on his truly remarkable chronicling of his own life's work has been available for nearly a half century, Joseph Klapper's *Der Erfurter Kartäuser Johannes von Hagen: Ein Reformtheolog des 15. Jahrhunderts*. Why did it have so little resonance?[52] Here one can at best offer only several hints at an answer.

52. A search of the OCLC database shows that the two-volume work is owned by approximately fifty libraries today, one-tenth the number of libraries owning contemporary monographs from the E. J. Brill Studies in Medieval and Reformation Thought series (1960s and early 1970s); perhaps one-sixth or one-seventh as many as leading monographs in the equivalent J. C. B. Mohr monograph series (Beiträge zur historischen Theologie).

In the 1950s and 1960s something of a Ladnerian circle led by Erich Kleineidam and Josef Klapper and others functioned at Erfurt (which had remained bi-confessional during the sixteenth-century Reformation)[53] in a small Catholic seminary that managed to survive in Communist East Germany. Kleineidam, well known in the West for his definitive histories of the University of Erfurt and its theological faculty, was less well known for his Catholic-oriented studies of Erfurt Carthusian spirituality and Bernard of Clairvaux's sapiential-affective theology.[54]

Perhaps the most important reason Klapper's truly remarkable monograph on Johannes of Hagen, published at the end of a long scholarly career that began before the First World War, had little resonance in Western European and North American scholarship was that it was very Ladnerian in a world in which historians were fascinated with "social history," with its attendant soft-Marxist assumption that history was driven by broad social movements, not calls to personal conversion and *reformatio*. Johann of Hagen could write all the tractates he wished and send them to all the rulers and bureaucrats of central Europe, but so what? Appeals to personal *conversio* as the key to church reform, we all "knew" back then, were futile, since they represented the discredited "great men" theory of history. Oh, yes, perhaps a celebrated preacher like Gabriel Biel or Johann

53. See Bob Scribner, "Civic Unity and the Reformation in Erfurt," *Past and Present* 66 (1975), 29–60.

54. Erich Kleineidam, *Wissen, Wissenschaft, Theologie bei Bernhard von Clairvaux*, Erfurter Theologische Studien, 1 (Leipzig: St. Benno Verlag, 1955); Erich Kleineidam, "Theologie bei Bernhard von Clairvaux," in *Bernhard von Clairvaux, Mönch und Mystiker: Internationaler Bernhardkongress Mainz*, Veröffentlichungen des Instituts für Europäische Geschichte Mainz, 6, edited by Jean Leclercq (Wiesbaden: Institut für Europäische Geschichte, 1953), 128–67; Erich Kleineidam, "Die theologische Richtung der Erfurter Kartäuser am Ende des 15. Jahrhundert: Versuch einer Einheit der Theologie," in *Miscellanea Erfordiana*, Erfurter Theologische Studien, 12 (Leipzig: St. Benno Verlag, 1962), 247–71; edited by and reprinted in Marijan Zadniker and Adam Wienand, *Die Kartäuser: Der Orden der schweigenden Mönche* (Cologne: Wienand Verlag, 1983), 185–202; Erich Kleineidam, *Universitas Studii Erffordensis: Überblick über die Geschichte der Universität Erfurt*, in 4 parts, Efurter Theologische Studien, 14, 22, 42, 47, 2nd ed. (Leipzig: St. Benno Verlag, 1985–88).

von Staupitz, to whose influence Martin Luther himself testified, might merit study in order to understand the era's movements, but not someone, so we thought then, who seemed to have dissipated himself with treatise after treatise on every subject under the sun, all written with a common goal of showing this prince or that town administrator how to live a genuine Christian life. Perhaps one of the reasons that Johann of Hagen has not been noticed is precisely that he worked with administrators ranging from provincial officials to papal legates but always behind the scenes, unheralded. Historians claim to have long since shifted from paying attention only to the celebrities to a concern with the story of the average practitioners of late medieval religion. In that light, Johann of Hagen merits new attention.

Moreover, Johann of Hagen's writings were not merely unedited but untranscribed. One would have to trust Klapper's extensive excerpts and thoroughgoing topical cataloguing of them, at least initially. To form one's own judgment on Johann of Hagen and his significance would have required years of tedious manuscript research. Yet Klapper's work is so thorough and organized that trusting him, at least far enough to become conscious of Johann of Hagen as a significant possible paradigm, would not have been unreasonable.

Finally, Johann of Hagen did not write in the formal genres of university scholastic theology, and in 1961, when Klapper published, students of the Reformation era were busily engaged in rehabilitating the late-medieval background to the Reformation but were still doing so (a) as background to the Great Reformation and (b) primarily as formal, scholastic theology. The movement to pay attention to piety and devotional life was still primarily a Catholic matter, going all the way back to Johann Janssen's *Geschichte des deutschen Volkes seit dem Ausgang des Mittelalters* (1876–1888)[55] but especially

55. Note Heiko Oberman's critique of "völkisch" approaches, whether that of the Catholic Janssen or the Protestant Johannes Haller in *Werden und Wertung der Reformation: Vom Wegestreit zum Glaubenskampf* (Tübingen: J. C. B. Mohr (Paul Siebeck), 1977), 10–11.

in the work of H. Outram Evennett and the *Archivio italiano per la storia della pietà*. Heiko Oberman's 1963 *Harvest of Medieval Theology* and his *Sonderforschungsbereich* for late medieval and Reformation historical theology at Tübingen focused intently on the heritage of scholastic theology in the late fourteenth and the fifteenth centuries, giving a clear, if subtextual, confessional Protestant reading to Gabriel Biel and others.

Oberman shifted to take account of "social history"[56] in the mid-1970s. After a dissertation on scholastic covenant theology, Berndt Hamm staked out new ground by successfully establishing the analytical genre of *Frömmigkeitstheologie*. Thanks to the appearance of Dieter Mertens's *Iacobus Cartusiensis*, Hamm became aware of Johann of Hagen and the Erfurt Carthusians to a degree that the Oberman school in general was not.[57] At Erlangen Hamm followed up with a focus on bourgeois "lay theologians" like the Nürnberg "Stadtschreiber" Lazarus Spengler.

But even Hamm's more recent and justly influential theory of the Reformation era as a time of "normative centering," in which

56. Heiko Oberman, "'Tumultus rusticorum': Vom 'Klosterkrieg' zum Fürstensieg: Beobachtungen zum Bauernkrieg unter besonderer Berücksichtigung zeitgenössicher Beurteilungen," *Zeitschrift für Kirchengeschichte*, 85 (1974), 301–16.

57. In *Frömmigkeitstheologie* Hamm was aware of Klapper's monograph on Hagen. He cited Hagen (at 62, 139, 176–77, 181–82, 187, 202, 314, 317–18) as an example of a writer of *Frommigkeitstheologie* and pointed out that the Augustinian Eremites (e.g., Johann von Paltz, and before him, Johannes von Dorsten) had very good relationships with the Erfurt Carthusians. He cited Kleineidam's articles on the spiritual direction of the Erfurt Carthusians based on their library catalogue (187). Hamm did not, however, recognize the degree to which Hagen had a thoroughgoing program of a "universal call to holiness," giving spiritual meaning to daily life. And Hamm was less aware of James the Carthusian, though he listed Mertens's book, only recently published, in his bibliography. Fascinatingly, at the end of the book (317–18), as he attempted to assess just how significant von Paltz and the Augustinian Eremite *Frömmigkeitstheologie* was, he noted that the question cannot be answered because far too little was known about how things stood in the other religious orders. He then pointed out that Johann of Hagen's tractate on original sin drew on two of Augustine's anti-Pelagian writings, works that seem to have been unknown to von Paltz, von Dorsten, and the Augustinians at Erfurt yet were the two works of Augustine that most interested Luther on this topic. Nestled within his concluding call to further research, this nugget remains ripe for further exploration, yet to my knowledge neither Hamm nor his students have taken it up.

the more complex theology of the medieval scholastics and "piety theologians" was transformed by bourgeois activists like Spengler into "sola" slogans, retains something of a scholastic approach and a Protestant subtext. As with Oberman's controverted claim that Gabriel Biel articulated a semi-Pelagian soteriology, so too with Lazarus Spengler in Nürnberg: despite similarities with late medieval Catholic authors like Gerson and James the Carthusian, in one or two of Spengler's specific phrases Hamm and his student, Sven Grosse, locate turning points, crossings-of-the-threshold from (1) Catholic salvation conditioned in some sense on human effort to (2) Protestant "unconditionality."[58]

Yet despite scholastically subtle attempts to pinpoint textually and *expressis verbis* clear differences between Lazarus Spengler, on the one hand, and Jean Gerson and James the Carthusian, on the other hand, with regard to the art of dying,[59] the texts of Gerson, Biel, and James the Carthusian *can* be read and interpreted differently.[60] Whether Biel and others like him were "Pelagians" or con-

58. See Berndt Hamm, "Was ist reformatorische Rechtfertigungslehre?" *Zeitschrift für Theologie und Kirche*, 83 (1986), 1–38; Peter Manns, "Zum Gespräch zwischen M. Luther und der katholischen Theologie: Begegnung zwischen patristisch-monastischer und reformatorische Theologie an der Scholastik vorbei," in *Thesaurus Lutheri* (Luther-Symposium, Helsinki, 1986), edited by Tuoma Mannermaa, Anja Ghiselli, and Simo Peura (Helsinki: Finnische Theologische Literaturgesellschaft, 1987), 63–154; reprinted in Peter Manns, *Vater im Glauben*, edited by Rolf Decot (Stuttgart: Franz Steiner Verlag Wiesbaden, 1988), 441–532. These themes are revisited in Hamm's *Lazarus Spengler* book.

59. Grosse, *Heilsungewissheit*, cited in note 4 above, 235–41, esp. 240–41; Hamm, *Lazarus Spengler*, 308–12, 330–36.

60. Francis Clark, S.J., already pointed this out in his review of Heiko Oberman's *Harvest of Medieval Theology*, "A New Appraisal of Late-Medieval Theology," *Gregorianum*, 46 (1965), 733–65; for Oberman's response, see *Werden und Wertung*, 168, note 20. William Courtenay, one of Oberman's first students, pointed out the influence of confessional commitments on how one read Gabriel Biel when he reviewed a book on Biel by Wilhelm Ernst, a member of the Erfurt Catholic circle. See *Speculum*, 53.1 (Jan. 1978), 138–40, at 139–40: "The problem here—and in part the explanation for the difference of opinion between Ernst and Oberman—is not simply differing interpretations of a fifteenth-century theologian, but interpretations that result to some degree from questions informed by the interests and perspectives of the sixteenth-century Reformations, both Protestant and Catholic. In his own time there is no question that Biel's views were orthodox. Whether they are orthodox by sixteenth-century standards or *sub specie aeternitatis Dei* is another issue and one that lies outside the historian's task in the strict sense."

ditioned salvation or solace in dying on "typical medieval Catholic" confidence in human works seems to depend largely on whether one has already internalized the "sola" slogans of a half-century later and applied them to Biel or James the Carthusian or Gerson. At Erfurt, Klapper's reading of Johann of Hagen and Ernst's reading of Biel placed these fifteenth-century authors firmly within the (Catholic and medieval) history of reform in general, not the history of the Reformation.

Awareness of the role played by cloistered Carthusians during the middle 1400s as they sought to address the very real, specific, complex questions posed by the lives of citizens in the world of business and government could help historians make better sense of the era that preceded the "centralizing" and "confessionalizing" forces of the early modern period. But uncovering and understanding the network of interaction between Johann von Hagen, James the Carthusian, and their bourgeois, court, and ecclesial correspondents could supply work for legions of doctoral students for decades, transcribing manuscripts and mapping networks of monks, court officials, *Bürgermeister*, and princes in the service of better understanding the idea of reform that animated a vigorous Christian populace during an era that, fortunately, no longer is merely dismissed as the decadent denouement of Christendom.

14

BLACK AND WHITE AND RE-READ ALL OVER

Conceptualizing Reform across the Long Sixteenth Century, 1414–1633

WILLIAM V. HUDON

Succeeding his 1959 treatment of the idea of reform in the age of the Fathers, Gerhart Ladner (1905–1993) planned for volumes that would cover the development of Christian reform throughout the early and later Middle Ages.[1] He seemed to envision analysis of this

My thanks to Christopher Bellitto, David Zachariah Flanagin, Morimichi Watanabe, Peter Casarella, and Gerald Christianson, the organizers of the Eleventh Biennial Conference of the International Seminar on Pre-Reformation Theology, which met along with the American Cusanus Society at the Lutheran Theological Seminary at Gettysburg, October 2008. I presented an abbreviated version of this essay as the F. Edward Cranz Lecture at that conference. My thanks also to the two anonymous readers for the Catholic University of American Press for their helpful insights and recommendations.

1. Gerhart B. Ladner, *The Idea of Reform: Its Impact on Christian Thought and Action in the Age of the Fathers* (Cambridge, Mass.: Harvard University Press, 1959), vii. For a fine study on the significance of Ladner's work, see Phillip H. Stump, "The influence of Gerhart Ladner's *The Idea of Reform*," in *Reform and Renewal in the Middle Ages and the Renaissance*, edited by Thomas M. Izbicki and Christopher M. Bellitto (Leiden: Brill, 2000), 3–17.

history at least up until the emergence of Martin Luther. While in some ways his hope for the analysis was fulfilled, his vision of companion volumes to his own was not. Scholars in the next two generations studied the idea of reform extensively, if not—as some social historians have suggested to me—*ad nauseam*. When looking through the later Middle Ages, across the sixteenth, to the first half of the seventeenth century, the situation is much the same: literally tons of collected erudition, but no satisfying synthesis. Lack of new synthesis consolidating the complex history of later reform ideology, as Ladner had done for the earlier, is bad, but what we early modernists face is, in some ways, worse. We struggle with a sort of intellectual failure to launch: failure to launch the results of the multiple methodologies used by scholars, of their changing categories, vocabularies, and understandings of early modern reform. We see the problem in a remarkable, even alarming amount of specialized literature, and nearly pervasive in textbook literature and popular media. Despite what Ladner hoped for, conceptions of the reform ideology and of the activity that ideology spurred in the early modern period—what is described here as the long sixteenth century—are truly still, at least in some quarters, quite black and white, despite having been thoroughly reread for the last fifty years.

Where's the proof? Well, one might begin by looking where any good Christian reformer would look: inside. When the phrases "church reform," or "Protestant Reformation," are used, what ideas, images, and words spring to mind? Many are embedded in popularized portrayals of the Reformation found in feature films and public broadcasting presentations. Take, for instance, the 2003 film entitled simply "Luther." The captions pasted over the dramatic images in the advertising trailer promise the tale of "one man," who "500 years ago," and apparently singlehandedly, "changed the world." The potentially apocryphal image of him pounding his Ninety-five Theses onto the door of the Wittenberg Church is front and center. The dialogue in the film appears even more one-sided. Luther is attacked by a finger-pointing cleric who identifies the German theologian as the cause of upheaval "just when we need unity." Luther himself questions a razor-wielding barber redoing his tonsure with the query, "Did you really think there wouldn't be a cost?" And with Joseph Fiennes as the title character—not to mention the beautiful Claire Cox as Katherine von Bora—the director, Eric Till, provides us with plenty that is pleasing to look at, way beyond the homely portraits by contemporaries of Luther, like Lucas Cranach, which we are used to seeing.[2]

Polarized interpretations with built-in blinders conveniently shutting out precedents and complicating factors should not surprise us. Religious leaders, polemicists, and politicians portrayed early modern religious events in dichotomous, polar opposite terms from the very beginning. In their sweeping overview of the history of reformation history, A. G. Dickens and John Tonkin noted how even in the mid to late sixteenth century, mostly Lutheran Protestant historians "canonized" the period from 1517 to 1555 as a self-sufficient one, requiring neither consideration of fifteenth-century precursors to Luther, nor the emerging Reformed churches in Switzerland, France, and England. Not to be outdone, of course, were Roman sympathizers like Johannes Cochlaeus (1479–1552), who treated Luther as a zealous outlaw with an evil purpose: the deliberate destruction of unity in central Europe.[3] This is not to say that more balanced assessments were completely lacking early on, as both Johannes Sleidan (1506–1566) and Cesare Baronio (1538–1607) rose above the muckraking tenor. They relied on archival sources at least, and sometimes used qualifying phrases when advancing interpretations that twenty-first century instructors in historical

2. *Luther*, directed by Eric Till (Halle, Germany: NFPteleart GmbH & Co., 2003). The theatrical trailer was available on YouTube at the time of this writing (May 2009): http://www.youtube.com/watch?v=SzFc7ilM7nw.

3. For the characterization of early Protestant historical analysis, see A. G. Dickens and John M. Tonkin, *The Reformation in Historical Thought* (Cambridge, Mass.: Harvard University Press, 1985), 9. For discussion of Cochlaeus, *ibid.*, 21–27.

methods courses would be proud to find in student writing. Still, the interpretative trend from the beginning has been to find heroes and demons in the story of early modern reform.

One need look no further than at artistic representations of the principal characters and events in the history for further evidence. Propagandistic broadsheets published at the mid-sixteenth century height of the polemics, now reprinted in works like Mark Edwards's *Luther's Last Battles,* in De Lamar Jensen's *Confrontation at Worms,* and in bits and pieces in most textbook accounts of the period, depict the two sides with great clarity. It was common to split images, either side by side or top-bottom to illustrate Luther and true religion on one side (or on the top) with the pope and his minions messing things up at the opposite point. Artists like Matthias Gerung and Lucas Cranach portrayed the Protestant side in these illustrations often by emphasizing the cross, baptism, communion, and simple preaching, usually with angelic accompaniment and sunny skies. He and others sometimes showed preaching on the papal side, but most often as God rained punishment, in one form or another, upon popes and their supporters. Priests show up, but viewers of the images observed them intently saying Mass, apparently oblivious to all the unsavory action taking place around them. In these illustrations, artists often depicted the pope, with demonic creatures as his assistants, greedily collecting cash even as the "preaching" continued. In other works, images evoking New Testament scenes—like Jesus clearing the temple or washing the feet of his disciples—were juxtaposed with pictures of nasty papal practices like indulgence trading and papal foot kissing.[4] Artists created some of the illustra-

4. Mark U. Edwards, *Luther's Last Battles: Politics and Polemics, 1531–1546* (Ithaca, N.Y.: Cornell University Press, 1983); and De Lamar Jensen, *Confrontation at Worms* (Provo, Utah: Brigham Young University Press, 1973). For some examples of such illustrations published in textbooks, see Merry Wiesner, Julius R. Ruff, and William Bruce Wheeler, *Discovering the Western Past: A Look at the Evidence* (Boston: Houghton Mifflin, 2008), 317, 319; and James D. Tracy, *Europe's Reformations, 1450–1650* (New York: Rowman and Littlefield, 1999), 62.

tions with still other messages in mind, as in one cartoon accompanying Luther's 1545 translation and commentary on Robert Barnes's *Lives of the Roman Pontiffs*. In the image, the pope was treading on the neck of an emperor apparently crying out in considerable pain. The sarcastic title was "How the pope, obeying Peter, honors kings." Cranach turned the tables on this image completely with a woodcut showing peasants defecating into the papal tiara, with the caption explaining that the pope has treated the kingdom of Christ "just as his crown is being treated here."[5]

And lest we think that it was Protestant polemicists who had all the fun, remember that Catholic artists did much the same. Richard Verstegen, for instance, showed "the horrible crimes perpetrated by the Huguenots" in a book illustration now often used in anthologies. He depicted a Catholic church in flames, with victims leaping to their death from its tower. If they weren't lucky enough to die in the fall, heretics were waiting below with large axes on long handles to finish them off. In the foreground of the picture, corpses of still other victims were being desecrated and burned.[6] Artists from Catholic territories joined in polemicizing that most infamous of "reform" organizations, the Inquisition. Pedro Bereguette (1450–1504) presented the Spanish version of the tribunal in a well-scrubbed, fairly heroic version, presided over by Saint Dominic himself. But in contrast, who could forget the dramatic nineteenth-century painting by Cristiano Banti illustrating perhaps the most famous early-modern trial of that infamous tribunal, the *processo* against Galileo? Here the accused Tuscan astronomer—who just happened to be a pretty virulent polemicist himself—became the hero. He dramatically confronted the court in this depiction, with chest and left foot thrust forward, his eyes firmly fixed on the crucifix hanging on the wall before him. Two of the three clerics lined up against him are hooded or appear to be lurking in shadow. There is no way that a

5. Edwards, *Luther's Last Battles*, plate 5, 194; plate 3, 192.
6. Tracy, *Europe's Reformations*, fig. 7.3, 104.

viewer, even knowing the broad outlines of the story, could believe that the digit-pointing friar trying in vain to direct Galileo's eyes to the text of the Bible even began to comprehend the truth lying immediately under his finger.[7]

In some ways, historians and other scholars have simply followed suit, and deviation from that pattern constitutes an exception, not the rule. As one great scholar of both reform and of the historiography of early-modern reform, John O'Malley, pointed out, by the end of the nineteenth century, interpretations of the Catholic version of early modern reform were driven by categories inseparable from a much larger question: how an institution like the Roman church related to all the bad things—or all the good things—that had happened in western Europe since 1450. He was referring, of course, to a debate in which the leading voices were German, and mainly Lutheran, like Christop Keller, Johann Stephas Pütter, and Moriz Ritter, with Catholics, like Johannes Janssen, Joseph Hergenröther, and Joseph Döllinger, reacting.[8] Their specific, not exactly "larger" question, it seems, was how badly did Catholics mess up the religious creativity and doctrinal clarity that lay behind the reform ideology delivered through and inspired by Martin Luther? The focus of their research was the front end of the period covered in this essay. When scholars examined the history of reform ideas for the hundred or so years after approximately 1520, the leading voices among them were not German, but Italian. Their specific question was how completely did the Catholics mess up not so much the religious innovation of Luther and his followers, as what was left of that Italian cultural efflorescence known as the Renaissance? "Completely" seemed to be the answer of literary critics and historians like Francesco De Sanc-

7. For the Bereguette illustration, Tracy, *Europe's Reformations*, fig. 7.5, 106. The 1857 painting by Banti is reproduced in Pietro Redondi, *Galileo eretico* (Torino: Giulio Einaudi, 1983; English translation by Raymond Rosenthal, Princeton: Princeton University Press, 1987), illustration 18.

8. John W. O'Malley, *Trent and All That: Renaming Catholicism in the Early Modern Era* (Cambridge, Mass.: Harvard University Press, 2000), 18–28.

tis and Benedetto Croce, plus others such as Guido Quazza, Gino Benzoni, and Albano Biondi. The approach of De Sanctis has been reprised recently by scholars like Gigliola Fragnito and Marina Roggero. The latter, like her predecessors, highlighted a climate of distrust, suspicion and "massive censorial intervention," that stultified the flourishing Italian editorial industry whose passing she lamented.[9] Anglo-American historians have weighed in as well, often reiterating the tired orthodox commonplaces. William Bouwsma and Frederic Lane did so when considering Venice, and describing it as a society heroically defending the Renaissance values of civic liberty and republicanism (values, they suggested, with which we should identify) against Spain and against a Catholic Church that threatened to demolish them. Guido Ruggiero and Judith Brown did so too when considering the sexual practices and legal realities under which early modern folk lived. Church-sponsored repression worked to obliterate expressions of sexuality—like lesbianism—via penalties like thirty-five years in solitary confinement, when necessary. In these works, historians tend to emphasize the repressive legislation and penalties rather than the deeper reality that the regulations were largely ineffective. Sensitive acknowledgment of complexities, as in Elisabeth Gleason's admission that the paragon good guy on the Catholic side of the Reformation, Gasparo Contarini, could be a proponent of "moral absolutism," are overwhelmed by the sea of eulogistic renderings—some coming from her own pen—of him and his fellow travelers. The real accomplishments of institutions and individuals who stood arrayed against Roman intolerance

9. For the classic statement of this position, see Francesco De Sanctis, *Storia della letteratura italiana*, 2 vols. (Naples: D. Morano, 1870). See also the following works of Benedetto Croce: *La Spagna nella vita italiana durante la rinascenza* (Bari: G. Laterza, 1917); Benedetto Croce, *Storia della età barocca in Italia* (Bari: G. Laterza, 1929); and Benedetto Croce, "La crisi italiana del Cinquecento e il legame del Rinascimento col Risorgimento," *La critica: Rivista di letteratura, storia e filosofia*, 37 (1939): 401–11. See also *Church, Censorship and Culture in Early Modern Italy*, edited by Gigliola Fragnito, (Cambridge: Cambridge University Press, 2001), 5–11, 13–48; and Marina Roggero, *Le carte piene di sogni: testi e lettori in età moderna* (Bologna: Il Mulino, 2006), 15–16.

were allegedly recognized only long after, in an age that could genuinely appreciate them, the Enlightenment.[10]

But surely all is not lost, as brave scholars have challenged the dominant interpretations, and for good reason. Historians reconsidering pre-Lutheran reform ideology, for example, found realities that do not fit traditional conceptions of the later Middle Ages. The standard interpretation of reform leaders and their initiatives in the fifteenth century at the councils of Constance and Basel finds prelates full of good intentions, but decidedly wanting when it came to action ... a rather complete failure. This picture has lately undergone serious reconsideration. Phillip Stump charted in careful detail the productive discussions and compromises reached at Constance (1414–1418) on fiscal reform, on filling vacant ecclesiastical offices, and on developing reform ideology. Thomas Izbicki recently reported on reactions to some of the decrees of the Council of Basel (Basel-Ferrara-Florence, 1431–1439). Those reactions, he found, were certainly complicated, if not altogether driven, by theological concerns quite separate from the competing, ideologically motivated claims of authority usually cited as the cause for the failure of late medieval reform. He found that those concerns had lengthy staying power—more than 100 years' worth, in fact—as they continued to generate heat right into the era of the Council of Trent. Stump went still further in his fine book, asserting that charges of failure applied to reform initiatives in this era were compromised by religious and

10. For a small sample of the host of relevant examples, see William Bouwsma, *Venice and the Defense of Republican Liberty: Renaissance Values in the Age of the Counter Reformation* (Berkeley: University of California Press, 1968), 52–54, 93–94, 624–28; Frederic C. Lane, *Venice: A Maritime Republic* (Baltimore: Johns Hopkins University Press, 1973), vi, 1–2; Elisabeth G. Gleason, *Gasparo Contarini: Venice, Rome, and Reform* (Berkeley: University of California Press, 1993), 162, 299–301; Judith C. Brown, *Immodest Acts: The Life of a Lesbian Nun in Renaissance Italy* (New York: Oxford University Press, 1986), 3–20, 132–37; Guido Ruggiero, *The Boundaries of Eros: Sex Crime and Sexuality in Renaissance Venice* (New York: Oxford University Press, 1985), 168; Constance M. Furey, *Erasmus, Contarini and the Religious Republic of Letters* (New York: Cambridge University Press, 2006), 4–8; and Camilla Russell, *Giulia Gonzaga and the Religious Controversies of Sixteenth Century Italy* (Turnhout: Brepols, 2006), 1–5, 209–11.

political commitments. Historians were looking, he suggested, for the emergence of constitutional monarchy and-or the beginnings of nationalism. Only such concerns—ones that amounted to complete anachronism, Stump correctly implied—represented for such historians the real difference between definitions of conciliar failure or success.[11]

Scholars recently examining the context in which late medieval and early modern—but still pre-Lutheran—reform ideology developed have located even greater complexity. That context, for lack of a better name, we might call Renaissance religiosity. In the traditional picture derived from Jacob Burckhardt in the mid-nineteenth century, there was nothing religious about Renaissance values at all. For him, the Renaissance was a cultural and artistic flowering with breathtaking productivity, plus a shift in political and civic values emphasizing the value of the individual, of civic engagement and of virtuosity. But as an intellectual change with religious implications, it was rather completely truncated. It began, in this common view, with religious skepticism, not commitment to religious reform, while any growth of the latter in southern Europe was decapitated, like the Renaissance itself, when a mid-sixteenth century combination of ecclesiastical intransigence and Spanish hegemony shut down the positive developments. That intransigence and hegemony were never thrown off again until, roughly speaking, the *Risorgimento*. Reconsideration of this picture, one might argue, began long ago. A partial change can be identified through a couple of well-known works identifying commitments among Renaissance religious leaders which resembled no part at all of Burckhardt's view—that is,

11. Phillip H. Stump, *The Reforms of the Council of Constance (1414–1418)*, Studies in the History of Christian Thought, 53 (Leiden: Brill, 1994); and Thomas M. Izbicki, "The Immaculate Conception and Ecclesiastical Politics from the Council of Basel to the Council of Trent: The Dominicans and Their Foes," *Archiv für Reformationsgeschichte* 96 (2005): 145–70. See also the numerous works of Nelson Minnich, some of which are now conveniently collected in one volume: his *Councils of the Catholic Reformation: Pisa I (1409) to Trent (1545–63)* (Burlington, Vt.: Ashgate, 2008).

clerics committed to humanistic learning well after their definitive "sacking"—plus prelates treating the churches they administered as inheritable property to be passed along to family members.[12] While this nineteenth-century idea of the "pagan" Renaissance has been challenged, scholars should be warned against any congratulatory notion that it is fully dead and buried. Beginning some forty years ago, historians like Donald Weinstein, Richard Trexler, and Ottavia Niccoli enriched our understanding of Renaissance religiosity through analysis of the many, varied purposes of public activities like devotional processions and popular preaching. The best of such works illustrate the complexity of early modern religion, as in Trexler's suggestion that the ostensibly religious rituals of Renaissance Florence were about politics and the political process, not religious ideas. The weaker treat novel religious expression in the age as a flash in the pan, quickly extinguished around 1530 by overbearing ecclesiastical regulations and the "end of liberty" progressing to an "age of repression."[13] In any event, anything Burckhardt or his modern successors would describe with the words "religiosity" or "reform" either appeared nowhere in the picture, or thoroughly squashed as liberty ended. How commitment to liberty—or to genuine religiosity—could suddenly emerge *ex nihilo* later on is, for those scholars who suggest it, an unasked, unanswered question. Others, stepping forward from the beginning of this reconsideration have either followed leads opened by scholars like Trexler and Niccoli or have cultivated related fields, to substantial positive effect. Hence, the fine recent work by Tamar Herzig on the later female devotees of the

12. John D'Amico, *Renaissance Humanism in Papal Rome: Humanists and Churchmen on the Eve of the Reformation* (Baltimore: John Hopkins University Press, 1983); and Barbara McClung Hallman, *Italian Cardinals, Reform, and the Church as Property* (Berkeley: University of California Press, 1985).

13. Donald Weinstein, *Savonarola and Florence: Prophecy and Patriotism in the Renaissance* (Princeton: Princeton University Press, 1970); Richard C. Trexler, *Public Life in Renaissance Florence* (New York: Academic Press, 1980); Ottavia Niccoli, *Prophecy and People in Renaissance Italy*, translated by Lydia G. Cochrane (Princeton: Princeton University Press, 1990). For the quotation, Niccoli, *Prophecy and People*, 189–90.

prophetic reform message of Girolamo Savonarola. Charismatic women outside of Tuscany she found ignoring expectations about female comportment to establish religious houses, to promote the cult of the heretical preacher, and to predict a coming divine chastisement for the ecclesiastical hierarchy. These women enjoyed the support of numerous Dominican friars and powerful noble laymen.[14] Recent work on religious women in early modern Italy has gone to demonstrate that despite the continuing seizure of their history by some who use it only to condemn ecclesiastical patriarchy and clerical institutions, others have contributed analysis that illustrates the multidimensional relationship between religious women and contemporary males.[15]

So, it is true that the religiosity of the Renaissance, and its reform initiatives, are now decidedly, as one scholar of the period recently put it, "out of the margins." A far more complex portrait has emerged. Roman religiosity—and experimentation with reform ideas—was vital and multifaceted, these scholars argue, not monolithic or stultifying. Connecting humanist revival of educational ideals with ideals of individual renewal and perfection that have the longest of pedigrees in the Christian tradition, Renaissance-era religious leaders helped to produce great complexity, even where we have been told we may not find it: in Spain and Italy. In both places

14. Tamar Herzig, *Savonarola's Women: Visions and Reform in Renaissance Italy* (Chicago: University of Chicago Press, 2008), 189–94.

15. For an overview, see *Women and Faith: Catholic Religious Life in Italy from Late Antiquity to the Present*, edited by Lucetta Scarafia and Gabriella Zarri (Cambridge, Mass.: Harvard University Press, 1999). For some additional, more specialized works, see Jodi Bilinkoff, *Related Lives: Confessors and their Female Penitents, 1450–750* (Ithaca: Cornell University Press, 2005); Sarah Gwyneth Ross, *The Birth of Feminism: Woman as Intellect in Renaissance Italy* (Cambridge, Mass.: Harvard University Press, 2009); Silvia Evangelisti, *Nuns: A History of Convent Life, 1450–1700* (New York: Oxford University Press, 2007); John Jeffries Martin, *Myths of Renaissance Individualism* (New York: Palgrave Macmillan, 2004); Patricia Ranft, *Women and the Religious Life in Premodern Europe* (New York: St. Martin's Press, 1996); Giovanni Romeo, *Esorcisti, Confessori, e Sessualità femminile nell'Italia della Controriforma* (Firenze: Casa Editrice Le Lettere, 1998); and Jeffrey R. Watt, *The Scourge of Demons: Possession, Lust, and Witchcraft in a Seventeenth-Century Italian Convent* (Rochester, N.Y.: University of Rochester Press, 2009).

there were broad, deliberate attempts, no doubt, to control, silence, and shut down religious innovation. There were also attempts by ecclesiastical judges, long before the conclusion of the Council of Trent, to legislate and enforce restrictions on socio-religious practices, such as marriage for instance, and in ways that some historians have described as "intransigent." But attempted repression and repression, like attempted murder and murder, are just not the same things. And the historical record shows us plenty of variations of the ecclesiastical theory operating in practice. We find canon law doctrine sometimes protecting allegedly "modern" values like informed consent in marriage, more effectively than either secular law or than actions taken by the families of marital parties. We also find early modern individuals skirting rules, avoiding prosecution, maintaining questionable "evangelical" attitudes while still undertaking reform assignments from allegedly "intransigent" prelates who supposedly were lined up against them, and subverting presumably domineering institutions like the Roman and Venetian inquisitions. When you add recognition of the strong popular support behind some ecclesiastical leaders that does not square with the image of a Renaissance shut down against the will of the people, we are now fairly compelled to look at this era in a different manner.[16] Arguably

16. For some works arguing for this revision, see David Peterson, "Out of the Margins: Religion and the Church in Renaissance Italy," *Renaissance Quarterly* 53 (2000): 835–79; Lu Ann Homza, *Religious Authority in the Spanish Renaissance* (Baltimore: The Johns Hopkins University Press, 2000); and Francesco C. Cesareo, "The Complex Nature of Catholicism in the Renaissance," *Renaissance Quarterly* 54 (2001): 1561–73. Studies of attempted repression, and of some celebrated cases tried in order to squash innovation, are legion. For a few, see Massimo Firpo, *Nel labirinto del mondo: Lorenzo Davidico tra santi, eretici, inquisitori* (Firenze: Leo S. Olschki, 1992); Massimo Firpo and Sergio Pagano, *Il processi inquisitoriali di Vittore Soranzo,* 2 vols. (Vatican City: Archivio Segreto Vaticano, 2004); Dario Marcatto, *Il processo inquisitoriale di Lorenzo Davidico (1555–1560): Edizione critica* (Firenze: Leo S. Olschki, 1992); and Adriano Prosperi, *Tribunale della coscienza: Inquisitori, confessori, missionari* (Torino: G. Einaudi, 1996). For examples of some recent literature identifying more specific realities that encourage thinking beyond the standard oversimplifications, see Cecilia Ferrazzi, *Autobiografia di una santa mancata, 1609–1664,* edited by Anne Jacobson Schutte (Bergamo: Pierluigi Lubrina, 1990); "Il diario di Giambattista Casale (1554–1598)," edited by Carlo Marcora, in *Memorie storiche della diocese di Milano* vol. 12 (Milano: Biblioteca Ambrosiana, 1965), 209–437; Giorgio Chittolini

the finest recent work in this vein—fine because of the celebrity of the case that is the subject and fine because of the breathtaking scope of the author's erudition plus the power of his argument—is Maurice Finocchiaro's *Retrying Galileo, 1633–1992*. Finocchiaro has demonstrated with compelling evidence that the virtually continuous retrial of Galileo from 1633, to his recent rehabilitation by John Paul II, is little more than a set of ruminations on whether or not the action taken by the Inquisition against him was legal, reasonable, justified, and "fair" or not.[17] There is nothing particularly historical about the analysis Finocchiaro surveyed. Instead, those ruminations constitute a form of moralistic breast-beating that may make entertaining plots for stage and screen, but as history, they do little to unshackle readers from anachronism and presentism. Indeed, they obscure rather than illuminate a fascinating episode, still more fascinating historical actors, and a complex early modern religious context.

Historians have found that comprehension of the human realities behind the Protestant Reformation has similarly still been hindered by traditional ways of thinking about early modern Germany, France, England, and its religious leaders. Twentieth-century histo-

and Peter Johanek, *Aspeti e componeti dell, identità urbana in Italia et in Germania (secoli XIV–XVI) = Aspekte und Komponenten der städischen Identität in Italien und Deutschland* (Bologna: Mulino, Berlin: Duncker & Humblot, 2003); Anne Winston Allen, *Convent Chronicles: Women Writing about Women and Reform in the Late Middle Ages* (University Park, Pa.: Pennsylvania State University Press, 2004); Elizabeth Teresa Howe, *The Visionary Life of Madre Ana de San Agustin* (Rochester, N.Y.: Boydell and Brewer, 2004); Bruno Léal, *La crosse e le baton: visites pastorals et recherché des pécheurs publics dans le diocese d'Algarve, 1630–1750* (Paris: Centre Cultrel Calouste Gulbekian, 2004); Bárbara Mujica, *Women Writers of Early Modern Spain: Sophia's Daughters* (New Haven: Yale University Press, 2004); Timothy J. Schmitz, "The Spanish Hieronymites and the Reformed Texts of the Council of Trent," *Sixteenth Century Journal* 37/2 (2006): 375–99; Massimo Firpo, *Vittore Soranzo vescovo ed eretico: riforma nella chiesa e inquisizione nell'Italia del cinquecento* (Rome: Laterza, 2006); and Cecilia Cristellon, "Marriage and Consent in Pre-Tridentine Venice: Between Lay Conception and Ecclesiastical Conception, 1420–1545," *Sixteenth Century Journal* 39/2 (2008): 389–418.

17. Maurice A. Finocchiaro, *Retrying Galileo, 1633–1992* (Berkeley: University of California Press, 2005). Those unwilling to tackle Finocchiaro's weighty tome can find a condensed version of the argument in his article "The Church and Galileo," *Catholic Historical Review* 94/2 (April 2008), 260–82.

rians of the Protestant Reformation redrew the heroized mantle, if not to say halo, rounded about Luther and his followers by the controversialists. They have passed it on quite recently, in works published by some major presses, apparently designed to reach both scholars and more popular audiences. Among them are not just the usual suspects like Roland Bainton, but also Diarmaid MacCullogh, Richard Marius, and even the justly venerated Hans Hillerbrand. Luther still, even in MacCullogh's view, was a "champion" of the "ordinary Christian" whose clear cry for simple reform delivered with "unmovable" commitment to finding truth in Scripture was spoiled by the actions of individuals and groups outside of his control. While in MacCullogh's picture Luther may not be quite the center of the reform story that he is for Bainton, Marius, and Hillerbrand, to get beyond the commonplaces we must tackle a seven-hundred-page monster of densely-packed type. Hillerbrand acknowledged that the Protestant Reformation was an interplay of religious, political, and economic forces, but still insisted that Luther "overshadowed everything and everybody else" in the history of this "greatest conflagration" of western Christendom. Even his title—*The Division of Christendom*—exposed his commitment to the standard interpretation.[18]

Late in the twentieth century, spurred no doubt by the use of anthropological and sociological method by the *Annalistes*, a very different, quite promising line of analysis was developed by Heinz Schilling and his students and collaborators. Their depiction of the "confessionalization" of Western Europe, which they say reached its apogee in the sixteenth century, has much to commend it. They reject pictures of the sixteenth century as a revolutionary schism, se-

18. The classic statement, of course, is in Roland Bainton, *Here I Stand: A Life of Martin Luther* (Nashville, Tenn.: Abington Press, 1950), 15–16, 300–302. See also Richard Marius, *Martin Luther: The Christian between God and Death* (Cambridge: Harvard University Press, 1999), 469–87; Diarmaid MacCulloch, *The Reformation: A History* (New York: Penguin, 2004), xxi–xxiv, 114–23; 143–49; and cf. also Hans Hillerbrand, *The Division of Christendom: Christianity in the Sixteenth Century* (Louisville, Ky.: Westminster John Knox Press, 2007).

cession, or separation from a mythical unified religious past. They insist instead that the reform developments of the long sixteenth century (both Roman and Protestant) were consistent with a much longer pattern of change, in a place where Christian theology had never really monopolized culture, where religion and society did not constitute separate spheres, where the separatist movements of Luther, Calvin, Henry VIII, and others were not a uniform, dynamic, purifying Protestantism in binary opposition to a static, corrupt Catholicism, but where, in the end, four churches were formed: Lutheran, Calvinist-Reformed, Anglican, and Tridentine. All claimed to be universal and in sole possession of the real connection with the old "evangelical" church of Jesus and his apostles, all wrote explicit confessions of faith, and all—including Tridentine Catholicism—were truly "new."[19]

Some new lines of interpretation that appeared promising have not, however, quite lived up to the hopes of either their proponents or their readers. Confessionalization, for instance, has not been consistently useful because the thesis, in the end, tells us a great deal about the systems designed to promote Anglican, Calvinist, Lutheran, and Catholic Christianization, but precious little about how effectively these systems operated in practice. Only further research through specialized study of specific communities—which finally will lead back to a consideration of individuals and their

19. An introduction to confessionalization can be found in Heinz Schilling, *Early Modern European Civilization and Its Political and Cultural Dynamism* (Hanover, N.H., and London: University Press of New England, 2008), 11–32. This book providing Schilling's Menaham Stern Jerusalem Lectures in May 2006 also contains a vast set of references to the related literature. See also Wolfgang Reinhard, "Reformation, Counter Reformation and the Early Modern State: A Reassessment," *Catholic Historical Review* 75 (1989): 383–404. For the situation in early modern England, covering Catholicism and the confessional interchange between contemporary English Protestants and Catholics, see Robert S. Miola, *Early Modern Catholicism: An Anthology of Primary Sources* (Oxford: Oxford University Press, 2007): 1–38. One of the most powerful challenges to the confessionalization theory was written by Marc R. Forster: *Catholic Revival in the Age of the Baroque: Religious Identity in Southwest Germany, 1550–1750* (Cambridge: Cambridge University Press, 2001), 241–44.

actions—will reveal whether the systems were efficacious or not. Gerald Strauss provided early contributions in this reconsideration, identifying the conviction of the magisterial reformers that they had failed in their objective to create Christians. Strauss began the study of visitation records which are now *de rigueur* for the examination of local implementation of reform. Scholars now study such records in intimate detail and they are finding, in the main, that implementation of directives about religious teaching and practice was slow, spotty, and often only minimally effective.[20] Historians have also provided less than persuasive evidence of the efficacy of contemporary "social disciplining," an allied but somewhat different concept. The basic tenets of the concept require not just recognition of plans to shape and control human behavior through centralized religious, political, legal, and social institutions, but also imply that the plans successfully cowed the early modern European population. The trend of specialized studies of individual inquisitorial proceedings goes, at least at the moment, toward illustrating the enormous creativity, bravery, and determination—if not to mention genuine deception and manipulation—employed by the victims of those attempting to do the disciplining. Diocesan studies, like that of Wietse de Boer, moreover, show that episcopal efforts aiming at moral reform through social control in the confessional had similarly limited consequences. For de Boer, Milan across nearly a century—the period with bookends represented by Carlo and Federico Bor-

20. Gerald Strauss, "Success and Failure in the German Reformation," *Past and Present* 67 (May 1975): 30–63; Gerald Strauss, *Luther's House of Learning: Indoctrination of the Young in the German Reformation* (Baltimore and London: Johns Hopkins University Press, 1978); and Geoffrey Parker, "Success and Failure during the First Century of the Reformation," *Past and Present* 136 (August 1992): 43–82. For some examples of the array of local studies that have followed, see C. Scott Dixon, *The Reformation and Rural Society: The Parishes of Brandenburg-Ansbach-Kulmbach, 1528–1603* (Cambridge: Cambridge University Press, 1996); James Kittleson, "Visitations and Popular Religious Culture: Further Reports from Strasbourg," in *Pietas and Societas: New Trends in Reformation Social History*, edited by K. C. Sessions and P. N. Bebb (Kirksville, Mo.: Sixteenth Century Journal Publishers, 1985), 89–102; and Marc R. Forster: *The Counter-Reformation in the Villages* (Ithaca: Cornell University Press, 1992).

romeo, roughly from 1564 to 1631—was marked by efforts at harsh repression, but the human capacity to resist was strong, and parish priests acted as mediators facilitating compromise. In Milan and elsewhere, the overwhelming evidence at the moment indicates that plans for social disciplining generated, at the most, highly limited, regional control.[21] Achievements were nothing even remotely close to the control the authors of such plans intended. If local administrators had in fact succeeded in some comprehensive disciplining, after all, we should have to explain how the cowed suddenly lost their yokes and overthrew religious and political authorities later on. The simpler, more reasonably human explanation is that no authorities—religious, political, legal, social, or familial; ancient, medieval, early modern, or modern—fully exercised anything close to the power they so vociferously claimed.

21. Carlo Ginzburg, *I benandanti: stregoneria e culti agrari tra Cinquecento e Seicento* (Torino: G. Einaudi, 1966; English translation by John and Anne Tedeschi (Baltimore: The Johns Hopkins University Press, 1983); Redondi, *Galileo eretico*; Carlo Ginzburg, *Il formaggio e I vermi: Il cosmo di un mugnaio dl '500* (Torino: G. Einaudi, 1976; English translation by John and Anne Tedeschi, Baltimore: The Johns Hopkins University Press, 1980); Massimo Firpo, *Inquisizione romana e controriforma: Studi sul Cardinal Giovanni Morone e il suo processo d'eresia* (Bologna: Il Mulino, 1992); John Martin, *Venice's Hidden Enemies: Italian Heretics in a Renaissance City* (Berkeley: University of California Press, 1993); Wietse de Boer, *The Conquest of the Soul: Confession, Discipline, and Public Order in Counter-Reformation Milan* (Leiden: Brill, 2001), esp. 53–83; 323–30; Lucia Bianchin, *Dove non arriva la legge: dottrine della censura nella prima età moderna* (Bologna: Il Mulino, 2005); *Heresy, Culture and Religion in Early Modern Italy: Contexts and Contestations*, edited by Ronald K. Delph, Michelle M. Fontaine, and John Jeffries Martin (Kirksville, Mo.: Truman State University Press, 2006). A recent review article identifies numerous studies of early modern confessionalization—or "confessionalism"—in Italy, Germany, and Spain, indicating that these have "unyoked" the theory from "teleogical narratives." These studies have pointed out the inability of the theory to explain complexities in popular response to efforts of contemporary authorities to shape behavior and belief. See Diarmaid MacCulloch, Mary Laven, and Eamon Duffy, "Recent Trends in the Study of Christianity in Sixteenth-century Europe," *Renaissance Quarterly* 59/3 (2006): 697–731, esp. 706–20. For other examples of the limited applicability of "confessionalization" to early modern Italy, see the works of Thomas Deutscher, including his "The Bishop's Tribunal and the Laity: the Diocese of Novara, 1563–1614," in *The Renaissance in the Streets, Schools, and Studies*, edited by K. Eisenbichler and N. Terpstra (Toronto: Centre for Renaissance and Reformation Studies, 2008), 183–209; and Oscar Di Simplicio, *Peccato, penitenza, perdona Siena 1575–1800: la formazione della coscienza nell'Italia moderna* (Milano: Franco Angeli, 1994), 13–16, 392–98.

And last, but certainly not least, scholars have found that concepts applied to Catholic religiosity in the early modern period—both those formerly considered pro-Catholic leaning and those with an anti-Roman, anti-clerical bent—are thoroughly suspect as misleading oversimplifications. The rethinking began in the 1970s with works by scholars like Paul Grendler and Eric Cochrane. This scholarly beat certainly goes on. For instance, Thomas Mayer not only complicated our picture of Reginald Pole with a recent biography in which he suggested that sources point toward homosexual relationships between the famous early modern English prelate and at least one of his cardinal familiars, but has also taken on the entire tradition of historical examination designed to find an acceptable generalization to apply to reform-minded sixteenth-century Italians who found Lutheran theology attractive. He considered the examination a distraction from the work of figuring out what really happened in the sixteenth century, and in a recent article only half-jokingly proposed "monkey in the middle" as a substitute name for one of the factions Italian historians like Paolo Simoncelli still like to identify in that age. Even Massimo Firpo, who had been one of the firmest in insisting that ecclesiastical repression squashed free thought in early modern Italy, admitted in a recent essay that "overly rigid categories" might not work in describing those we presume to have been victims of repression in the sixteenth century. Neither do rigid categories work when applied to those long considered one-dimensional repressors, like the inquisitor Ambrogio Catarino Politi (1484–1553). Giorgio Caravale recently argued that the Dominican's theology was complicated, even innovative, when considering the matter of justification. Paul Murphy wrote one of the best new works in this vein, a wonderfully contextualized portrait of Cardinal Ercole Gonzaga (1505–1563), a thoroughly complex early modern reformer impelled toward his work by a fascinating range of motivations. Ingrid Rowland, moreover, just published a stunning portrait of Giordano Bruno (1548–1600), the heretic considered such a martyr to free thought that even today his death at the stake is commemorated as a yearly civic event in Rome. Rowland found him a curious blend of traditional scholasticism, Platonic poeticism, and stubborn independence who nonetheless appealed repeatedly for reconciliation with the Roman church while traveling in northern Europe after his excommunication.[22] The complexity Rowland identified so thoroughly demolished the usual picture of Bruno that the reviewer of her work in *The New Yorker,* apparently set to report on an updated version of the standard martyr-hero image, seemed completely flummoxed. All she could do was to suggest that perhaps poor Rowland could not understand Bruno's philosophical works.[23]

This substantial reconsideration and rethinking is certainly a positive development, but as demonstrated above, it is only partly making its way into scholarly literature. The reconsideration is making its way to an even lesser extent into textbook literature, and not at all, of course, into popular media. Even while taking a more sophisticated approach to cultural change, urging students—for instance—to see religious growth in religious institutions as affect-

22. Paul Grendler, *The Roman Inquisition and the Venetian Press, 1540–1605* (Princeton: Princeton University Press, 1977); Eric W. Cochrane, "Counter Reformation or Tridentine Reformation? Italy in the Age of Carlo Borromeo," in *San Carlo Borromeo: Catholic Reform and Ecclesiastical Politics in the Second Half of the Sixteenth Century,* edited by John M. Headley and John B. Tomaro (Washington, D.C.: The Catholic University of America Press, 1988), 31–46; William V. Hudon, "Religion and Society in Early Modern Italy: Old Questions, New Insights," *American Historical Review* 101 (June 1996): 783–804; Thomas F. Mayer, *Reginald Pole: A Biography* (Cambridge: Cambridge University Press, 2000); Thomas F. Mayer, "What to Call the *Spirituali?*" in *Chiesa cattolica e mondo modern: scritti in onore di Paolo Prodi,* edited by G. Brizzi, A. Prosperi, and G. Zarri (Bologna; Il Mulino, 2007), 11–26; Massimo Firpo, "Lorenzo Lotto and the Reformation in Venice" in *Heresy, Culture and Religion in Early Modern Italy: Contexts and Contestations,* edited by Ronald K. Delph, Michelle M. Fontaine and John Jeffries Martin (Kirksville, Mo.: Truman State University Press, 2006), 21–36; Giorgio Caravale, *Sulle trace dell'eresia: Ambrogio Catarino Politi (1484–1553)* (Florence: Leo S. Olschki, 2007), 117–27, 206–15; Paul V. Murphy, *Ruling Peacefully: Cardinal Ercole Gonzaga and Patrician Reform in Sixteenth-Century Italy* (Washington, D.C.: The Catholic University of America Press, 2007); and Ingrid Rowland, *Giordano Bruno: Philosopher/Heretic* (New York: Farrar, Strauss & Giroux, 2008).

23. Perhaps it was the reviewer who failed to understand Rowland. See Joan Acocella, "The Forbidden World," *The New Yorker,* August 25, 2008, 76–80.

ing not just the culture in which the religion grows, but altering also the religion itself, many textbooks simultaneously present the Reformation in simplistic terms, as spurred—again for instance—by the controversy over indulgences and very little else. Others, in the space of a brief chapter, voice complete contradictions by discussing the loose, fragmentary nature of the medieval church and just a few pages later delivering the Reformation as a "movement that shattered the thousand-year unity of Western Christendom." Many still find the beginnings of modern nationalism, social relationships, and secular states—in short, the emergence of our world—there in sixteenth-century achievements.[24] When turning to motion pictures we see, time and again, directors who have adopted tired commonplaces about the era, even if reworked slightly to incorporate early twenty-first century concerns, having omitted genuine updating and contextualization of the past. Contextualizing and complicating portrayals of history might be the right scholarly thing to do, but of course, there is no connection between this and box office sales, as anyone would readily admit. So the commonplaces come back, heroizing attractive figures from the past who then look just like we do, or to be slightly more accurate, who look just like we wish we looked. Thus, Queen Elizabeth of England in the cinematic portrayal of her "golden age," doesn't just sound like a powerful, determined woman who could stand up to any arrogant religio-political fanatic

24. For the quotation and contradiction, see Mortimer Chambers, et al., *The Western Experience*, 8th ed. (New York: McGraw Hill, 2003), 435–46. See also Lanny B. Fields, et al., *The Global Past* (Boston: Bedford Books, 1998), 497–505; 699–727. David Ringrose presented a somewhat more sophisticated and global approach to early modern history, but the only complexity added in his view of the Reformation is the political factor behind some examples of religious dissent: see his *Expansion and Global Interaction, 1200–1700* (New York: Longman, 2001), 42–53. For some who continue to emphasize the emergence of modern western ideas and values in the early modern period and in changes stemming from the Reformation, see Judith G. Coffin, et al., *Western Civilizations: Their History and Their Culture*, 16th edition (New York: W. W. Norton, 2008), 487–516; Marvin Perry, et al. *Sources of the Western Tradition*, 5th edition (Boston: Houghton Mifflin, 2003), 305–7; Margaret L. King, *Western Civilization: A Social and Cultural History*, 2nd edition (Upper Saddle River, N.J.: Prentice Hall, 2003), 444; and J. M. Roberts, *The New History of the World* (New York: Oxford University Press, 2003), 547–97.

like Philip II. Cate Blanchett played the part, and in a striking scene she literally shouted down the Spanish ambassador, delivering withering determination, not to mention ribald double-entendre. "I fear neither him, nor his priests, nor his army," she insisted, adding that if Philip wanted "to shake his little fist," she would insure that in the long run he would "wish he had left his hands in his pockets." There is no doubt that we are to believe the "hurricane" she described within herself was the real cause of the wind that wrecked the Armada. Blanchett may look and sound severe, but she's also beautiful, despite the odd sixteenth-century costuming. And when, in a moment of self-examination after mercilessly teasing Sir Walter Raleigh, she takes her clothes off, the effect is at least as breathtaking as the hurricane speech. Such storyboarding brings people to the box office, as does the portrayal of blazing "Armada beacon" bonfires—which end up looking like the sixteenth-century equivalent of homeland security operations.[25]

But the effect of some such portrayals, in terms of historical understanding, is even worse than the impact of scholarly repetition of tired commonplaces, or of simplified textbook accounts. In the end, all have fallen short of incorporating complexities revealed, albeit gradually, in the fifty years since Ladner wrote. Perhaps simplifications are needed by audiences that may go no further in pursuit of historical truth. Perhaps this is just the way sophisticated history is always treated in popular culture, and there is nothing very serious to worry about. But historical truth, which is inherently complex and elusive, gets watered down at best, and its understanding is fully compromised at worst, in the process. Should we care? As students, teachers, and scholars—indeed, as thinking human beings in a complex world—all of this should matter deeply. We prefer our heroes—

25. *Elizabeth: The Golden Age*, directed by Shekar Kapur (University City, Calif.: Universal Studios and Motion Picture Zeta Produktionsgesellschaft mbH & Co., KG, 2007). The theatrical trailer was available on YouTube at the time of this writing (May 2009): http://www.youtube.com/watch?v=meCoQ2u_oVo&feature=related.

whether religious, cultural, or political—to be one-dimensionally reflective of the "us" we hope to be. We prefer our demons—again, whether religious, cultural, or political—to be one-dimensionally reflective of the "other" we turn away from in shudders. That is not a particularly sophisticated way of thinking about human beings, but it remains natural, and it clouds contemporary understanding of history: the history of the Reformation, the history of other civilizations, the history of ourselves. We are, it seems, immersed in such images.

Without comprehending the genuine attraction of these easy simplifications we can neither properly guard against them nor properly understand history. We also cannot explain embarrassing battles among otherwise highly intelligent people, like one published recently by the Historical Society, a self-proclaimed scholarly reform society. From its foundation in 1999, the leaders of the organization have professed a goal of counteracting what they consider the dangerously politicized American Historical Association. In a skirmish published in their 2007 newsletter, John Headley, a truly wonderful scholar of early modern Europe, composed a rather goofy piece on "Western exceptionalism," where he said, among other things, that in the last several decades the earlier, valued, virtuous portrayal of the Renaissance has been lost. It has been lost, he said, in the fashionable push to "heap condemnation and blame" upon Western civilization in deference to an incompletely understood set of other civilizations—like the Islamic—that opposed Western hegemony. His essay was then followed by three others, by Sanjay Subrahmanyam, Constantin Fasolt, and John Hobson. These other three challenged one or another part of Headley's essay, with goofiness virtually all around. To suggest that a "tradition of fundamental thought and concern" about inherent human rights "stretches" in "sustained, continuous concern" in the West "from the initial Stoic-Christian statement through the Middle Ages to the present," as Headley did, is no better or worse than the assertion that as a category, Western civilization is "a figment of Christian and lapsed Christian ideology," as Subrahmanyam did. Both are caricatures, not human portraits. The exchange is entertaining, but decidedly polemical, and at least hostile if not dangerously inflammatory. Subrahmanyam tossed off Headley's arguments as the product of "no more than an ideologue," and Headley responded in kind, insisting that the positive features of Western civilization are "almost forgotten" by an "establishment" that is "drunk, if not drugged with Derrida, Foucault, and political correctness."[26]

That debate serves to illustrate what can be at stake when caricatures and oversimplifications about history, culture, and politics are posited and defended. As professional historians we would never recommend basing historical conclusions about the 2008 presidential candidates one hundred years from now, whether in scholarly literature, textbooks for students, or movies for popular consumption, on the sort of candidate caricatures that appeared in that election cycle. Yet we seem to have little aversion to the persistence of caricature images of the early modern past. We might chalk up the problem to a few out of touch scholars, or the nature of textbook literature, or "par" for the cinematic course. Regardless, these images obscure the historical truth about the Reformation and its people. Sadly, these caricatures also keep some of us, but even more so the students and public we are also supposed to serve, from understanding change and continuity in history. In the final chapter of his magisterial work on historiography, Ernst Breisach said that we have "the history of historiography to caution [us] that no simplifications, regardless of their sophistication, can make the writing of history's fundamental theoretical problems disappear."[27] The fundamental

26. "Recentering the West: A Forum," *Historically Speaking: The Bulletin of the Historical Society* IX/2 (Nov./Dec. 2007): 9–19. For the quotations, see in the same issue John M. Headley, "Western Exceptionalism and Universality Revisited," 11; Sanjay Subramanyam, "Beyond the *Sonderweg*," 13; and Headley, "Response," 19.

27. Ernst Breisach, *Historiography: Ancient, Medieval and Modern*, 3rd ed. (Chicago: University of Chicago Press, 2007), 429.

theoretical problem in the history of reform, it seems, is to explain the relative importance of change and continuity in that history. The movement, and the characters who took part in it, are especially attractive to those who prefer to make moral and religious judgments and conclusions—as opposed to historical ones—about the past. But without rejecting and seeking to counteract simplified characterizations of the human universe wherever we find them—in literature on the ideology of reform; in cardboard caricatures of leaders, of followers, or of the civilizations in which they lived, past and present—we cannot live up to the promise of our calling as historians to seek fuller truth about the past. Neither can we live up to our present responsibilities as human beings in a complex world.

CONTRIBUTORS

DAVID ALBERTSON is assistant professor of religion at the University of Southern California in Los Angeles, Calif.

C. COLT ANDERSON is dean of the Graduate School of Religion and Religious Education and associate professor of spirituality at Fordham University.

ANN W. ASTELL is professor of theology at the University of Notre Dame.

CHRISTOPHER M. BELLITTO is associate professor and chair of the History Department at Kean University.

INIGO BOCKEN is associate professor of philosophy and director of the Titus Brandsma Institute for Spirituality at Radboud University in Nijmegen, The Netherlands.

GERALD CHRISTIANSON is professor emeritus of church history at Gettysburg Lutheran Seminary.

LESTER L. FIELD JR. is professor of history at the University of Mississippi.

DAVID ZACHARIAH FLANAGIN is associate professor of theology and religious studies at Saint Mary's College of California in Moraga, Calif.

KEN A. GRANT is lecturer in history at the University of Texas Pan American.

JOHN HOWE is professor of history (medieval) at Texas Tech University.

WILLIAM V. HUDON is professor of history at Bloomsburg University of Pennsylvania.

WILLIAM P. HYLAND is director of the Center for Norbertine Studies at St. Norbert College.

DENNIS D. MARTIN is associate professor of historical theology at Loyola University in Chicago, Ill.

LOUIS B. PASCOE, S.J. is professor emeritus of medieval history at Fordham University.

PHILLIP H. STUMP is professor emeritus of history at Lynchburg College.

MICHAEL VARGAS is assistant professor of history at the State University of New York at New Paltz.

INDEX

Reassessing Reform: A Historical Investigation into Church Renewal was designed in Arno with Requiem display and typeset by Kachergis Book Design of Pittsboro, North Carolina. It was printed on 55-pound Nature's Natural Recycled and bound by Sheridan Books of Ann Arbor, Michigan.